TAILS OF THE FIFTIES

AN ANTHOLOGY OF
AVIATION MEMORIES

PUBLISHED BY:
Cirrus Associates (S.W.),
Kington Magna,
Gillingham,
Dorset SP8 5EW, U.K.

The copyright of each chapter belongs to the author of that chapter apart from the following:

Chapter 3: International Auster Club
Chapter 6: 'Aeroplane Monthly' magazine
Chapter 8: 'Flight International' magazine
Chapter 10: Air-Britain (Historians) Ltd.
Chapter 11: International Auster Club
Chapter 17: 'Flight International' magazine
Chapter 28: Air-Britain (Historians) Ltd.

ISBN 0 9515598 3 4

PRINTED IN ENGLAND BY:
The Book Factory,
35-37 Queensland Road,
London N7 7AH.

PHOTO SCANNING BY:
Castle Graphics Ltd.,
Nunney,
Nr. Frome,
Somerset,
BA11 4LW.

SOLE DISTRIBUTORS:
Cirrus Associates (S.W.),
Kington Magna,
Gillingham,
Dorset SP8 5EW.

COVER PHOTOS:
Aircraft tails: Peter G. Campbell
Cloud background: Flt. Lt. Tullach (via the Met. Office)

EDITOR'S ACKNOWLEDGEMENTS

I would like to acknowledge with grateful thanks the help of the following (in purely alphabetical order), without whom this book could not have been completed:

Peter Amos, John Bagley, Eric Bell, Lewis Benjamin, Chris Button, James Campbell, Jack Da-Costa, Chris Dearden, Barry Dowsett, Tim Foster, Denis Fox, Mervyn Fox-Pitt, Ted Gould, Ken Hamilton, Roy Hough, Bill Ison, Archie Jackson, Michael Jones, Denis Kirkham, Fred Lynn, 'Ladi' Marmol, Bernard Martin, Mark Miller, Rex Nicholls, Ron Paine, Richard Riding, Edwin Shackleton, Mike Stroud, Ann Tilbury, Alexander Timmis, Charles Tomkins, Tim Webb and Allan Winn.

I hope I've not forgotten anyone . . .

CONTENTS

PREFACE

by

PETER G. CAMPBELL

Why has this book been put together? I suppose I would have to start by admitting that 'it seemed a good idea at the time.'

As we get older the concept gradually dawns on us that we don't have as much time to look forward to as we have to look back on. We need to hold our nostalgia in check by acknowledging that we can't live in the past, only remember bits of it (hopefully the more pleasant bits).

But, to be honest, who of us, of whatever vintage, hasn't yearned for the days when life was so much simpler, we could trust people, a pound was real money, we were younger and fitter . . . ? And so it goes on. It's probably true for most of us that our favourite period for reminiscing about is the one we would perhaps call 'the formative years,' our growing-up time when we were old enough to appreciate the offers and challenges that the world held out to us, without having so many responsibilities that we felt unable to accept any of them.

And so, for me, I remember the decade of the fifties with affection. In particular I love the memories of that time because it was then that I became involved with small aeroplanes, many of which are still flying today (which helps greatly to keep the illusion of youth alive!). In those days, flying was indeed a lot simpler in many respects: few instruments, fewer radios, very few restrictions. But it still seemed to drain your pocket just as fast!

I hope that as you read this book, to which so many aviation personalities have contributed their memories of this period, you will agree that for pilots and owners of small aeroplanes it was a truly unique time, carrying on to a large extent the principles and practices of the pre-War years, before the lifting of import restrictions made possible the influx of more modern (and mainly American) aircraft to these shores.

As was bound to happen, I suppose, not everything in this book is strictly concerned with the fifties; where it seems sensible I have allowed for slight digressions into both the forties and the sixties, which I hope you will excuse.

Also I am very grateful for being allowed by copyright holders to include some previously published material, which to me seemed too significant to leave out of a book reviewing the fifties.

So to get in the right frame of mind, just sit back, close your eyes and imagine a warm summer's evening with the fragrance of newly-mown grass in your nostrils; very soon you will be bound to hear the unmistakable sound of a Gipsy Major in the distance . . .

FOREWORD

by

MICHAEL JONES

(President of the Tiger Club)

I learnt to fly in the mid-fifties on Tiger Moths at that busy little Surrey airfield, Fair Oaks, then all grass and without a runway marker in sight.

I can well remember my father Norman driving me to the airfield for the first time in an open Lagonda sports car (which was even then a 'classic'). I can also remember the excitement I felt at seeing the sky alive with circuiting Tigers well before we reached the airfield itself, which was then concealed by trees.

My father had his own special reasons for taking me to Fair Oaks that day. He wanted to get back into private flying after a gap of more than twenty years, and he needed a few hours instruction to regain his Licence.

As it turned out, we both had as our instructor the CFI, a wonderful man called Cyril Arthur, known to all as the "WingCo". He was rumoured to have taught himself to fly during the First World War without the benefit of an instructor. The "WingCo" seemed to spend all the daylight hours strapped into the front cockpit of a Tiger, and had the uncanny knack of imparting to his pupils all the arts and skills required to fly and land a Tiger without the need for verbal communication.

The fifties were an important decade in the history of British aviation because they saw the renaissance of private and sporting flying after the restrictions of the war years. Racing, rallying and aerobatics became popular again, and most of the pre-war grass airfields were still available. An undoubted stimulus was the ubiquitous Tiger Moth, and it was during these years that a serviceable machine could be bought and flown from an RAF Maintenance Unit for less than £100. Also, although it was not until the end of the decade that restrictions on the import of foreign-built aircraft were finally lifted, the fifties saw not only the first arrivals in Britain of Pipers and Cessnas but also some marvellous all-wood French designs, of which the Jodels proved to be outstanding. Finally, there was the single-seat VW-powered Turbulent, which was first built in Britain in 1958 under licence from its French designer and was to prove, both then and now, an inspiration to all young pilots. It was in 1960 that Prince Philip demonstrated his long-lasting committment to private flying in Britain by piloting a Turbulent himself at White Waltham.

In this book Peter Campbell has brought together a wonderful collection of anecdotes and reminiscences from over twenty different authors, illustrating many aspects of aviation in the fifties. It will appeal not only to all *aficionados* but also to the general reader.

CHAPTER 1

DOING IT YOURSELF

by

LEWIS J. BENJAMIN

To be honest, flying in the fifties was very little different from the late thirties and forties, or for that matter, the early sixties, but there was no question the period covered was for us, the merry participants, an unforgettable time. The reason of course for the blurring of the decades both before and after centred on the machines we flew and a hang-over thirties bureaucracy still reeling from the return to their ranks of enlightened ex-servicemen, and we were to benefit from this delightful confusion. That is until a sterner civil service management began rebuilding their hierarchy in their own image rather than the public's, who, poor fools, still believed them to be their servants.

But back to that first essential – the aircraft we flew. Everything we touched had previously been through the hands of the RAF/ATA training and communication units. I tell a fib. That's not entirely true. There had been many aircraft that had remained in civilian hands, for not every source was commandeered for war service. Believe it or not, a limited amount of buying and selling did go on throughout the war. You only have to see the 'For Sale' and 'Wanted' columns in both 'THE AEROPLANE' and 'FLIGHT' to arouse your interest. And yes, they were flown, positioning flights and airtests were permitted, plus of course the inevitable bit of flying on the side, but fuel was tight. The prepared answer, "Oh, it's fuel we still had in the tank," must have worn a little thin as the years went by. The chances were that most of the fuel was scrounged from the service aircraft that often shared in common both servicing and hangar space.

The belief that wartime servicing left a lot to be desired was far from the truth. Aircraft released at the war's end were usually in top-line condition with log books right up to date. When one considers their war years utilization the aircraft available in 1946 when civil flying first restarted were in excellent trim. Even the pre-

10

1939 examples seemed none the worse after six years of impoundment. Their airworthy condition, indeed their very existence, owed a great deal to regular maintenance from the RAF and ATA. Put to rest the myth that the servicemen fitters and riggers were a slapdash lot, believe me there was a high standard of ongoing maintenance on all machines, and it showed on every ex-service machine I ever saw or flew. Mark you, I speak of light aircraft. If there were surplus service types available on the civil market just after the war, and I believe there were, they would have been hideously expensive to run. Consequently they didn't figure in our thinking, which was inevitably how much and how cheaply. Nothing changes.

For me, civilian flying began even before my demobilisation and at Shoreham, one of my all-time favourite airfields. Another was Redhill where I was to fly with the Tiger Club from 1960 onwards, but more of that later.

In July of 1946 I joined the South Coast Flying Club. It was much the traditional sort of club. I was still in the RAF, but I lived nearby in Hove and on my leaves I would go to Shoreham and do the one thing the RAF wouldn't let me do: take my civilian friends flying. The Club fleet consisted of Tiger Moths, and the CFI was the most remarkable of men. Cecil Pashley, or 'Pash' as he was known far and wide, was a legend in his own lifetime, and about the most famous of all flying instructors. He'd been around a long while too. He had built, and flown with his brother, his own aircraft before the first World War, and in 1946 had around 18,000 hours instructing to his credit. Even with my current flying practice – and I was actually doing a refresher course on Tigers at Brough in Yorkshire – Pash insisted on showing me around the Tiger as though it was the first aircraft I'd ever seen. When I offered to swing the propeller for him he was horrified.

"No," he said firmly, "always leave things like that to qualified engineers, never do it yourself."

We climbed in and awaited the engineer. When no one turned up Pash began to fret. Impatiently he climbed out of the front cockpit, his long leathers flapping in the wind (I thought irreverently of Grumpy of the Seven Dwarfs for he was scarcely five feet tall), snorted around to the front and reached on tiptoe to grasp the propeller.

"Contact," he shouted.

The engine caught first swing and the Tiger nearly ran him over. He'd forgotten the chocks.

"Let that be a lesson to you, Benjamin," he barked, as he disappeared back into the front cockpit. He was a great man and loved by everyone.

Flying was quite unrestricted immediately after the war. There were almost no recognisable regulations, and even getting an 'A' Licence, as the private pilots' licence was then known, presented no problems. Eight hours solo was all the experience needed, a simple oral exam plus a flying check which was observed from the ground. Civil flying officially began again on January 1st 1946 and the first post-war licences were issued that very week, and mine was amongst them. Since I was RAF-trained I was allowed to skip the flying test; all that was needed of me was to take the oral exam. I presented myself for this at the Royal Aero Club premises in Piccadilly on January 6th 1946, in company with a fellow RAF pilot. The Secretary General had a bit of a cold that day, so his second-in-command, Colonel Preston, officiated.

We stood before 'Mossie's' desk like recalcitrant pupils before the Head. Needless to say we hadn't a clue what questions he was going to ask us. We'd swotted up on a pre-war publication, and had an idea about the positioning of lights on a balloon cable, but little else.

He first turned to Dicky and snapped: "What's a Customs Carnet?"

Dicky was game for a try. "Isn't it something you need if you leave the country?"

Mossie growled and then turned to me. "And you, Benjamin?"

"I agree with Dicky," I said loyally.

He looked at both of us for a moment or two, gave an imperceptible shrug and a shadow of a smile appeared.

"I can see you two know b*****-all about it. Here, give me the papers."

We were in and out in five minutes.

We left behind a pound, I think it was, and came out with the prospect of a licence soon to be in the post, and clutching an aviator's certificate, which cost us five bob. I still have that little blue book with its behest in several languages that all who read this give the holder of this document every help. And all written in the most beautiful copperplate. It was worth five bob of anybody's money. An idiotically earnest boy looked out from the accompanying photograph.

I stayed with the South Coast Flying Club for over a year. They were a jolly lot and led by Duncan Davis, surely one of aviation's most irrepressible and cheerful stalwarts. Duncan was known as 'Drunken Davis' among the regulars. I expect if he knew his soubriquet, and he probably did, he'd have approved.

I remember one evening when Duncan was really drunken he

decided to go flying with two pretty girls. The Club manager was in despair, and shot out ahead of him to urge the engineer to fix the Proctor so that Duncan couldn't fly. Anxious to help, I held up the cowlings with one eye on the club doorway whilst the engineer, doing the best he could at short notice, hurriedly opened up something or other and inserted a piece of paper between two contacts.

"That'll never start," he muttered.

We had no sooner fixed the cowlings back when Duncan staggered out, pushed his giggling passengers into seats and clambered in after them. "Clear," he shouted to the world at large, pressed the starter and the engine roared to life; and before anyone could stop him – were that even possible – he rushed away and took off. White faced, stunned, we watched him fly, tensed against the enormity of what could happen. The engine continued heartily and Duncan came back safe and sound, as good a pilot drunk as sober. Greatly shaken, the other two went inside, presumably to get as drunken as Duncan.

*　　*　　*

But I was restless with their slow and cautious approach to getting airborne; there seemed no room to progress to better things, and more important, there was the expense of it all. The more I thought about it the more convinced I became that the cheapest way to get flying was with an aeroplane of one's own. I put the idea to Duncan.

"Excellent idea," he roared. "Count me in to help."

So encouraged I began to scout around, but every avenue I explored had the same dead end. No money. That wasn't surprising. I had now left the RAF (May 1947) and had promptly spent the next six months sitting on a beach in a summer of brilliance such as one could only dream of. I got wonderfully brown, I swam, had parties, danced and made merry. I was nearly twenty-two. I had been in the RAF four years, and I wasn't going to do a thing until I was ready, and whilst I had some gratuity money left and parents who were glad to have me home again, I certainly *wasn't* ready. Two things finally made me think of work as autumn drew on. I'd run out of money, but worse, there was the threat of the then current Control of Engagement Order. It gave layabouts like me a choice of finding work smartly or being conscripted to the coalmines. I capitulated and went to work for a friend who had a wholesaling toy business. I was the office do-all, I tried to keep the books, collected and sold toys, but my mind was always out of gear. All I could think about was flying and owning my own aeroplane.

Then one night a brilliant idea came to me. What was wrong

with a tiny share, I asked myself, as opposed to a larger one like a half or a quarter? There was no more sleep that night for me as I furiously extended my germ of an idea. I followed the idea up immediately. I put an advertisement in the local paper, the Sussex Evening Argus, announcing the first meeting of the Enthusiasts Flying Club. Pay £10 a head, I declared, and given fifty members we would have enough for an aeroplane with a bit left over for luck and the insurance. But money, even at a tenner a time, was hard to come by. I'm not sure I believe in coincidences, but right on schedule my grandmother died, and with the few hundred pounds that came my way I bought, in quick succession, a big share in the aeroplane, an old open Armstrong Siddeley car of 1931 vintage and a new BSA Bantam 125 c.c. motor bike.

The Club I founded late in 1947 at Shoreham eventually became known as the Brookside Flying Group, and we operated a Miles Magister which we bought from Rollasons for £325 complete with a year's Certificate of Airworthiness. We did everything ourselves to the immense joy of the members and the alarm of others. We set up camp on the north side of the airfield and Duncan wasn't amused at all. When I reminded him of his offer of help he grumbled that he didn't think I meant it. But he eventually relented and proved a good friend. Incidentally it was the first community flying club in the South of England. We were beaten to being the first ever only by a short head when Jill Donnisthorpe started a similar club in Reading; neither knew of the other's existence at the time.

The fun we had is a story in itself, but a little background is important to get the feel of club flying in the immediate post-war years. For instance, anyone could instruct and anyone did. Take me for instance. The insurance policy I negotiated was fully comprehensive: it covered any member under instruction or otherwise, and all for only an incredible seventy pounds a year. That would take some beating today. It also listed me, a complete unknown, as the Club's Secretary, and one authorised to check out others. I did so, often. Even to putting on my most serious face when, as it once happened, I was called upon to give an A1 qualified Wing Commander instructor an initial check. If Wiggie ever reads this, I hope he'll forgive me the indignity of calling for another circuit because I wasn't satisfied with the first.

* * *

In those days I kept a small diary, and a browse through it conjures up a picture far removed from present times. In a life that has been dominated by a conviction that one should only look forward, I'm only tempted to glance back encouraged – as if encouragement were necessary – by the words of a screen goddess with whom I was in love at the age of seventeen, that in looking back one should only remember the good things. Too true.

The Brookside Flying Group was arguably the PFA's first Strut. The Popular Flying Association celebrated its 50th anniversary last year (1996) but in its first few years it was known as the Ultra Light Aircraft Association and my outfit joined the ULAA in 1947. We didn't call it a Strut then for the PFA's word for a branch didn't come into existence until much later, but in all events it was the same Association. If ever there was a DIY flying group it was ours. It wasn't all easy going.

That first Strut, if first Strut it was, sought no outside help. We did our own maintenance. In my mind's eye I can still see us pushing our Maggie out of her tatty blister hangar, her silver sides wet with dew, and eyeing her critically. If she looked lopsided we'd boost her ego and sagging wing with a car footpump and so replenish her seeping pneumatics, and when she looked spritely again, there was a wiggle of controls, a count of plugs, and we were away, often flying before the club on the south side had even opened. The stillness and innocence of those early morning flights are the sort that memories are made of.

Our Miles Magister G-AKRJ arrived on April 17th 1948, some six weeks after we confirmed our order with Rollasons. Part of the delay could be thus accounted:

25/3/48: "No women, no money" (things must have been desperate).

And then:

27/3/48: "Wrote Lord Nathan – protest." (Lord Who?)

10/4/48: "ULAA meeting, Londonderry House. Spoke to Col. Preston. Could hardly say we saw eye to eye."

Quite what we were fighting for all those years ago is now obscure. Permission to operate probably, not everyone wanted us. Nothing changes, does it? Certainly there was no trouble with the Air Ministry, then custodians of the airfield. I well recall phoning the department that looked after civil airfields. The someone at the other end was very supportive. What did I need?

"Well, hangarage first, I suppose, our Maggie is due soon."

He countered: "Is there anything suitable on the north side?" (The south side housed the SCFC who viewed our arrival with dismay bordering on panic.)

I told him of the two blister hangars; the better one of the two already housed Hamilton's Auster, but the farther one, the one nearest to the old gunnery dome, was empty.

"Sounds the thing," he said; "what's its condition?"

Reply: "There are no side screens, cattle use it, and there is some loose roofing."

There was a pause for thought. "Would twenty-five pounds a year fit the bill?"

I agreed.

"What else?"

"Well, there's a large hut not far away which would do nicely for a club house."

The hut (at a guess it was about 35 ft x 30 ft) looked out over the billiard table that was always Shoreham, and was perched just beyond the peritrack and a little stream bridged by a plank.

"Make it fifty pounds," he suggested. "OK?"

His final words could well have marked the zenith of common sense. "Perhaps you would be good enough to let the resident Ministry police know of our arrangement."

I assured him I would. On the anniversary of that verbal agreement I used to send off seventy-five pounds, at least until 1952, no reminders, a simple understanding that worked. The police, a friendly lot, promised to keep an eye on things for us.

I guess I won't be the first to reflect how, once upon a time, a few civil servants did so much, so efficiently and for the common good, and yet still had time for a friendly word.

The hut had once been, so the tale goes, the flight office of a Free French fighter squadron. I recall I painted our name in vast white letters on its side. Until a few years ago the faded inscription could still be seen on a part of the old hut where it had been repositioned alongside the railway line. The last time I looked, I looked in vain. I shrugged; it amazed me that that little bit of history had lasted so long.

But we had fun, we had tragedy too, and bought another Maggie 'KRM to replace the first. We instructed, sent off solos, no one was paid, no one was qualified in the bureaucratic sense, and no one suffered. We occasionally took orphans under our wing. People would just leave them with us. For instance an Aeronca stayed for ages, and it was joined at times by a Fairchild Argus.

One last entry – 29/4/48: "Obtained some 1,300 gallons for three months. We all retired to the [looks like] Hobbled Goose to celebrate."

At a time when motorists were strictly rationed, sometimes only a gallon or two a week, this was a princely allocation. Before making the application I had blithely calculated an annual utilization of five hundred hours (I don't think we ever bettered two hundred). I multiplied that by seven, she was a thirsty beast. It did look an awful lot. With trepidation I visited the Allocating Officer and put my case. He nodded, thought it wouldn't be enough, and upped it.

On reflection we must have been living in cloud cuckoo land but it all happened.

*   *   *

Characters were drawn to our Club like Moths to Woburn. One I recall turned up at Shoreham early in 1949 in a Percival Proctor G-AIIP. Correction: two turned up.

"Come and have a flight/fright," said the first one, Mike Conry.

The second appeared to be his personal pilot, a Persian nicknamed Sinbad. I'd known Mike some time, albeit vaguely. I doubt he held a licence right then, which would account for Sinbad's presence. Mike had earned some infamy a year or two back having crashed a BAC Drone, and the poor fellow had come off badly. He wasn't a hero, but he was treated with a degree of awe at his audacity in even flying the thing. The crash investigators conceded the near-glider, underpowered with its Scott motorcycle engine, hadn't been in an airworthy condition. Apparently that was a calculated understatement. Rumour had it that they had found a bicycle chain and a dead rat in the petrol tank. There was more, but it made a good story at the time.

The Proctor flight, a series of erratic circuits and bumps, was highly different. I thanked them, grateful to be down in one piece, and off they flew to adventures new. Once in a while I wonder what happened to Mike; whatever it was it would have had an Errol Flynn ring about it.

Memories are a bit like characters, they hang around to be recalled with delight at the touch of a log book. One such moment arrived a year earlier.

We hadn't had our Maggie a week before we decided to aerobat it.

"What will it do?" we asked the only person we knew who'd flown one.

Poor Chadwick (he who had collected it for us from Rollasons of Croydon) was a bit nervous in recommending too much. He was a steady fellow, ex-ATA, and I doubt he'd done much experimenting with the aircraft he'd ferried.

"Well," he began, "it doesn't like spinning but it does everything else."

If he'd had the nerve he'd have added "I think."

The year was now 1948, we were young and the spring sunshine brought Shoreham's lush green billiard table of grass to life inviting us to aviate, nay, willing us to get airborne with an urgency that left

17

us breathless.

Our Group's Magister G-AKRJ sat happily just the other side of the little brook beyond our clubroom over on the north side of Shoreham, isolated from the well-established South Coast Flying Club by a nearly unused airfield. All ours. There was no Air Traffic, one just sniffed the grass-scented air and took off, usually from where one clambered aboard.

'KRJ, clad in a simple all-over silver respray, still had the Gosport system of intercom, but even in '48 there was the beginning of a shortage of helmet tubes. I recall I had bought a bundle of thirty pairs from Phil's surplus radio shop off Leicester Square for 1/6 a pair.

"Don't know what they are for," said Phil.

I didn't enlighten him, I figured he'd only have asked more the next time. I sold them on at 3/6 a time. My first business venture, if you discount my distribution of laboriously written copies of a disreputable Byron poem at the age of fourteen.

This isn't really a digression, for the shortage of Gosports led to our first experiment with electric hats. To start with we lashed two huge Leclanché cells into the locker behind the rear seat. (Leclanché cells? Well, I haven't seen one in forty years but they resembled mortar shells, weighed nearly as much and gave out 1½ volts – or was it 3 volts? – just about for ever. People were throwing them out around then as better door-bell systems took their place. Ours – free of course – were probably young in the first World War.) We had yet to wire in the new-fangled electric hats, i.e. standard RAF helmets, so the proposed trip was intercomless, the usual pair of Gosports short.

We promptly took off. A shared trip, this one. The under-standing was that I'd do ten minutes aeros and then Baggy Woodward in the back seat would do his stint. It was a lovely day. Sufficient height, a quick swing 180° either way and nose down for the first loop. The Maggie felt heavy as I heaved back. As we went over the top there was a heavy clunk. I levelled out at the same time Baggy yelled. I throttled back and Baggy's excited voice came forward.

"Something hit me."

I thought, a bird? What on earth could have hit him?

His breathless voice added, "It hit me on the head, I think it's on the floor." A far away voice yelled, "I can see it. I'm undoing my straps, keep it steady."

With a twisting of the head I couldn't repeat today, I peered back and saw his head reappear. He was holding up a black object I recognised – one of the two black cells.

His face was wreathed in a wide grin. "It came through the hole behind my head," he explained. "Hang on while I do my straps up again." Baggy's thumbs-up encouraged me to proceed.

Nose down, I put on speed and again pulled through. There was a second resounding bang. I levelled out and waited for Baggy's voice.

"Bloody hell," he yelled above the slipstream, "it's the other one. I'll pick it up."

"Got it!" he shouted triumphantly.

Now presumably he held a cell in each hand. The two loops were easy, thought I, let's go for a slow roll.

I dived the Maggie firmly to about 120 m.p.h., the air shrieked over the cockpit in protest. Up came the nose, I paused with it just above the horizon – artistic touch, that – and moved the stick firmly to the left and a little forward. I got on ten degrees, clearly heard two thumps and the stick went solid. I couldn't move it in any direction. Bewildered, I throttled back and became aware of someone shouting. The stick eased central and stayed there. I didn't force it but something must be awfully wrong, there was still this strange resistance. The shouting was renewed.

"Stop, stop," Baggy was yelling, "I haven't done my straps up."

We flew back, Baggy had a cell again in each hand ready to drop them at a moment's notice to grab the controls, but I flew gently. He wasn't the only shaken pilot. And yes, we scrapped the cells idea. Providing you can get Gosport tubes the old way is the best.

*   *   *

A few months later, there was another diary entry.

The log book records the date as September 11th 1948, and the remarks column suggests it was a glorious day. A young woman hesitantly approached our Group with a strange request. She carried a sleeping baby in her arms and told us the baby had developed whooping cough. Somewhere, somehow, she had heard that altitude cured whooping cough, tops of mountains and suchlike, and asked if it was true. None of us could answer her for sure but we assured her, if we could help, she'd come to the right place. Her glance upwards and back to our faces said it all. No time like the present, we all agreed.

The still-sleeping child was cocooned in blankets and placed on Joan Wood's lap in the open front cockpit, up near the warmth of the engine. I climbed into the rear and carefully took off and climbed and climbed and climbed. At 9,000 feet both Joan and I were frozen, but the baby, who had rosy cheeks and was cosy in the blankets, slept peacefully. My log book reveals the baby's name to be Pat Lock, boy or girl heaven knows, and I've often wondered what happened to him or her and did the mother one day tell him or her about us. We cruised for a while at this, for us, great height, and then slowly drifted downwards in big gentle spirals into warmer air, the engine noise now muted and rhythmic; it lulled our senses while Pat slept on.

Back safely on the ground Mrs Lock received her still sleepy child back with heartfelt murmurs of thanks and the Group members clustered round happily. Young Pat hadn't coughed the entire trip. Wasn't that proof enough of a cure? We thought so.

It was only later that the thought of publicity entered into our minds and Joan Wood offered to go around the next day to see the Locks and to report straight away to the 'Evening Argus'. A couple of days later Joan returned, somewhat subdued.

"Was Pat better?" we asked excitedly.

She just shook her head and said "'Fraid not; you see, it seems not only has Pat still got whooping cough but the doctor says the child now has pneumonia as well."

*   *   *

One thing general aviation at our end seldom had was the use of a radio. I can't recall any light post-war aircraft with it as standard. No doubt commercial flights used them and even then it was confined to the heavies. Local, and, indeed, European taxi and freight flights flew cheerfully around obeying the simple rules of sound airmanship. Joining circuits was an established procedure dictated by the signals square and an eye open for an Aldis lamp.

There was also a universal understanding that pilots commanded their aircraft. Air Traffic was there to assist. Naturally one obeyed their directions whilst within their orbit: it made sense. Don't forget this is a review of the fifties as seen from a fairly narrow perspective. One could for instance ask what the weather would be like at one's destination and if it was duff the controller would only suggest it wasn't a good time to aviate. The decision was always the pilot's.

It's near pointless discussing the present set-up. Even at a lightly-used aviation centre like Shoreham one must ask these days for permission to start and taxi. Too many weary by-passed airfields have channels filled with radio gabble from groundlings, all busy enjoying the sound of their voices, not the soundness of common sense. No one can turn the clock back, all I can sadly do is tell it as it was. Common sense? What of the American small field friendliness of their communal channel? Open when called for, a sensible back-up, but no substitute for circuit awareness and a pair of eyes. But I digress, let's go back again forty-odd years.

*　　*　　*

Along with a draughty cockpit bare of radio there wasn't much in the way of navigational help. A fifties pilot relied on compass and a well-worn wartime half-million map indecently nude of over-printing. True, there were occasional prohibited areas to fly around, usually small, mostly firing ranges. Even airfields en route were overflown at 2,000 feet. I seem to recall that below that height we had to give the circuit a three mile clearance. Generally we drew a line to our destination with ten minute interval marks and set off to follow it. A simple obvious method in fine weather. If the weather looked duff we could fly with certainty up and down railway lines because our maps showed every line clearly marked single or double track. They went everywhere. Nowadays they are a forgotten species and those that are left are outdated by ADF and GPS. Incidentally we always flew between 1,000 and 1,500 feet along the right hand side of any track – road, rail or river – essential to avoid the fellow coming the other way. Interesting to note we automatically adopted the European right of the road in spite of mere drivers below keeping to their left.

One flight, non-radio and in this case with little help from the map, comes to mind. For me it conjures up the spirit of flying then. My log book records it was in the June of '48.

I was asked by Danny Taylor, who suddenly felt like visiting his friends and family in Scotland, if I'd fly him up there, and would yesterday be too soon? Danny was a tiny man who ran an amusement arcade in Brighton, and he and his sister-in-law, Eileen, were firm supporters of our small club. As usual it was a case of 'no sooner said than done.'

We flew north in our open two-seater, and after stops for fuel at Sywell and Yeadon we pressed on into the gathering dusk above Yorkshire. By now, I'd flown off the South of England map. I hadn't been able to find a North of England map before we left, but Danny's logic that you couldn't miss the Firth appealed to me, and we left without one.

Darkness closed gently about us. There was a full moon and the evening was beautifully still. The land beneath us was ghostly in its pale whiteness, and our Maggie flew herself and her contented passengers into a dreamy state. Sure enough, some two hours after leaving Yorkshire we saw the Firth of Forth in the moon's reflected light, found the bridge, and turned westwards to Grangemouth, our destination.

I had reckoned to arrive in the early evening, but we'd stopped for a chicken supper at Yeadon and it had put our timing back a bit. It was dark over the airfield, but I could just discern the even darker triangle of runways below, but as I dropped lower, I saw too the big white crosses painted on the ends of them. Unserviceable.

Just after the war airfield runways were often used to store munitions, bombs and the like, so no way was I going to land blind on one of them. I eased the throttle and set up an approach on the runway up-moon, aiming to land on the grass alongside. The Maggie sank softly below the tree line, and the moon, low on the horizon, vanished. It left us in Stygian blackness. The grass couldn't have been 80 feet beneath us, so I closed the throttle and eased the stick into first a glide, and then when I thought the moment was right, eased the stick further back . . . and back, and finally right back.

Nothing happened. I could see nothing, there was no instrument lighting, nothing. All I was aware of was the rhythmic bark of the engine up front ticking over. I held the stick fully back and waited. Still nothing happened. Perplexed, I shut off the engine. The black stillness of the night embraced us.

A voice from the back said: "Are we down?"

"I don't know," I said.

We sat there a bit longer and the voice said: "I'll climb out and see."

I said: "Be careful."

There was a sound of Danny undoing his harness and fumbling around.

"I think we are down," he said; "I'm going to jump."

I waited with bated breath. He was only a little bloke, even shorter than me, and the wheat we'd landed in came up to his chest.

From afar came voices and flaming torches as Danny's friends and family ploughed their way to our rescue. I slept soundly that night in a showman's caravan, woken only once, when someone implored me to stop Danny, who couldn't fly, from going on another flight. The full moon was overhead now and probably affecting Danny as much as the whisky.

* * *

The second phase of my fifties flying came about when I finally realised that my company would one day transfer me from the easy reach of Shoreham and the happy weekends spent there. So in good time I offered myself to the RAFVR, confident in the belief that no matter where M & S would send me there would always be a VR airfield within reach.

An unknown W/Cdr. checked me out in a service Tiger – the log book only records it as number 622 – at Woodley, near Reading, in the January of '51. The understanding in the VR was that one flew whenever one could. I seem to remember an annual target of about thirty hours, of which fifteen or so hours was continuous training, a yearly two-week break at the centre of your choice. Board and lodging free and paid to fly into the bargain. Uniforms were seldom worn; it was certainly a golden period.

Since I was now working in departmental stores down in Devon I chose to fly with 10 FTS at Exeter which operated a mixture of Tigers and Chipmunks, aircraft we flew with equal abandon.

Early mornings, and way before the CO was about, we'd wheel out the aircraft and all go bouncing around the dew-covered grass of the airfield collecting mushrooms. I can still hear the staccato roar of Gipsy Major engines bursting on my ears as we flew around in our D.H. Chipmunks, like so many grasshoppers, a few feet from the ground, mushroom spotting, and abruptly the sudden silence broken only by a diminishing whistle as the aircraft sank to rest beside the crouching delicacy, then the rush to clamber over the side to be the first to pick and stuff them down battle-dress blouses. About 8 o'clock we'd be back in the mess urging sleepy white-coated stewards to take our treasure back out to the cook to have them reappear on our plate along with the eggs and bacon.

In 1954 the RAFVR closed down for flying and although the VR staggered on in a grounded form for a couple more years the fun was over. I had put in over a hundred hours in the three years of paid bliss and now I was out on a limb.

The sorry years between '54 and '57 of an ever-travelling assistant M & S manager can be summed up in a total of less than twenty hours. Not that they were dull. With the brief exception of moments in a Dart Kitten and a Proctor they were all Auster time and included two adventures to France. The second was from Croydon to Paris. Even in '57 it was still just get in and go . . . and no radio. The Auster G-ANIL had a Lycoming 125. It needed all of its 125 horses with four of us crammed in.

All I remember of the trip was that we shared the cheapest room we could find in Paris. There were only two beds. I claimed one as the pilot, they tossed for the other. We reckoned what little money we were allowed to take out of the country was better spent in food and fun. We got plenty of both . . . but not much sleep.

CHAPTER 2

BISH YOU WERE HERE

by

CHRIS DEARDEN

[Reproduced from the Miles Magazine No. 5, Vol. 1, March 1993, by courtesy of the Miles Aircraft Collection.]

[NOTES ON THE AUTHOR: Chris Dearden was born at Southsea, Hants on 19th April 1926. During the summer of 1929 the family moved to Crowborough, Sussex and he grew up in the magic expanse of Ashdown Forest – though it was confidently predicted that "the poor little weed won't make adulthood."
Oh, yes?
In 1943 he was apprenticed to Avro in Manchester where he substantially hindered Lancaster bomber production. But poor health cut the arrangement short (no doubt to Avro's relief) and he moved back south to recuperate. After some adolescent indecision and a deal of desperation he took a job as a draughtsman in the Civil Service. On his very first day there he incurred the displeasure of the boss and was tartly advised to seek alternative employment pronto. He found it in the drawing office of the Mullard Research Laboratories at Salfords, Surrey.
About this time (1947) he joined the Redhill Flying Club and in the spring of 1948 gained a pilot's 'A' licence on Miles Magisters (the PPL was introduced the following year and was automatically granted to 'A' licence holders).
Soon he returned to his first love of aeroplanes and went to work for Tiltman Langley Ltd. at Redhill aerodrome. TLL were engaged in contract design work variously for Supermarine, Avro, Blackburn, Vickers, Auster-Beagle etc. Happy days! In addition, the Popular Flying Association invited him to join their gang of volunteer 'design consultants' to help amateur aviators with any design problems; some bizarre ideas had to be looked at sympathetically and then tactfully sunk!
When aircraft design work significantly evaporated he became

Experimental Engineer at a small firm making recording tapes. However, an unexpected take-over, and the resulting office politics, killed off that nice little number rather abruptly. Further desperation took him into civil engineering, where he fitted in about as well as a snowball in Hades. No future there.

In the late 1960s he enjoyed a brief spell of financial independence, so he chucked engineering in favour of writing; he found virtually no financial reward in it but did regain the ability to sleep at nights.

He married in 1970, having met his bride-to-be in 1961 when he took her for a trip in a Tiger Moth – "Tiger Moths can seriously damage your batchelorhood!"

Dorothy and he now live in Worthing where their love story continues.]

It was a lovely afternoon for lounging in the grass and doing nothing. And that's exactly what I was doing. Nothing. The day was 7th July 1951, the place Redhill aerodrome.

The Flying Club was hosting a tea patrol, so, naturally, anyone who was anyone in the club had booked an aeroplane, ready to zoom off and defend the honour of Redhill. 'Seven aircraft seven days a week' was the club slogan and, as I recall, there were five of them on the flight line: three Magisters and two Auster Autocrats, the latter strictly for the criminally insane.

Anyone who was anyone? Well, that left me out for a start. I was a pale youth and the sprog of sprogs. Besides, I couldn't possibly afford to fly that week (so what was new?). I was a poor draughtsman and short of money as well.

So there I was, nought feet, flat on my back in the grass and letting it all happen. Hustle and bustle all around. Expectation. The smell of grass and aviation spirit. Glorious stuff! It's not easy now to convey the atmosphere of a flying club in those days. But even as late as 1951 there was still (for good or evil) a lingering 'wizard prang' feeling in private flying. It was much in evidence at Redhill that afternoon. The place fairly bristled with characters sporting vast moustaches and loud voices – not forgetting the male members of the club as well: 'Tommy' Thompson, Budge, Max, Doc . . .

And then there was Bish, alias C. Nepean Bishop. There was always Bish at week-ends. This time he was whizzing around like a supercharger in a sailplane and singing in a falsetto voice, as he was wont to when he was feeling cheerful – which, mercifully, wasn't very often.

On highdays and holidays, and this was a highday, Bish would amaze the assembled multitude with his party piece of landing a

Magister straight off a stall turn. He'd wait until the circuit was completely clear then beat up the 'drome, downwind and right on the deck. At a precisely judged instant he'd chop the power, pull up steeply over the hedge, stall turn and flop the thing onto the ground with a little blip of throttle. It was a harrowing spectacle, particularly for those who knew how the Magister turned itself into a product of 'The Instant Brick Co.' when it ran out of airspeed (quite unlike the benevolent Tiger Moth). No margin for error with Maggie, and no future for anybody who made one in such a situation.

Not that anyone else was ever likely to try it. Flying discipline at Redhill in those days was strictly enforced. Even to be seen taxying with flaps down was to risk being invited to go and join another club. On an early lesson, preparing to take off, I once left about six inches between the aeroplane and the end of the runway.

Budge's voice, in incredulous mode, came through the Gosport: "You're surely not thinking of taking off from here, are you?"

"Well . . . er . . . um . . . er . . . I was."

Oh no I wasn't! I was made to do a three hundred and sixty degree manoeuvre, reposition the aeroplane 'properly' across wind and go through the 'vital actions' again before I was cleared. They were as tight as that on it. But Bish was . . . well, Bish. There was a different rule book for him. And as far as I know, the fact was never resented by anyone.

Meanwhile, back to the 7th July. Zero hour was approaching. Our defenders had taken off and were dispersing to patrol their allotted areas. A temporary hush had settled on the 'drome. Even Bish had gone quiet. Only the faint burrrr of departing Gipsy Majors ruffled that hallowed air (the Cirrus Minors were, as always, beyond the range of human understanding).

Just one aeroplane remained on the ground. It was a privately-owned Magister, G-AIUA, looking superb in cream finish with scarlet flash and lettering. I wondered idly about it, though I was more concerned with the happy anticipation of the invaders who'd shortly be arriving. A Redhill 'At Home' generally attracted quite a large and varied selection. I continued to lounge in the grass; 'nothing' seemed like a good thing to continue doing just then. But not for much longer!

Suddenly Bish came bombasting by at about Mach 2. Without even pausing or glancing in my direction he pointed and called to me: "Oi, you! You great long streak, get yourself in the back of 'IUA."

Blunt? Certainly. Rude? I think not. Firstly, I am just a nadge short of six feet and in those days weighed well short of ten stone –

26

yer actual British Standard bean-pole; a longish streak, at least. And secondly, Bish was really being very generous in taking pity on me and offering me a free ride (for people like me the offer of a free ride in an aeroplane was – and is – so rare as to be of historic proportion). This was Bish being kind. It was just his abrasive manner which made him not always easy to love. His falsetto singing didn't help either.

But it was neither the time nor the place to split hairs on the matter of manners – or of music! I jumped gladly to it and had strapped and plugged myself into the back of 'IUA before you could say "Fred loves Blossom." Bish duly made his majestic way. In imagination I heard a fanfare of trumpets . . . 'His Royal Nepean-ship will shortly be boarding.' He dumped himself heavily (how else?) in the front seat, a minion wound up the elastic, the routine checks were done, and we were away in search of 'bandits.'

It was an education just to sit there as a passenger and watch. Well, that was it, really; there seemed nothing to watch. The economy of movement on the controls was almost uncanny. And yet we flew, we climbed, we turned. 'IUA not only performed like an angel, she seemed to become an angel in the hands of a master. Sickening!

Bish had decreed that he would patrol the Woodhatch area of Reigate (never mind what anyone else thought), so Woodhatch it was. We stooged and circled and stooged a bit more. Eventually I spotted something and was really only speaking my thoughts aloud when I muttered, "There's something over there . . ."

I was interrupted by a sharp pain in my helmet.

"'Over there'? What do you mean, 'over there'? 'Over there' doesn't tell me anything."

"Er . . . um . . . sorry . . . ten o'clock, level. Estimate range about three miles."

My Lord Bishop turned his mighty gaze in that direction. And 'IUA, as if by divine guidance, turned also. But no trade. It was a Piper Cub, probably from Gatwick, not apparently interested in our caper at Redhill. No need to chase. And so it went. No trade. No invaders chose to fly through our particular patch of sky – a plain truth for which, I think, Bish held me personally to blame!

We'd now been airborne for about forty minutes, and the time slot for the invaders had expired. Everybody home for tea! I could see two or three of the other patrols coming in from various directions to join the circuit. But Bish was still standing off: three, four, five minutes. A horrible thought crept up on me. He's not going to, is he? Not with a delicate sprog on board? He is, you know! The circuit at Redhill was now clear.

'IUA began curving in towards the upwind side of the field, shedding height rapidly, the increasing hiss from her wings saying more than the A.S.I. could ever say. Here she bucked gently through a patch of turbulence, there she responded instantly to a tiny correction from Bish. She was on her tiptoes and dancing downstairs to the music of the wind: a Leading Lady making her entrance.

And what a picture she must have made as she thrashed across the 'drome among the daisies on that summer's afternoon! I wished only that I could have been there on the ground as well to have seen it . . . ! Now, the merest hint of a wiggle with the change of directional trim as Bish chopped the power. It was decidedly past-life-flashing-before-the-eyes time. The downwind hedge was certainly getting prominent before the eyes. Anyone for freshly-chopped firewood . . . ? Then whoops! I seemed to be flat on my back again, a faceful of sky. 'IUA shuddered briefly – or was it me? Sky and earth violently changed places; earth much too close for peace of mind, now dead ahead. There was that hedge again, only going the other way this time.

Then that familiar little kick as the flaps went down, one smooth sweep of the stick, a blip of throttle, and 'IUA hit the ground with all the ferocity of a falling feather . . . The mandatory left turn, flaps up, trim fully tail-heavy and taxi in.

I thanked Bish sincerely for his kindness in having taken me along with him. He grunted and went on his way. After that I had a spot of tea in the clubhouse, then once more lounged on the grass to watch some more of our friendly invaders taking their leave of us. And after that I bicycled back to my digs in rather thoughtful mood.

CHAPTER 3

THE AUSTER THEN AND NOW

by

MIKE STAPP

[Reproduced from International Auster Club News Vol. 2, No. 1, 1979, by kind permission of the Club.]

I first met the Auster at the tender age of 13. I was just big enough, with the aid of cushions, to reach its pedals and see a little of where I was going – or hoped to be going. I discovered a neat little grass airfield and a Flying Club at a Nissen Hut, run by Mr Vic Nightscale and aided by his wife, who made the place homely and did some catering *[this was of course Denham – Ed.]*. They had two Taylorcraft 'D's, a Tiger Moth, a Magister, a Proctor and a (or was it *the*) D.H. 60G Moth Major, with folding wings. All were survivors of the recent war. Flying cost no less than £3 per hour, and there was, soon to disappear, a tax rebate on aviation fuel. Airways were no more than a threat to light aviation, a sort of creeping ivy-like proposal which was to set up places you couldn't fly, and the most common commercial types you met in the sky were the DC-3 or the Viking. Rumour had it that extremely rich people could fly to America from Heathrow, but that was another world. Heathrow still had pleasure flights in Dragon Rapides, just for the record. Even Luton was a pleasant grass airfield, with its bounding hares ... and Tiger Moths. A good place to go for a cross-country. Or perhaps to *Croydon*, the mecca of aviation, where my mother watched Amy Johnson fly home to England.

I bought a pleasure flight in a 'D' and the disease took hold of me. I would learn to fly this thing which had widened my horizons beyond anything I had imagined previously. So I ran errands, mended fences, got a paper round and all sorts of other things. My parents were horrified beyond belief, although my father had actually built Swordfish for Messrs. Fairey at nearby Hayes. Flying was something different, apparently. By the time I was 14, I could somehow get the 'D' off the ground, round a circuit and down within the confines of the airfield. My instructor, Lew Pond, a former racing cyclist of some Olympic fame, survived all this without nervous breakdown. He went on to enter the Daily Mail air race [in 1959 – Ed.], making the cheapest time from London to Paris by bike and Turbulent, about 30/-. Of course, I could not think of going solo for years, but I did my spins in the Tiger Moth and remember seeing in the distance a D.H. Comet, which everyone said would change the whole aviation scene. By this time, I was reasonably proficient on the 'D', not having to bother about flaps, radio, or anything beyond its very few instruments and the manner in which it hit the ground. We were called "Bucks Flying Group" and the parties in the Nissen Hut were unparalleled anywhere else, certainly not since.

A firm called Rotax actually sponsored employees to learn flying! Imagine that now. I bought a big cumbersome Dalton computer from the Club and set about learning to navigate, along with a book, reduced to 2/6 on W.H. Smith's stall. It was called "Teach Yourself to Fly" and centred on the super-new Chipmunk. About that time someone flew an Auster under Tower Bridge, G-AJZH, I think. Can't be sure [it was actually G-AGYD, G-AJZH was a Hawk Trainer – Ed.]. Ours were G-AHUG & G-AIIU, which was written off (I soloed 'HUG).

The management were prepared to risk me cleaning their aircraft and even help the late Herbert Lawrence maintain them in a small way. So I learned about the innards of the Auster airframe and the Cirrus Minor engine. When I was 16, it was considered a good idea for me to do some gliding, since I could theoretically solo a whole year before that was possible on the 'D'. It took a winter of saving up from my paper round for a week's flight course at London Gliding Club, Dunstable, which had recently been a POW camp. It cost me all of £13 and as soon as I was 16, I was spending it, learning on the barge-like T.21. I eventually soloed, having also become an ATC cadet and risen to gliding by that route also. The ATC, by the way, was a really air-minded affair in those days, and cadets droned about the sky for hours in the right-hand seats of Ansons, just for the asking. There were also a lot of Chipmunks, replacing the aged Tiger, and many 'desk-job' officers were anxious to keep flying. In fact, almost all the instructors and pilots of the day were very experienced on a lot of military types and this reflected in the Clubs, too.

The magic day when I would be 17 approached. It was a horrible winter and it rained so much that the airfield disappeared beneath a sheet of water. Members spoke of fitting floats to the hard-working 'D's on which the basic instruction was almost always done. I was 17 and 3 weeks when the airfield would bear the weight of an aeroplane. One day, I was sent flying with a Gp. Capt. Carey, who appeared in a very authoritative RAF flying suit and sat quietly while I did my best to convince him of my abilities. I managed three landings and broke nothing. I was still rather surprised when he got out, saying something about my chances of survival, then walked away across the field without looking back.

"He can't do that to me . . . I'm not ready to fly this thing on my own . . . well, perhaps I might manage it . . . it's almost the same as if he was in this very empty-looking seat beside me . . . am I going to sit here all day with this engine ticking over, and everyone looking at me? Got to do something . . ."

And so I brought the various nerves under command and taxied back to the marker on the fence. I don't know what Gp. Capt. Carey weighed, but the 'D' leapt into the sky in about half the previous distance. I was taken totally by surprise, reaching circuit height long before I really wanted to. Some voice in my ear was saying "Watch your airspeed" quite often, as I tried to follow the same route as before round past gravel pits, the railway and the golf course. About that time, it occurred to me that perhaps I was just a bit hasty in taking off, and had I really considered that it was totally up to me how I came down again, and where? I got lined up on the approach, the few checks done. "Be very careful about trimming," prompted a voice from my previous few hours instruction. I groped with the little lever between the seats and the 'D' was happy at about 55 m.p.h. I passed the boundary and floated . . . and floated. It never did this before. This airfield really was *small*. Could a 'D' without two people in it really be fitted into such a space? Of course it could, Carey would never have sent me to do anything impossible . . . or was he just growing two little horns and a forked tail, grinning at me from the Clubhouse, holding a trident? I'd show him. *Next* time, this thing would land, not just land, but gracefully. I roared skywards, trying to look as if I was using the discretion of maturity, not just correcting a horrible, juvenile mistake, a difficult air to put over from the noisy confines of a 'D'. How much fuel left?

"Suppose I *can't* get this down, what then . . . ? Course you can, its only a glider with an engine. You've soloed a glider, so what's different about this? Its heavier, it ought to land better, not this horrible floating on for ever. Why doesn't it have flaps or something? Should I try the approach slower? No, they said 50 m.p.h. only for very calm and hot days, not much like today," so 55 it was, and I aligned the thing again on a much longer, delicately adjusted, approach poised on a razor-edge of nervous hope. I was a bit lower over the fence, seemed to hang in the air for ages, but the wheels touched; stick right back to that big triangular metal clip in the Sutton harness, and then . . . the rudder worked. Light as a ballet-dancer, they said it had to be. I did Swan Lake, Les Sylphides and other choice selections whilst rather consciously running out of airfield. "*Mustn't* use the brakes hard, propellers are terribly expensive!" But it stopped. Waves of relief had to be put aside, as I still had to taxi in to the pumps, trying to look as if I had done this hundreds of times. I parked into wind like a good student should and went into the Clubhouse, a real pilot at last. They were very nice to me about it.

I later went on to learn about the Chipmunk, at vast public expense, in which instructors had to be called "Sir" and wrote highly confidential reports about you to those who had the power of flight or earth-bound condemnation over you. For ever after, however, the Taylorcraft 'D' has a very special place in my memory and log book. It was the aeroplane in which my ambition grew from hope to achievement.

In later years, when teaching students on all sorts of Austers, the very nicest thing about it is to pass that on to the next generation of pilots, and the next . . .

Of course, other students, learning on Cessna and the like, say: "It must be so *difficult* learning on that . . . how do you manage it?" I think back to when I was only 14 and the Americans could not export to the UK. The Cessna 150 hadn't been invented. We flew the 'D' because it was there. It wasn't difficult or easy, by any standards we knew about. It was just there . . . to be flown and mastered. Some day we might be allowed to fly a Proctor (which cost around £300 surplus) or even a *Gemini*, with two of those (fortunately) infallible Cirrus engines. Ah . . . ambition!

CHAPTER 4

THE TALE OF TWO MAGGIES

by

TIM WEBB

It was early in 1950 and I had just begun a three-year Diploma course at the College of Aeronautical Engineering in London. My fellow students were a mixed bag, some, like myself, recently demobbed after doing two years or so with the RAF, while others were from overseas from places like India and Pakistan.

We used to forgather at a little pub in the King's Road, Chelsea, and one evening a familiar face emerged from the crowd. It was Chris de Vere, whom I had known from school days at Lancing College in Sussex. He and I had been fellow aeroplane spotters watching the 'planes at nearby Shoreham, but I had not seen him since. We exchanged pleasantries, but little did I guess how that chance encounter would lead to a fascinating chain of events.

Several weeks later we met again at the same pub and Chris announced that he would shortly be joining me at the College of Aeronautical Engineering. But more importantly he had this plan to recover a certain Miles Magister G-AJDR, on which he had learned to fly at the Gloucester Flying Club in 1948. It seemed that the Club at Staverton had fallen on hard times, and that the Magister had been sold to a local scrap dealer, H. Buckland, where it was sitting in his yard with its wings stacked nearby.

Chris wanted to get it to Blackbushe, where he had formed an association with Doug Bianchi of Personal Plane Services. Chris already had another Maggie G-AKMU at Blackbushe, but it had been damaged in a night landing at Weston-super-Mare in November 1949. I think Chris was motivated to get 'JDR for spares more than anything as it was going for a song.

So a very devious plan was hatched that night to drag 'JDR tail-first on its wheels all the way to Blackbushe! A friend had offered the services of his Wolseley and he was sure it had the power. The fact that the Maggie was considerably wider than the car across the centre section did not seem to worry anyone. Time was the essence

33

of the plan as the scrap dealer wanted the space and was planning to torch the Maggie, so early the following Saturday the Wolseley headed out of London bound for Staverton. There were four of us in the team: Chris, myself, and two of his friends whose names I have long since forgotten. However some photos of the trip have survived and one day the identities may be revealed, although Chris himself is no longer with us. I suppose we would have been dubbed 'irresponsible students' at the time, but the story of the trip still makes good reading. We reached Staverton without incident around noon and found 'JDR still intact on its wheels. However the wings were in such poor condition we decided to abandon them.

Interestingly, in the same yard there was a Miles Martlet on a trailer, minus wings, and I took a photo for the record. However I have to admit that I did not recognise it at the time as a Martlet, and it is only recently that I have rediscovered the photo which shows that it was G-AAYX, which is now being rebuilt by the Shuttleworth Trust.

We hitched 'JDR onto the Wolseley's boot with rope around the tail wheel, the rudder was put into the cockpit and off we went. At first things went well, with 'JDR following faithfully behind us much to the interest of all. However it was a winter's evening and all too soon we began to run out of daylight. Crossing the Marlborough Downs out of Swindon, we pulled up to fit a bicycle lamp covered in a red cloth as a makeshift rear light for 'JDR. We were just about to start off again when a car came racing up behind us and very nearly collided with 'JDR. The driver roundly abused us for poor lighting, but then drove on. It was sheer madness to continue, but there was nowhere to park 'JDR, so we pressed on. After Newbury we took to the side roads, striking cross-country for Blackbushe down narrow country lanes. Just ten miles short of our destination we rounded a bend to encounter the local policeman on his bicycle approaching us over a narrow bridge. Our driver accelerated past the policeman and I looked back just in time to see him topple from his bicycle over the bridge parapet! Needless to say, we did not stop until we entered a darkened Blackbushe airfield, with 'JDR miraculously intact.

Next morning Doug Bianchi found he had acquired another Maggie overnight, albeit without wings. The perpetrators of this bit of skulduggery had left the area for London fearing enquiries from the local police, but none ever came.

Work began on 'JDR soon after and my task was a rebuild of the tail wheel attachment where the glued joints had failed in the structure. All the next summer we slaved away, and it was a real labour of love in our 'hangar,' a former wartime Nissen Hut. As students we had very little money but enormous enthusiasm, and I used to ride a bicycle all the way from London to Blackbushe and back most weekends. Such dedication!

Doug Bianchi had a Magister G-AIUE which was flown by all and sundry including his mechanic 'Titch' who was theoretically undergoing *ab initio* training. As part of his solo experience he used to fly over to Woodley (where he lived) for lunch, and a 'quickie' with his wife, as he put it! No doubt this was logged as a solo local flight, but eventually Doug got a call from someone in the Ministry of Civil Aviation and 'Titch' had his wings clipped somewhat.

David Ogilvy (now of the Shuttleworth Trust) was a frequent visitor in those days and he often flew G-AIUE. If I remember correctly he even offered to teach me to fly if I paid for the petrol, but I was just too poor at the time. It was an opportunity that never came my way again . . .

G-AIUE was to distinguish itself with a forced landing on the hallowed turf at Sandhurst, as recounted in an article by George Hilder in the *'Miles Magazine'* of October 1996.

One of the other events which occurred at Blackbushe at around this time was the return to the U.K. of the famous Mew Gull G-AEXF which had belonged to Alex Henshaw before the war. Doug Bianchi had organised a rescue mission to Lyons in France where the Gull had been hidden from the Germans during the war. The engine had to be re-installed and nobody knew if it would even run. But they got it going and the new owner, Hugh Scrope, decided to fly it back to Blackbushe for a complete overhaul although he had never flown the type before. We waited for him to arrive with mounting tension, but finally he was seen approaching and circled the airfield with a very interested audience. He made a good approach but 'porpoised' it onto the ground much to our alarm; however he finally made it down in one piece. My photo of its arrival made it into 'FLIGHT' the following week.

Back to 'JDR. Eventually it was decided to use the wings of 'KMU to get 'JDR completed, and I secured a photo with the composite 'plane with dual registrations. The aircraft was then transferred by road (on a lorry this time) to Redhill where Chris and I were both doing the practical sections of our Course.

Things progressed fairly rapidly at this stage and the first test flight loomed. 'JDR looked resplendent in a silver respray and one of our fellow students, by the name of Paul I think, offered to carry out the first flight as Chris was away in Spain on holiday. I should have resisted the temptation to see it fly and waited for his return. But I was persuaded that it would be just a quick circuit to check out systems.

The take-off was faultless and he climbed away in style. The aircraft performed beautifully and our pilot did some mild aerobatics before returning. At the top of a stall turn the motor cut, and, despite his best efforts, would not restart. We could not see what had happened and the first indication of trouble was his rather low approach. In fact he was trying to stretch the glide to reach the airfield, but had to put down in a hay field just outside the boundary. The subsequent encounter with a thick hedge at the end of the field pulled him up safely but did enormous damage to both leading edges. Our pilot had left the 'plane by the time we found it and we had a few anxious moments searching the hedgerow for him!

Once more 'JDR was towed home on the boot of a car, with the wings strapped along each side: a sad little procession into Redhill and the end of our endeavours. Subsequently the Redhill Flying Club bought the remains and as the fuselage was relatively untouched the registration G-AJDR continued on as one of the Redhill fleet.

CHAPTER 5

MEMORIES OF A NATIONAL SERVICEMAN AT CHRISTCHURCH

by

PETER AMOS

[NOTES ON THE AUTHOR: Peter Amos was born at Redhill in Surrey on the 7th August 1930 and his lifelong interest in aeroplanes started at the tender age of nine when he persuaded his father to take him to the last Empire Air Day to be held at Kenley in May 1939.

Following demobilisation from National Service he spent a year as a junior draughtsman with de Havilland Aircraft in their Regent Street, London, Drawing Office working on 'production-ising' the Heron, followed by eight very happy years at Redhill aerodrome with Tiltman Langley Laboratories Ltd. working on the Ambassador, Swift, Supermarine 545 and 525. Then with Avro on the S.A.A.F. Shackleton Mk.3 and Vulcan. Work on the Saro Skeeter took him to Hamble where in 1959 he joined Sir W.G. Armstrong-Whitworth Aircraft Ltd. to work on the Avro 748. After A.W.A. amalgamated with Follands in 1960 he joined Flight Development at Chilbolton working on the Gnat Trainer for the RAF before moving with the Department to Dunsfold in 1961. After 14 years at Dunsfold he left the aircraft industry for pastures new and eventually found a niche in general insurance.

His love affair with Miles aircraft can be traced back to the last Miles Open Day at Woodley which he attended on Sunday, 20th July, 1947. A member of Air-Britain since its formation in 1948, he is an active Specialist Member on Miles Aircraft, the ATA and Folland Aircraft for more years than he cares to remember.

On 29th March 1993 he was instrumental in forming the Miles Aircraft Collection which is dedicated to the preservation and restoration of aircraft built by Phillips and Powis Aircraft Ltd. and Miles Aircraft Ltd.]

To start at the beginning – always a good place when you don't how to. At the prime of my life when I should have been seriously thinking of carving out a career for myself, it became obvious that I would have to do at least 18 months in the service of His Majesty's something-or-other, so I began to give serious thought as to how it could be done without wasting the time completely.

The RAF was still full of pilots left over from the war so there was little chance of becoming a National Service pilot and I had no desire to be a cook or nondescript aircraft hand just to be near aircraft, so somewhat against my better judgement I signed on for the Army, a desperate and sobering thought!

In those far off days, it was considered essential by the 'powers that be' to declare at least three choices of regiment and, having finally decided that I would eventually like to become an engineering draughtsman, I put my first choice as the Royal Electrical & Mechanical Engineers with the trade of Mechanical Draughtsman, but with about as much hope of fulfilling either of those aims as becoming a pilot. I can't remember my second and third choices now but they were probably the Royal Engineers and the Royal Army Ordnance Corps.

Be that as it may, I signed on at the Labour Exchange sometime after my 18th birthday in August 1948. I duly had my medical examination somewhere later and then waited in fear and trepidation to do my duty for King and Country – although on reflection, how I could have been expected to influence world events I just could not imagine. I wasn't particularly looking forward to joining up anyway and I waited and waited and waited for the dreaded brown OHMS envelope to drop on the doormat.

Autumn gave way to winter and eventually the brown envelope arrived. To my amazement, I had been granted my first choice of regiment! I was to report to the No.1 Training Depot, REME at Blandford in Dorset on 6th January 1949 to commence my six weeks basic training and induction into the ways of the British Army. I was to be a 'Pongo' or 'Brown Job' as we were affectionately called, and was to spend the next six weeks in abject misery in the middle of a very cold and frosty winter, perched on the top of a very high hill in the middle of nowhere, being shouted at and treated as though I had arrived totally unnecessarily into this world without the benefit of parents! This from a relatively sheltered life as an only child was something totally unexpected. I thought that I had prepared myself for this change of lifestyle by Youth Hostelling all round the country on a bicycle and 'roughing it' during the previous year but how wrong I was! It is difficult to imagine such a place could ever have existed in that day and age.

The significance of having been kept waiting was to become apparent during the period at Blandford when we were told that we were to be the first National Servicemen to get caught, not for two years continuous service but for eighteen months straight service and four years on the 'Supplementary Reserve' as it was to be called. This not unnaturally concerned us, as after eighteen months we wanted nothing further to do with the bloody army – and we had not even started yet!

What it actually meant was that after demob we would have to keep most of our kit and return to 'active service' for two weeks each year for a further four years – we were definitely not amused!

Imagine my surprise therefore when, after having been finally kitted out at the Quartermaster's Stores, bundled unceremoniously into an ancient wooden hut with both arms full of all our 'essentials' and allocated a bed space near a window, I saw on the far distant skyline a row of Lancastrians. Was I hallucinating already? Was there after all within eyesight, something to help me to keep my sanity in this concentration camp?

Although I had not realised it, Sir Alan Cobham's Flight Refuelling Ltd. had moved to Tarrant Rushton airfield in 1948 and it was his Lancastrian tankers which I could see from my window. Flight Refuelling Ltd. had been heavily involved in the Berlin Air Lift since it started on 28th June 1948 and as it was still in full swing I realised that if I wasn't very careful, I could so very easily find myself caught up in part of the 'cold war' and I didn't fancy this one little bit! On the very first Sunday that we were allowed out of camp I hot-footed it to Tarrant Rushton, which had played such an important role in the invasion of Europe nearly five years earlier.

The Lancastrians had looked relatively close when viewed from the window of my hut but to get there entailed descending to the bottom of a valley, crossing the river Tarrant and then climbing to the plateau on the next hill on which sat the airfield. In a hangar was the red and silver Hornet Moth G-AESE, but unfortunately I could not go round the hangars due to the presence of the company police.

After Blandford I was posted to No.27 Command Workshops at Warminster in Wiltshire where I was to spend the next few months, during the course of which I was promoted from Private to Craftsman Class III on 25th May 1949, having passed my first Trade Test.

On 12th June 1949, whilst on a 48-hour pass, I managed a visit to R.A.F. Kenley where the Surrey Air Pageant was taking place and amongst the events were 'Flying demonstrations by JET aircraft' – quite a novelty in those days – this consisting of three Gloster

Meteor F.3s from West Malling! The ATC also gave gliding displays and some Spitfires arrived, probably from Biggin Hill.

Back in camp and still very 'browned off' with my lot, I thought that the time had come to get the hell out of Warminster and its hostile populace. So on Sunday 10th July I boarded a Royal Blue coach and departed to Bristol with Filton being the ultimate goal. After a long bus ride from town I was somewhat disappointed not to see the 'Brabazon' but there were Bristol Freighters, a number of near-derelict ex-RAF Beaufighters, a few new RAF Brigands and one of only two Brigands for the Pakistan Air Force.

Then quite unexpectedly, when I had just about given up any hope of ever escaping from Warminster, my posting was announced on Standing Orders, along with one other of my breed, Draughtsman Mechanical, Class III: I was to be posted to the SRDE (MOS), Christchurch, Hampshire.

This posting intrigued and excited me but no one could throw any light on the meaning of the initials, let alone what might be entailed by the job there. The good news was that there were no known military 'concentration camps' in the vicinity of Christchurch and it was certainly not a garrison town. MOS obviously stood for the Ministry of Supply, who were running all the military technical establishments at the time, so it had to be a civilian establishment, presumably with a military detachment. Detachments were considered to be the ultimate posting as usually discipline was more lax!

Now, for all of you who are wondering what all this has to do with the title of this epistle, your patience is about to be rewarded!

Friday, 26th July 1949 – the big day – dawned. I was about to leave the dreaded Warminster for sunnier, and hopefully, happier climes. I had completed over 6 months of my 18 month 'sentence' and I felt that perhaps, after all, my lot was about to improve – it certainly could not get any worse! The day got off to a bad start however when some thieving swine stole our last week's pay packets before we left Warminster, but eventually we arrived at Bure Homage, a delightfully run-down Georgian mansion at Mudeford situated just off the eastern edge of what we were soon to discover was Christchurch airfield. This was not at all what we had expected; there we were, clean, smart and bloody useless when all of a sudden we were moved back in time. Bure Homage was a requisitioned and very shabby mansion that didn't look as if it had ever been cleaned since God knows when. The cookhouse (kitchen) was closed and in those days we were always hungry, so we took the Duty Corporal's advice and went home for the weekend.

Before we left however, with admittedly not too many ideas as to how we were to cover the 100-plus miles home, we did discover the meaning of the initials SRDE These stood for Signals Research and Development Establishment and this was a very top secret place engaged in . . . ?? We would have to wait until after the August Bank Holiday to find out!

On our return to Bure Homage we were introduced to a seasoned REME Corporal whose first question was: "I hope that you two are Draughtsmen (Electrical) as we are desperately short of them to assist in the preparation of new service instruction manuals for the new signals and communication equipment which is being developed here."

At least we now knew what they did if nothing else! When we told him we were Draughtsmen (Mechanical), he nearly threw a fit. For a terrible moment we thought that he would have us sent back but they were desperate so he decided to keep us. Perhaps they should have requested Draughtsmen (Mechanical), then they would probably have got what they wanted.

We cycled to work round the northern outskirts of the airfield as the SRDE, although sharing a corner of the airfield with Airspeeds, did not have any entrance onto it. It is interesting to relate that Bure Homage, which adjoined the airfield and which was connected to it by a rough track, had once been home to the officers of the 405th Fighter Group, 84th Fighter Wing of the 9th Tactical Air Command, USAAF, who had flown P.47 Thunderbolts from there during the summer of 1944.

I soon became interested in both the activities of Airspeeds over the other side of the airfield and what appeared to be a flying club operating out of a couple of old wooden army huts on the southern edge of a copse, which divided the airfield into two parallel sections running roughly north-south. The longer grass N/S runway on the eastern side had been laid down in 1943 by the U.S. 833 Engineering Battalion to give the P.47s a slightly better chance of becoming airborne with their 2,000 lb bomb loads. The other original N/S grass strip in front of the Airspeed works and the E/W strip at the southern end were far too short for such heavy fighter-bombers.

During this long hot, glorious summer, Airspeeds were busily engaged in the flight-test programme of their new post-war airliner, the Airspeed Ambassador. This was without doubt a most beautiful looking, twin piston-engined, high-wing, triple-finned job, which was also their first excursion into the design and manufacture of large metal aircraft, having previously built the Oxford advanced trainer, Horsa glider and latterly the de Havilland Mosquito which were all of wooden construction.

41

I felt it a privilege even then, I remember, to witness the beginning of the trials and tribulations of the entry into service of a brand new airliner, and Airspeeds certainly had their fair share of them. I remember one incident very well when I heard the first prototype Ambassador, G-AGUA, passing over with its normally smooth and sweet-running Bristol Centaurus engines (an unmistakable sound) making a different noise which drew our attention to the fact that all was not well. I recall that we saw flames streaming from the starboard engine to a considerable length behind the wing, but a faultless landing soon followed. George Errington, the Chief Test Pilot, and Ron Clear, his assistant, were both of exceptional ability and we heard nothing further of the incident. All in a day's work and we noted that G-AGUA was soon flying again.

Airspeeds were also overhauling Horsa gliders, but their biggest problem in flight-testing them was the lack of communication between George Errington and Bob Milne, who generally flew the Halifax A.9 Tug, and Ron Clear who usually piloted the Horsa. Hair-raising stories were told to us of an incident which had occurred only a few months before our arrival at Bure Homage, in which an undercarriage leg from a Horsa (which was 'fixed' for these trials, although it was jettisonable in service) parted company shortly after it had become airborne. Ron realised what had happened immediately but he could not communicate with George as the R/T was unserviceable. Their flight plan, which had been worked out months before and used many times with no problems, unfortunately took no account of such an eventuality as the inadvertent jettisoning of an undercarriage leg. So, despite much wing-waggling at the end of the line in an attempt to attract George's attention to his plight, Ron was towed inexorably to the predetermined point of drop and released.

What neither pilot knew at this stage was that the heavy undercarriage leg with wheel attached had fallen onto the edge of the airfield and bounced, landing the second time on a school, penetrating the roof. The pupils were lucky not to have been underneath the ensuing wreckage and no one was injured. Ron was then left with the prospect of landing the Horsa on two wheels because, needless to say, the nose wheel and the other main leg refused to jettison, but this he carried off apparently with no problems or damage to himself or the Horsa.

The locals must have been very wary of the activities at Christchurch by this time, because in 1944 a fully laden USAAF Thunderbolt had attempted to take off on the newly-laid runway, run into difficulties and crashed into a bungalow on the southern boundary of the airfield.

However, the summer of 1949 could only be described as idyllic. The weather was perfect and the evenings and weekends were spent swimming in the bay, cycling around the locality and getting to know the place: late suppers in 'Joy's Café,' just at the junction of Mudeford Lane with the main Christchurch Road (now a Little Chef and hardly recognisable) or 'Bert's,' if one got fed up with the flavour of the egg and chips – we were always hungry!

On consulting my old diaries I note that I did not see many aircraft visit Christchurch, but this was due to the fact that apart from tea and lunch-breaks I was slaving away over my drawing board in a Nissen Hut. I have since discovered, looking through the airfield log books, that many movements were in fact recorded in connection with both Airspeeds and visiting aircraft.

Airspeed Oxfords, Consuls (including G-AHEF) and de Havilland's Leopard Moth G-ACMN were frequent visitors on business from the Portsmouth and Hatfield factories of the company. The first visitor I recorded was Intava's Percival Proctor 5, G-AHZY, which called on 13th August 1949. On 14th August I visited Hurn where BOAC had their training facility and, as the new Canadair C-4 was being introduced into service, these were to be seen grinding round the circuit all afternoon. The Speedbird Flying Club, for members of BOAC, BEAC and BSAAC, had a section based there with the two Hawk Trainers, G-AKKS and G-AKKV, and these were usually to be seen 'circuit bashing'. BOAC were also experimenting with new colour schemes and had painted their York G-AGJC midnight blue overall with white registrations. It landed while I was there but the colour scheme never caught on and it reverted to silver later.

The Autocrat G-AIBM was noted, but not having the benefit of binoculars in those days, I missed a Gemini painted in Miles' cream with green trim, three silver Yorks over on the BOAC side on the western perimeter, two Lancastrians and two Canadairs, all belonging to BOAC.

Christchurch on 17th August 1949 produced the Miles Falcon G-ADFH and I noted about this time the Horsa RN343. The Halifax A.9 tug I later discovered to be RT935. The fuselage of Horsa RN371 appeared on the airfield about this time and it was rumoured to have been for use as a clubhouse, but for whom I never discovered.

After work on the 17th I cycled over to Hurn where I noted no less than four BOAC Yorks, one Tudor (in storage), one BOAC Lancastrian, four BOAC Canadairs, five MCA Consuls, one Dove and the two Hawk Trainers of the Speedbird Flying Club.

On 21st August 1949 I decided to cycle to the Air Races at Thruxton, which was some 40 miles away, a mere local run for a keen, fit(?), young and very enthusiastic 'Life Member' of the new Air-Britain. It was well worth the trip and brought back memories of my first visit there the year before when a friend and I had cycled and Youth Hostelled to Land's End (and back) over the course of a fortnight, taking in as many airfields as possible on the way. Gone now were the 48-plus Horsa gliders which had been abandoned by the RAF off the western perimeter, but it was a good event witnessed by some 6,000 spectators.

The main event was the Thruxton open handicap race over a 72 mile course from the aerodrome to Totland Bay in the Isle of Wight and back. The winner, out of a field of 23 aircraft, was D. Jemmett in a Miles Magister, which averaged 140 m.p.h., second was Tommy Rose flying a G.A. Cygnet and third was Flt. Lt. J. Thompson in another Miles Magister. The fastest time was set by Ron Paine in his Miles Hawk Speed Six with an average speed of 188.75 m.p.h. and the runner-up was Ian Forbes in the Miles Nighthawk at 155.75 m.p.h. There was also a race for Miles Magisters and this was won by Ron Paine. The Air Display included a parachute descent by Gwynn Johns, the Skeeter flown by H.A. Marsh and a Sikorsky flown by an army pilot. Ranald Porteous gave his usual demonstration of aerobatics and a cross-wind landing in Auster's demonstrator fitted with a Goodyear castoring undercarriage.

It was also during that summer that I discovered SHULAC. These wondrous initials stood for the South Hants Ultra Light Air Club, and this, it transpired, was the flying club in the army huts. They used an Auster J/1 Autocrat, G-AIPX, which was owned by J.C. Hayland, a member of the club, but on Sunday 18th September 1949, whilst I had been over to Hurn to see what was going on, tragedy struck. Mr. Hayland was being taught to fly by an instructor who was apparently not over-endowed with patience and, on reflection, must therefore have been a lousy instructor. On this particular occasion the owner, having made a mistake or not fully understanding his instructions, had had the control apparently wrested from his grasp by the instructor (whose name escapes me), probably with words being spoken such as "I'll bloody well show you how to fly and I have control" and who then promptly, from far too low an altitude, proceeded to put the Autocrat into a spin (by accident or design) from which it never recovered. Autocrats were essentially touring aircraft and were not cleared for aerobatics, and should not therefore have been spun in the first place, but in the ensuing crash onto the airfield, in full view of the remaining members of the club and a few of the mob at Bure Homage who were watching the performance, the two occupants lost their lives and G-AIPX was written off.

It was about this time that I discovered a small hangar just off the southern edge of Christchurch airfield, at the end of Warren Avenue. This had once been the flight shed for Portsmouth Aviation Ltd who had been refurbishing Oxfords for the RAF during the war. It was now being used by No. 171 ATC Squadron who numbered amongst its cadets one John Pothecary, although I did not realise it at the time.

Also in residence was Pat Parker, a charming Licensed Ground Engineer who had been in the A.T.A. during the war. She was working on several aircraft including the Avro Cadet G-ADFD which was owned by Flt. Lt. Ron E. Hayter, C.O. of the ATC Squadron and Alec C. Leith, an ex-RFC pilot who worked at Airspeeds, and it was Alec who had been instrumental in forming SHULAC a couple of years earlier. However the Cadet was destined never to fly again.

I seem to recall that another inmate of this hangar also receiving Pat's attentions was a Cub-type aeroplane which could have been the Taylorcraft Model A G-AFJP. This was later to achieve fame with SHULAC as being the most successful non-flying aircraft ever to have been owned by the club!

My diary recorded a big event in the West Country on the 4th September 1949 when the giant Bristol Brabazon G-AGPW made its maiden flight from Filton. Then on the 17th September I cycled to R.A.F. Beaulieu in the New Forest to attend the last Battle of Britain Display to be held there before it closed.

Beaulieu was home to the Airborne Forces Experimental Establishment who put on a very good display and the Command fly-past consisted of Yorks, Lincolns and Meteors before the American Superfortresses arrived. Sqdn. Ldr. 'Jeep' Cable showed what could be done with a Bristol helicopter, including engine-off landings, and seen for the first time in public was the new technique developed by Flight Refuelling Ltd. when one of their Lancaster tankers appeared with a Meteor linked by the refuelling hose. The Meteor then broke away overhead the airfield.

The famous circus of performing Hoverflies disguised as elephants was put through its paces, and at the end of the act the Cierva Air Horse arrived and disgorged a herd of pantomime ponies, which after amusing the crowd with their antics were lassoed and taken round to collect for the RAF Benevolent Fund. High-speed aerobatics by the Meteor and Vampire were contrasted with low-speed aerobatics by the Hawker Tomtit and Comper Swift.

45

Mike Lithgow then arrived at high speed and nought feet in the swept-wing Supermarine 510 before putting it through its tremendous paces. A great day and well worth the ride.

Monday 19th September saw Viking VL247 of the King's Flight fly into Christchurch from Hurn with the Duke of Edinburgh on board, presumably to visit Airspeeds. Then on Sunday the 2nd October the Zaunkoenig G-ALUA arrived for appraisal by SHULAC Group No.10. It was owned by the Ultra Light Aircraft Association and was doing the rounds of the ULAA clubs. SHULAC's pilots weren't very impressed by the performance of this aircraft which was exceedingly safe but oh! so slow. One pilot complained that, although he didn't mind being overtaken by an Austin Seven in the New Forest, he felt a mite put out when he was overtaken by a brace of inquisitive ducks! The Christchurch log records that a 'German Moth' was flown by George Miles and George Errington on 6th October so it can be assumed that they must have flown the Zaunkoenig also. It was also during the autumn of 1949 that Tommy Marshall and Ted Gould appeared on the scene and began breathing new life into the dispirited and aeroplaneless club.

At 10 a.m. on Monday, 7th November, 1949, a strange noise caused us to lay down our pencils and rush outside to peer into a bright blue sky for the source of the sound. This materialised as the eight Centaurus engines of the Bristol Brabazon G-AGPW and it made a very impressive and majestic sight as it crawled across the sky, looking for all the world like a winged airship. On Sunday 13th November I decided to cycle to Stoney Cross airfield in the New Forest. The cows were grazing between the runways but I recall a T.2 hangar on the western side which was full of Auxiliary Fire Fighting Trailers, although little evidence of its previous occupation by the Stirlings of Transport Command remained. I did however find an instrument panel in a ditch behind one of the hangars but could not identify its owner.

It was whilst cycling down the main runway that I received the fright of my life: a jet noise caused me to look over my shoulder to find one of the blue Canberra prototypes diving at high speed, apparently directly at me! I was off that runway like greased lightning and I swear I could see the grin on the pilot's face as he returned to Boscombe Down, from whence he had obviously come.

Wednesday 16th November brought Argus G-AJST to Christchurch while a Boeing B.29 Superfortress 9781 flew over, being air-to-air refuelled by Lancaster III tanker G-33-2 (ex-PB972) 'George Two' of Flight Refuelling Ltd. from Tarrant Rushton.

The rest of 1949 was quiet, but following Christmas leave I returned to Bure Homage on 1st January 1950 wondering what the

New Year would bring. The Brabazon flew over again on the 16th but the big event of the month was to occur on Saturday the 28th when, having calculated that it would still be possible to eat, I presented myself to the clubhouse of SHULAC with the avowed intention of learning to fly. I was now being paid £2.10s (in real money) per week – what can you get for £2.50 today?

Persistent rumours had been flying around Bure Homage that the going rate was just 35/- per hour, so the temptation was too much. I walked across the main runway with the intention of confirming these rumours and immediately became a bit of a novelty as they were all civilians, most working at Airspeeds. Ernie Weston the club secretary confirmed the rate, and the following Friday, 3rd February 1950, I enrolled and was accepted as a fully paid-up member.

Following the loss of its only aircraft, the club was reconstituted and now boasted a light blue Taylorcraft A, which could move at high speed across the grass but could on no account be persuaded to make the final effort and actually fly. This caused intense frustration among the members and it wasn't until someone had the bright idea of opening the cowlings in an effort to find the reason for this laggard approach to the job for which it had been designed that the problem became apparent. Examination then proved that the head gaskets had gone and it was only firing on two cylinders. I actually experienced one of its high-speed attempts at take-off and was frankly very pleased that it didn't, because at the end of the longest runway we were still firmly attached to the ground.

Green novice that I then was, with just 15 minutes passenger joyriding time behind me (in Autocrat G-AHCL from Elstree on 20th July 1948), I remember feeling distinctly uneasy about the whole thing. Added to this was the overweight problem (not me!) caused by the aircraft being kept outside in all sorts of weather, and this became apparent upon its moving when it was noticed that copious quantities of water would pour from the trailing edges of the wings! Following the fitting of new gaskets the Taylorcraft finally took off on Sunday, 12th February, with most of the water drained and with two up. I never did get a flight in it but ignorance was indeed bliss and even I was not sorry to see it finally depart for fresh fields.

On the day before this epic event, one of the members from Airspeeds took me round their flight shed where I saw, in between the prototype Ambassadors G-AGUA and G-AKRD, their hack Consul and Ron Clear's beautifully restored Comper Swift, G-ACTF, painted silver with red trim. The Halifax was parked outside, as I seem to remember it was too big to go into the hangar.

The Swift brings back very happy memories of one very idyllic summer's evening when I first saw Ron give the most spontaneous and exhilarating display of aerobatics that I had ever seen. He obviously enjoyed it and literally made G-ACTF 'talk': ah! the sweet nostalgia of it all.

There was little purpose in keeping the club going with no aircraft and something had to be done and quickly. Ted Gould very generously came to the rescue and lent his Taylorcraft Plus D G-AHUM to the club and flying instruction then began in earnest. The next problem was common to all clubs, too many pilots and only one aircraft, which meant waiting around for many hours just to get the odd half an hour in; but the atmosphere was great – just being with the flying fraternity in those heady post-war days in such delightful surroundings seemed to make up for the little flying we managed to get.

On 25th February 1950, I nearly made my first flight with the club; it was a glorious day but the winds were too strong and flying was cancelled. Being in such close proximity to the sea, Christchurch airfield suffered from some extraordinary and rapid changes in the weather. An episode that I witnessed one evening brought this home in a dramatic fashion. Mr Fisher took off in his Monarch G-AIDE into a sunny sky to the north for a local flight but as he left the ground a sea mist rolled in at about the same speed. He had built the aerodrome before the war so he knew the score, and within a few minutes we heard his engine in the mist and the Monarch touched down right on the centre line of the runway that he had just left. Realising the situation as he got airborne, he flew a circuit pattern, timing each leg to a nicety which he knew would bring him down safely, but it *did* impress us.

On Sunday 12th March 1950 the second prototype Ambassador G-AKRD developed undercarriage problems, which were not uncommon in those days, and decided to belly-land at Hurn where there were better facilities. Whilst a goodly slice of the bottom fuselage was ground off in the ensuing landing, working parties were despatched post-haste, the aircraft was jacked up, the undercarriage lowered and locked, the bottom of the fuselage tidied up and faired over with plywood and the aircraft flown back to Christchurch for more permanent repairs on Saturday 25th March. I also seem to recall that an Ambassador carried out a belly-landing sometime earlier at Holmesley South, another disused wartime airfield in the New Forest.

On Sunday 18th March 1950 I assisted in the destruction of two B.A. Swallows, G-AEAV and G-AEGN. In view of my current preachings on the preservation of British aircraft I hang my bald head in shame! I was young (that's my excuse), and given a fireman's axe I entered into the spirit with the rest of them and, when we were done, tossed the remains, engines and propellers included, into the sandpit in the south-east corner of the airfield where they joined some Mosquito wings. In all fairness, they were both waterlogged and rotten, having spent many years in open storage in an open-ended blister hangar on the west side of the central 'island' (how they avoided impressment beats me), but even allowing for the birds' nests in the leading edge of the wing in one of them, I now bitterly regret having been involved in the incident and feel that at least the engines and propellers should have been salvaged.

Bournemouth Flying Club's premises in the south-west corner of the airfield were still in evidence but did not look as though they had been used for many years. They now housed Mr. Fisher's five dismantled Hawk Trainers G-AICD, G-AICE, G-AIUF, G-AKGR and G-AKGS all looking immaculate in their silver and red colour scheme but presenting a forlorn sight reminiscent of sardines in a tin, and I was taken to see these on Saturday 25th March. His efforts to reform the club had come to nought and these aircraft were destined never to fly from Christchurch.

Two months after my experience with G-AFJP the great day dawned and on Saturday 22nd April 1950 I received my first flying instruction, 30 minutes in G-AHUM with Eddie Livermore, the CFI of the club. I managed another 25 minutes the next day and also undertook my first instruction in the noble if somewhat frightening art of propeller-swinging! Events at the club were now really beginning to hot up with the arrival of Tommy Marshall's Auster 4 G-ALYH on Saturday 29th April. We now had two 'serviceable' aircraft, or so we thought.

It was about this time that we heard a wondrous story about a problem which had been experienced by a new crew whilst converting to the Canadair at Hurn. Although doubtless embellished in the telling, the tale related to an undercarriage problem which had occurred after selecting 'down' when only the two main legs locked. No amount of persuasion could apparently get the nose leg to lock so the flight engineer suggested that he went forward to see if he could rectify the fault. There was only one snag to this idea – there was no entry to the nose section from the cabin. This did not deter our keen type who then proceeded to gain entrance with the aid of the fire-axe. The story goes that not only did he manage to smash his way through but he also managed to lower and lock the offending leg. On reflection it was considered that the aircraft

49

would have probably suffered less damage if they had landed with the nose leg retracted!

I saw all the BOAC Canadairs as they passed through Hurn and a few of the new Handley Page Hermes 4s which were in use by the Corporation's Development Flight from January 1950. By March, some five Hermes were in residence but the stored Lancastrians, which were destined never to fly again, were awaiting the scrapman's axe and this fell later that year and early in 1951.

Meanwhile, back at the club, things were moving apace, and on 30th April I saw clouds from above in G-AHUM for the first time. I should just mention that our C.F.I. Eddie Livermore was a rather short (both in stature and temper) ex-RAF flying instructor but was at heart, a frustrated Spitfire pilot! Apparently, while he was being taught to fly during the war he had shown a natural aptitude for flying so had been 'streamed off' to become a flying instructor. Having seen no active service he had become a very frustrated man and this had made for a rather acid and somewhat sarcastic character. However he did have a peculiar sense of humour, as I was to find out on the afternoon of Saturday 6th May.

We had been having trouble with the slow running on G-AHUM's Cirrus Minor engine; we always seemed to be having problems with something in those days but we took off that Saturday on what was to be a local 'circuits and bumps' flight without a care in the world other than trying to make a decent landing or two. Imagine my horror when, having closed the throttle on finals, the engine just stopped and for the first time in my flying career I saw a stationary propeller up front. Up till then the only time I had seen this phenomenon was on the ground: it was most disconcerting to say the very least! It also went very quiet. Eddie immediately took control and executed a perfect forced-landing on the runway in use. We stopped very short, needless to say, well out of sight of the clubhouse which was a long way to the south of us and screened by the trees in the centre of the airfield.

"Let's casually stroll into the clubhouse and see if anyone has noticed that we are no longer on the circuit," said Eddie as we climbed out of G-AHUM.

This idea also appealed to my perverted sense of humour. Whilst the club members were a great bunch with a genuine love of flying, I had noticed even with my limited experience that perhaps they were treating this flying game rather casually, especially remembering their abortive attempts to get G-AFJP airborne when it was obvious that there was something the matter with its engine.

Anyway, we had been in the clubhouse for a few minutes when one of the more 'with it' members suddenly noticed us and with some bewilderment said: "But didn't you two take G-AHUM off a few minutes ago?"

A deathly hush descended on the room as Eddie silenced the babble of conversation with a withering glance and in a very loud voice said: "Due to that !!!***!!! useless lump of metal on the front of that aircraft, we've had to force-land on the golf course on the other side of the road!"

The golf course, by the way, was to the north-east of the airfield more or less in line with the runway in use and was well-known for its downdraughts which caught out many on finals, often necessitating a little extra bit of throttle to clear the fence. The members, by now somewhat nonplussed, were then treated to a tirade about keeping a watchful eye on the activities while flying was actually in progress – a rare enough event as it was. A recovery party was then organised and as they couldn't see G-AHUM, they naturally believed him – you didn't argue with Eddie, they were all in the wrong anyway. Off we all tramped to get it back, but when we turned the corner of the trees G-AHUM came into view and they realised that they had all been 'had'. After that a watch of sorts was kept when we were flying.

Tommy Marshall owned two Austers, a Mk.4 G-ALYH and a Mk.5 NJ635 which was registered G-ALZM on 31st March 1950 although it was residing in a loft in one of his barns at his home when I saw it. G-ALYH had been overhauled and given its first C. of A. by Doug Bianchi at White Waltham and it was with great interest that we awaited its arrival at Christchurch.

One evening it appeared out of the inevitable blue sky and shortly after, on the 29th April, I managed to scrounge a ride in the third seat while one of the members took it up for a test flight. Unfortunately, in its present state it turned out to be a bitter disappointment. The controls were very stiff, especially the ailerons which made it very hard work to fly, but it boasted a full C. of A., so what could be the problem? Following much debate, Ron Clear was asked to test-fly it and write a report of his findings. I seem to recall that this report highlighted a few problems and it was finally agreed that Flightways, Viv Bellamy's company at Eastleigh, would put it right and it was collected by one of his pilots on the 13th May. On the 11th June I flew to Thruxton in G-AHUM with Ted Gould piloting and in strict accordance with his earlier training there landed downwind because that was what the landing 'T' said we should do! The windsock was in total disagreement with this and needless to say Ted was not amused! The upshot was that the wind had apparently been changing dramatically all morning and they had got fed up with changing the 'T'. The lesson was learned but

51

"we didn't half use up a lot of the main runway!" I returned to Christchurch with Tommy in G-ALYH, overflying Boscombe Down ("It's alright, I know the C.O.!") and turning left at Salisbury Cathedral.

The pre-production Ambassador G-ALFR made its first flight on Thursday 18th May and the following day G-AKRD took to the air again following its fuselage repairs.

On Sunday 21st May I made my first flight with Paddy O'Sullivan, a charming if slightly eccentric Irish part-time flying instructor who I hadn't recalled seeing before. We flew in G-AHUM and I recall that he was a natural; I won't go into what he did with that Auster as it might revive painful memories for some of the locals, but it was "a joy to behold, that it was!"

G-ALYH duly returned fully restored and pronounced fit to fly, and was promptly pressed into service to help with the backlog of would-be pilots. It had just one minor and somewhat irritating problem that we never could cure, which seemed to be inherent in the basic design of the engine, and that concerned starting the thing from warm. From cold it was just about acceptable but when hot, it was a b******! We finally reckoned that the problem was due to oil draining into the rear two cylinders and wetting the plugs. Being an American engine, it also went round the wrong way, which made starting an extremely difficult procedure as it was not natural to swing a large propeller anti-clockwise.

By now, my eighteen-month sojourn was drawing to a close and it was becoming obvious that serious efforts would have to be made to find suitable full-time employment. I could have gone back to the Gas Company as the personal assistant to the Chief Engineer with whom I had worked since leaving school, but my appetite was now whetted for a career in aviation. On the 13th June 1950 I wrote to the Chief Draughtsman of Airspeed Ltd at Christchurch in the hope that they might have a vacancy for a junior draughtsman. I received a pleasant reply two days later but unfortunately they had no vacancies at that time. So, after a 10 minute flight in G-AHUM with Eddie in the calm of the evening of Monday 19th June 1950, I made preparations for my impending departure from Bure Homage, which had become my second home.

Suddenly I didn't want to leave: I would miss the bonhomie, the balmy evenings swimming and flying, and just being with aeroplanes. What had the army done when they posted me to SRDE in 1949?

On reflection, I suppose that this was the event which was to shape my future destiny. Looking back, would I have changed anything? Probably not – just rounded off some of the sharper edges with the benefit of hindsight. I left Bure Homage for the last time on Thursday 22nd June 1950, but before I left I hatched a plot with Derek Goddard, a club member, that was to bring me back to Christchurch for a day within a very short space of time. But that, as they say, is another story.

CHAPTER 6

THE 1951 'DAILY EXPRESS' SOUTH COAST AIR RACE

Edited by

PETER G. CAMPBELL

[Most of this chapter is reproduced by kind permission of Richard Riding of 'AEROPLANE MONTHLY' from the August 3rd, August 10th & September 28th 1951 editions of 'THE AEROPLANE' magazine. All the additional material, which comes from various sources and has been written or collated by the Editor, is printed in italics and within square brackets to differentiate it from the official reports – Ed.]

[Air Races in the fifties were popular with both pilots and spectators, who flocked in large crowds to the various vantage points around the course (although the crowds were perhaps not as large as in pre-war days). Nevertheless, races were prestige events and attracted a large number of competitors, who doubtless took part for the pleasure and excitement of it all as much as for the cash prizes. The King's Cup had always been the 'premier' race, with most honour attached to winning, but the races sponsored by the "Daily Express" offered five times as much in prize money!

The 1951 race was due to be run on the 6th August. In a preview, Tony Cole (one of the would-be competitors) had written in the August 3rd edition of 'THE AEROPLANE':]

Without a doubt, the "Daily Express" race on August 6th will be the greatest to be held since the war. Not only is it the longest, 186 miles, and worth the most money, £2,255, but it will be the race that will require the most skill . . .

There will also be the greatest number of competitors from abroad to fly in any post-war race. Let them be given the welcome they deserve. Some are old friends. Captain Christie is here again, this time with a mysterious Klemm in place of the little Beauty he had last year. J.G. Lignel is again flying the machine of his own design that he used last year, F-BCZJ.

And from the wild parts comes R. Matthews-Naper, who flies his Messenger in true Irish style. The other visitors are newcomers to racing in England, though everyone will know L.C. Marmol, flying a Belgian-registered Proctor, renowned for his superb glider flying.

One thing of great interest is the team of two Ambrosinis entered from Italy. It is the first time in post-war racing that we have seen a team entered, unless possibly we have such in the TBU! *[The story behind the TBU is told in another chapter of this book – Ed.]* But here are two supposedly identical aircraft, and we should get some surprising results. The Italians always go in for internal-combustion-engine-powered sports in a big way, and they do not do things by halves!

It is very pleasing to have the race from Shoreham Aerodrome. Apart from being a delightful field it will be a most suitable welcome to the return home of F.G. Miles. A deserved honour, as F.G.'s machines in races always outnumber those of other firms, and often outnumber the remainder put together! Shoreham has a splendid past, which we hope to see revived in the hands of the 'old' master!

The 'Throttle Benders' are out in full strength, minus Geoffrey Alington, with the same old machines, although a few new mods may be seen here and there. Nat Somers has now recovered from a bent neck, and will get his own back on the twin throttles of his King's Cup-winning Gemini.

[However optimistic the race forecast may have been, the weather on the 6th August, the one factor which was entirely unpredictable, deteriorated rapidly through the day, and despite one or two postponements made with the optimism that surely things would improve, things in fact did not improve and eventually the inevitable decision was made to cancel the race that day and try to re-run it again at a later date.

In the 10th August edition of 'THE AEROPLANE,' in an article entitled 'No Racing Round the Coast,' the anticlimax was summed up thus:]

High hopes of what had promised to be a most exciting afternoon's racing were dashed on August Bank Holiday Monday when the *"Daily Express"* Air Race became the second major event in this year's racing calendar to fall victim to the unpredictable whims of our weather. Low cloud, rain, and very low visibility, all along the 186-mile course – particularly in the region of the coast – brought about its final cancellation and proved a bitter disappointment to the organisers, the competitors, and to the tens of thousands of would-be spectators along the course from Shoreham to Whitstable and back round the coast.

[One of the competitors who was not too concerned at the postponement of the race was Hugh Scrope, who when arriving in the Percival Mew Gull G-AEXF a day or two before had overshot and run on into one of Shoreham's famous ditches. Ron Paine (in the Hawk Speed Six) and Hugh had been coming in at the same time; Ron was flying down the valley on the normal approach line with Hugh to the right of him, and wondered how he was going to get down safely, which he didn't! Fortunately the aircraft was not written off, and as on many occasions since that time, it was rebuilt with loving attention and given a new lease of life.

The re-run was scheduled for the 22nd September, which fortunately was blessed with somewhat better weather. It was a little bumpy over land, but otherwise not at all bad. Visibility was between six and ten miles, although there was a slight haze which emphasized the need for first-class navigation.

The course of 186 miles was the same as had been planned for the previous occasion: from Shoreham to Brighton & Newhaven, then inland and across country to Whitstable, and then back along the coast to Hythe, Rye Harbour, Hastings, Eastbourne, Beachy Head, finishing at Brighton West Pier.

As has been already mentioned, the event was an international handicap race, and, being open to aircraft of up to 10,000lb in weight, it was possible to legitimately enter aircraft like the Spitfire and Hurricane.

The 63 entrants for the race were as follows:

Aircraft	Reg.	Entered by/Pilot
Ambrosini S.7	I-BOZI	Count Leonardo Bonzi
Ambrosini S.7	I-EFFE	G. Ferrari
Auster J/1 Autocrat	G-AJEK	Capt. R.J. Crossfield
Auster J/1B Aiglet	G-AMIH	T.W. Hayhow
Auster J/4	G-AIPG	B.F. Francis
Auster 5	G-AJVT	R.G. Pilkington
Avro Avian 4M	G-ABEE	Capt. R.E. Gillman
Beechcraft Bonanza	HB-ECS	P. Genin
Chilton D.W.1	G-AFGI	H.M. Kendall
Chilton D.W.1A	G-AFSV	D.D. Dempster
Comper Swift	G-ABUS	Plt. Off. A.L. Cole
D.H. 60G Gipsy Moth	G-ABAG	P.M.A. Hull
D.H. 60GIII Moth Major	G-ADHE	Plt. Off. D. Norman
D.H. Moth Minor Coupé	G-AFOJ	W.P.I. Fillingham

D.H. Moth Minor	G-AFRY	W.T.S. Buchan
D.H. Puss Moth	G-AAZP	H.E. Scrope
Fairey Tipsy Junior	OO-ULA	J.O. Matthews
Hawker Hart	G-ABMR	Flt. Lieut. G.F. Bullen
Hawker Hurricane 2C	G-AMAU	Sqn. Ldr. F. Murphy
Hawker Tomtit	G-AFTA	Sqn. Ldr. N.F. Duke
Klemm KL.35D	LN-OAV	Capt. J.H. Christie
Lignel 46	F-BCZJ	J.G.L. Lignel
Miles Aries 1	G-AMDJ	Hon. M.A.R. Cayzer
Miles Falcon Six	G-ADTD	G.C. Marler
Miles Falcon Six	G-AECC	Sqn. Ldr. J. Rush
Miles Gemini 1A	G-AKKB	F. Dunkerley
Miles Gemini 3	G-AKDC	J.N. Somers
Miles Hawk Major	G-ADMW	A.E.H. Coltman
Miles Hawk Speed Six	G-ADGP	R.R. Paine
Miles Hawk Trainer 3	G-AITO	E.A. Ross
Miles Hawk Trainer 3	G-AIUE	J.T. Basnett
Miles Hawk Trainer 3	G-AKMN	Mrs J.H. Ashton
Miles Hawk Trainer 3	G-AKRH	Plt. Off. M.R.T. Chandler
Miles Hawk Trainer 3	G-AKRV	E. Day
Miles Hawk Trainer 3	G-AKRW	Flt. Lieut. P. Raymond
Miles Hawk Trainer 3	G-ALFE	J.H.G. Turner
Miles Messenger 2A	EI-AFH	R. Matthew-Naper
Miles Messenger 4A	G-ALBE	E.W. Westbrook
Miles Messenger 5	G-ALAC	Lieut. P.G. Lawrence
Miles Monarch	G-AIDE	F.C. Fisher
Miles Nighthawk	G-AGWT	I.A. Forbes
Miles Whitney Straight	F-APPZ	Unknown
Nord 1203 Norécrin	F-BEBL	J.J. Garnier
Percival Proctor 1	G-AGWV	HRH Prince Alexander of Yugoslavia
Percival Proctor 1	G-AHDJ	W.W. Lyle
Percival Proctor 1	G-AHES	J.H. Sauvage
Percival Proctor 1	G-AHNA	A.S.K. Paine
Percival Proctor 1	G-AHVG	H. Wood
Percival Proctor 1	G-AIEB	Wg. Cdr. R.H. McIntosh
Percival Proctor 3	G-ALJH	Capt. C.B. Wilson
Percival Proctor 3	G-AKWV	J.P. Crowther
Percival Proctor 3	G-AMCO	D.J. Bennett
Percival Proctor 3	G-AMGE	R.A. Peacock
Percival Proctor 4	OO-INT	L.C. Marmol
Percival Proctor 5	G-AGTC	Gp. Capt. H.A. Purvis
Percival Proctor 5	G-AHGR	D.J. Bennett
Percival Proctor 5	G-AIET	Mrs Z. Irwin
Percival Vega Gull	G-AFEA	Dr. D.F. Little
Supermarine Spitfire 22	PK542	J.K. Quill
Taylorcraft Plus D	G-AHKO	Mrs Y.M. Grace
Taylorcraft Plus D	G-AHSB	D.G.S. Cotter
Taylorcraft Plus D	G-AHUG	Gp. Capt. G.F.K. Donaldson
Wicko G.M.1	G-AFJB	Miss E.L. Curtis

Hugh Scrope flew Puss Moth G-AAZP in place of the still-damaged Mew Gull, and D.G.S. Cotter flew Taylorcraft G-AHSB in place of Auster G-AGXT. The Bonanza HB-ECS was ex-NC90572, and the Marmol Proctor bore unmistakable traces of its former British registration G-AJWN.

Three entrants scratched at the last moment, the Miles Aries, the Messenger EI-AFH and the Ambrosini I-EFFE (which was at Redhill undergoing radio tests), so sixty aircraft lined up for the start, which was scheduled for 2.30 p.m. First off, at the drop of Phillip Mayne's green flag, was Capt. Gillman's Avro Avian G-ABEE. The scratch man was Jeffrey Quill flying the silver Spitfire PK542, who took off almost 77 minutes after the Avian!

To complete the record of the day as far as is possible, the other aircraft seen on the field or overflying during the event are listed below (with thanks to Fred Lynn):

Resident aircraft:

J/1 Autocrat G-AJXS (burnt out in a hangar fire on the 5th September), Cierva C.30A G-AHLE (dismantled early in 1950), Hawk Trainer 3 G-AITS, Messenger 2A G-AIBD, Proctor 5 G-AHBI, B.A. Swallow 2 G-AFHS, Taylorcraft Plus D G-AHCI (burnt out in a second hangar fire only four days previously, on the 18th September).

Visiting aircraft:

J/1 Autocrat G-AGYM, G-AGYN, G-AHAY, G-AHHR & G-AJAS, Auster J/4 G-AIPR, J/5F Aiglet Trainer G-AMKF, Cessna 170 N1383D, Chipmunk G-AJVD, Cub Coupé G-AFSZ, Gemini 1A G-AIDO, G-AJWF, G-AKDB, G-AKFY, G-AKHJ, G-ALZG & F-BFPP, Gemini 3C G-AKGE, Hawk Trainer 3 G-AMBM, Hornet Moth G-AELO, Messenger 2A G-AJWB & G-AKAN, Proctor 1 G-AIED, Proctor 4 G-AJMH, Proctor 5 G-AHGJ & G-AKDZ, Tiger Moth G-AMIE (on its first outing from Croydon, with a C. of A. only three hours old!), Whitney Straight G-AERV.

Overflying aircraft:

Ambassador G-AKRD, Anson 1 G-ALUM, Attackers (RN formation), Comet 1 G-ALZK.

And so to a report on the re-run race itself, which is reproduced in full here from 'THE AEROPLANE':]

A RACE WITH A MORAL

Taking a second bite at any cherry is likely to prove a somewhat unprofitable occupation, but – if such a metaphor can be applied – the September 22nd bite at the "Daily Express South Coast Air

Race" cherry was the exception which proved the rule, and more than made up for the indigestible morsel of August 6. Indeed, favoured by good weather – or more precisely, a weak sun, cool easterly wind, reasonable visibility and no rain – and a healthy entry list, the event provided much good sport for the 55 contestants who were fortunate enough to stay the course.

First man past the post and winner of £1,000 and the "Daily Express" Challenge Trophy was Hugh Kendall, encased in his diminutive Chilton monoplane. Considerable ingenuity on the part of the owner-pilot, aided and abetted by all of 30 b.h.p. from the Carden-Ford power plant, enabled this remarkable team to achieve the astonishing average speed of 129 m.p.h.

So taken aback were the rest of the field by this performance that the next man home – Hayhow in the Auster Aiglet – was seven minutes behind the Chilton. And being out of sight of it throughout the race, he thought that he had won, but found on landing at Shoreham his prize money had been divided by two.

A visitor from abroad, Capt. J.H. Christie, relaxing from the cares of flying large airliners, was third past the post in a venerable Klemm, whose conversion into a single-seater for the race and sporting coupé top helped it to achieve an average speed of 132 m.p.h. in moving up from being 16th off. For this creditable performance he received £250.

Compared with the original list of entrants for the race, the field this time was stronger by eleven, including, we were glad to note, two additional foreign entries. Although G. Ferrari in one of the Ambrosini S.7 monoplanes scratched, the other foreign entrants all turned up, including this time the Swiss Bonanza, 'Ladi' Marmol's Belgian-registered Proctor, a Whitney Straight from France and the Tipsy Junior from Belgium.

Another of the aircraft previously entered but only now appearing for the first time was the Bombardier-engined Messenger G-ALAC, the subject of much polishing throughout Friday afternoon. This being the first occasion in which a Bombardier has been raced, this aircraft was the subject of much interest, and was regarded by many as something of an unknown quantity.

All in all, the field of starters we judged to be one of the most interesting in any post-War air race, with the emphasis very much on private-owner and sporting aeroplanes. Here we had representatives of what can now almost be termed a bygone age, in the Avian, and the Moth: we had ultra-lights – the Junior and two Chiltons: we had the 'stock' Austers, Messengers and Geminis: we had the out-and-out racing craft of Tony Cole, Fred Dunkerley, Ron

Paine and Jimmy Rush: we had the foreigners – an Ambrosini, a Bonanza, a Norécrin, the Lignel and Jan Christie's diverting coupé-top Klemm: and for good measure we had the Hurricane and Spitfire.

THE RACE FROM BRIGHTON

We have already described, both on the occasion of last year's race for the "Daily Express" Trophy and in dealing with the frustrated attempt earlier this year, the arrangements at Brighton West Pier, which was the finishing and control point. Reports from the observers at turning and observation posts around the course were all passed back to the control point for the benefit of the commentators, the race 'tellers,' and those who, like ourselves, were endeavouring to build up an intelligible picture of the progress of the race.

The nature of the course and the field of entrants, however, combined to make it virtually impossible for this well-devised system to be a complete success and despite the gallant attempts of the hard-working team of observers, it was inevitable that one or two aircraft should slip past a point here and there without their passage being noted on the progress chart. It was also inevitable, that as the field of 60 starters began to bunch up at the end of the course, recording the position of each aircraft at each point should become impossible.

As usual, Peter Masefield, Peter Brookes and the Goodhart brothers were hard at work with their assorted calculating machines and charts with a view to forecasting the result of the race. And in this respect they were an unqualified success, for they correctly forecast Hugh Kendall as the winner only some ten minutes after his take-off. By the time he had reached Newhaven and turned on to the cross-country leg, in fact, his speed already showed him to be a likely winner, finishing three minutes ahead of his handicap.

At this point, Kendall was still lying ninth, in which position he took off with a handicap of 8 mins 20 secs. On the long cross-country leg, however, he got out in front and was the first competitor to reach the coast again at Whitstable. This meant that he was not only forecast to win on his speed so far, but was also physically in the lead, and could be caught only if another aeroplane also managed to beat its handicap.

This, of course, did not happen and with clockwork regularity the number 7 appeared at successive points on the indicator. With the benefit of a brisk tail wind on the latter part of the course,

Happy Brookside Flying Group members with Magister G-AKRJ at Shoreham in the summer of 1948 (L.J. Benjamin)

The Mew Gull G-AEXF at Blackbushe at the end of Hugh Scrope's epic flight back from France in 1950 (T.M.A. Webb)

The 'Maggie' G-AJDR in the Gloucester scrapyard before recovery in 1950 (T.M.A. Webb)

The same aircraft (well, sort of!) after rebuild (T.M.A. Webb)

A sad end at Redhill to G-AJDR's first flight after rebuild (T.M.A. Webb)

The reluctant-to-fly Taylorcraft A G-AFJP at Christchurch in 1950
(P. Amos)

One of only two Brigands built for the Pakistani Air Force, seen at
Filton in 1950 (P. Amos)

Airspeed's 'hack' Consul G-AHEF, based at Christchurch in the early
fifties (P. Amos)

The forlorn Mew Gull G-AEXF hangared at Shoreham after its landing
mishap on August 2nd 1951 (P. Amos)

An evocative shot before the rerun of the 1951 'Daily Express' race at
Shoreham, with Savage's Proctor 1 G-AHES, Lignel F-BCZJ and
newsreel-film vehicle (P. Amos)

Hugh Kendall taxies in his winning Chilton G-AFGI after the 1951
'Daily Express' race (P. Amos)

Record-breaker Tom Hayhow with his Aiglet Trainer G-AMOS at
Fair Oaks, 1952 (P.G. Campbell)

The RAE (Farnborough) Flying Club's Tiger Moth G-AMCM
at the 1954 Goodyear Trophy meeting at Shoreham (P. Amos)

Herts & Essex Aero Club's Hornet Moth G-ADOT (T.R.V. Foster)

Proctor 4 G-ANYC at Croydon (T.R.V. Foster)

'Maggie' G-ALIO ('Pongo') of the Experimental Flying Group
(T.R.V. Foster)

Kendall increased his lead all the way and actually finished seven minutes ahead of the second man home. Without a doubt this is the easiest win of any post-War air race in this country, although there was a similar happening in the 1930 King's Cup.

At Newhaven, few changes had occurred in the order of the field, although as we have said, Kendall was already well up on speed. The only changes worth noting were that Prince Alexander and D.J. Bennett, both in Proctors, had each slipped back some five places.

[As was to be expected, the Avian was the first to arrive at Newhaven, some ten feet above the sea, and went into a steep climbing turn round the lighthouse. In contrast, Marler's Tiger Moth took the turn at about 200 ft. Cotter's Taylorcraft was so low that from a vantage point about 30 ft above sea level the onlookers were actually looking down on the aircraft. Francis brought his Auster J/4's wingtip within some ten feet of the framework.

According to 'FLIGHT' magazine's report, Miss Curtis' Wicko and Fillingham's Moth Minor caused some concern by 'swooping on to the lighthouse like two seagulls after the same piece of fish; it rather looked as though the Wicko pilot had not seen the other aircraft turning below.'

Two Proctor pilots had problems, even at this early stage: McIntosh's aircraft was emitting a trail of black smoke, and the engine of Purvis' was misfiring.]

Considerable sorting out had occurred by the time the aircraft arrived at Whitstable, however, and after the first 40 had passed this point, the 'tellers' forecast the first five places as going, respectively, to Kendall, McIntosh, Marmol, Christie and Bowles. In fact, three of these were among the first five home. Capt. Gillman in the Avian was still clinging grimly to Kendall's tail, followed by Hull in the Gipsy Moth. These two managed to stay among the first ten as far as Hastings, but on the last stretch were passed by many of the faster machines.

At Margate, Geoffrey Marler, in the lone Tiger Moth, was found to be still in the picture in second place, with the Avian third and Cotter having moved up to fourth.

One or two significant changes at Margate included Jan Christie, who had come up from 16th at take-off to 11th place, and Hayhow in the Aiglet from 18th to 10th. For some reason, the Aiglet kept disappearing, as far as we in the control room were concerned, and it did not receive serious consideration, although the 'tellers' did mention it at one point.

At Deal and again at Folkestone, Christie and Hayhow had both moved up and McIntosh was now in the picture and coming up well. From 33rd at take-off he moved up to 20th at Folkestone, and was the first of the more powerful aircraft seriously to challenge the lighter types up front. Among those not doing so well at Folkestone were Derek Dempster in the other more heavily handicapped Chilton, back from 17th to 22nd, and Matthews from 13th to 26th.

However, with the three 'fast' aircraft – the Ambrosini S.7, Hurricane and Spitfire – away, excitement began to mount. Number 7 went up on the Hastings column of the indicator, while the bulk of the field was still being checked through Margate, Deal and Folkestone, and then suddenly, almost unbelievably, Kendall was reported at Beachy Head. This was at a minute or two before 16.00 hrs, and it was clear that the race would finish quite some time before schedule.

In due course, then, Kendall appeared, completely un-challenged, and flew happily by, having thoroughly confounded the handicappers. There then followed the aforementioned pause of seven minutes, after which aircraft began to appear in quick succession. The next speck materialized as Hayhow in the Aiglet, followed by Jan Christie and R.H. McIntosh, who we might mention here is the oldest active pilot with a "B" licence and flew H.P. 0/400s on the Cricklewood/Paris service in 1920-21.

Fifth to arrive was Cotter, still climbing up and down the waves. Marler, of New Zealand, did well to keep his Tiger Moth so near the front, and finished sixth. Then came 'Ladi' Marmol in his Proctor, followed by Pat Fillingham, Bowles and Wilson. Eleventh home was Mrs Y.M. Grace, who was the first woman to finish and was suitably rewarded.

As prizes were awarded to the first fifteen finishers, Eddie Day, Miss E.L. Curtis, E.W. Westbrook and Capt. Gillman also qualified, having finished in that order. The gallant Avian was just 'pipped at the post' by Westbrook in his Messenger, but managed to earn its pilot a reward.

Several entrants had to retire during the race, but fortunately no injuries nor serious damage to aircraft ensued. P.G. Lawrence made a forced landing in the Bombardier-Messenger *[near Faversham, when an airscrew blade came adrift]*, and Ian Forbes, who was going well in the Nighthawk, retired at Redhill *[with a burnt-out vacuum pump. Jeffrey Quill landed his Spitfire at Tangmere with fuel trouble, Peacock retired his Proctor at Lympne, and Fred Dunkerley retired his Gemini for some reason.*

There was just one disqualification: the R.O.C. reported that Wilson's Proctor had passed inside a turning point – he would have taken ninth place.]

WATCHING AT WHITSTABLE

From the end of Whitstable's short jetty – the official observation post, and the changeover point from the over-land to the over-sea portion of the course – the race certainly can be said to have 'had its moments'; although, in the main, it was little more than a fairly steady procession of aircraft.

However, spacing of the contestants was sufficiently uneven to hold the interest; and on several occasions a number of aircraft could be seen approaching more or less in a bunch. The fact that the aircraft were coming 'out of the sun' and that there were a number of yachts and fishing boats in the middle distance, all helped to add to the general excitement of identification before they passed the end of the jetty.

Unfortunately, a lack of information, regarding the handicap times and the final starting order, made any real attempt at assessing individual performances difficult.

As a prelude to the race we were treated to the passage of the Ambassador followed by the arrival of the Comet and later on by the Attackers which flew over the town as they set course for Brighton. (They were quite oblivious of the fact that they had been disqualified by the Whitstable observers for failing to pass within 500 yards to seaward at the end of the jetty!)

From then until the time when the first aircraft was due to appear, there was a period of impatient waiting which, toward the end, produced the usual crop of false alarms – of a type that can only be described as ornitheroptic prematurity on the part of the ROC. However, after at least two official 'any minute now' announcements, separated by long pauses, three aeroplanes – a monoplane and two biplanes – could be seen coming out of the mist across the water.

Much to everyone's surprise, the monoplane turned out to be Kendall's Chilton, which was going quite fast and must have overtaken quite a number of its rivals. The Chilton was well out in front of the other two, which were the aged and gallant Avian and Marler's Tiger Moth.

After the race ended at Whitstable, but before the telephones had been dismounted, we learned that Kendall had held his leading position in the Chilton, and that the Aiglet that we had seen so obviously catching up the field had managed to get to second place.

THE FIRST FIFTEEN

Racing No.	Pilot	Aircraft	Reg.	H'cap M:S	St Order	Fin	Average Speed
7	H.M. Kendall	Chilton D.W.1	G-AFGI	08 20	9	1	129 m.p.h.
27	T.W. Hayhow	Auster Aiglet	G-AMIH	09 20	8	2	135.5 m.p.h.
40	Capt. J.H. Christie	Klemm Kl.35D	LN-OAV	18 00	16	3	132 m.p.h.
80	W/C R.H. McIntosh	Proctor 1	G-AIEB	32 05	37	4	158 m.p.h.
10	D.G.S. Cotter	Taylorcraft D	G-AHSB	04 25	5	5	113.5 m.p.h.
31	G. Marler	Tiger Moth	G-AMHP	02 30	2	6	111.5 m.p.h.
62	L.C. Marmol	Proctor 4	OO-INT	31 35	35	7	155 m.p.h.
50	W.P.I. Fillingham	Moth Minor Coupé	G-AFOJ	21 40	22	8	135.5 m.p.h.
35	W.P. Bowles	Messenger 2A	G-AJYZ	22 00	24	9	136 m.p.h.
8	Mrs Y.M. Grace	Taylorcraft D	G-AHKO	03 30	3	10	110 m.p.h.
68	E. Day	Hawk Trainer 3	G-AKRV	31 35	35	11	151.5 m.p.h.
48	Miss E.L. Curtis	Wicko G.M.1	G-AFJB	21 20	21	12	132.5 m.p.h.
28	E.W. Westbrook	Messenger 4A	G-ALBE	16 35	15	13	125.5 m.p.h.
3	Capt. R.E. Gillman	Avian 4M	G-ABEE	00 00	1	14	105.5 m.p.h.
52	E. Ross	Hawk Trainer 3	G-AITO	20 00	20	15	130 m.p.h.

[Prizes:
1st: "Daily Express" Challenge Trophy and £1,000 – H.M. Kendall.
2nd: £500 – T.W. Hayhow.
3rd: £250 – Capt. J.H. Christie.
Best performance by a woman pilot: £50 – Mrs Y.M. Grace.]

CHAPTER 7

SWEET CHARIOT

by

CHRIS DEARDEN

[Reproduced from the Miles Magazine No. 5, Volume 2, September 1993, by courtesy of the Miles Aircraft Collection.]

It's absolutely brilliant to have to start by saying, "I can't remember the date and I don't know the registration letters!" (Enthusiasts stop reading here.) But the aeroplane was a Magister, belonging to the Redhill Flying Club. That much is certain. (Ah! At least the fool knows something about it. Progress!) If I had to make a guess I'd say the letters were 'IYB. But even the combined talents of the Spanish Inquisition and the West Midlands Squad would not persuade me to sign a statement on it. *[Actually 'IYB was written off in 1952, so as this was now 1953 the aircraft was almost certainly 'IYD – Ed.]*

The reason I can't confirm the information is simply that I have no log book entry to cover it. And the reason for that is simply that my P.P.L. was suspended on medical grounds at the time. Thus I wasn't even entitled to log the trip as P.2. Legally I was just a passenger – a truth for which I became quite glad as it turned out.

I'd had a modestly successful crash with my motorcycle and done myself a bit of no good. Everything had mended up pretty well, except my right ankle. It was locked solid.

"You'll have to come in some time and have that seen to," the hospital people had said. "It's not urgent. We'll let you know."

Don't ring us, that sort of thing! So I'd shoved it to the back of what I laughingly call my mind. But technically I was still 'under the quack' and that's why the Min. of Civ. Av. wouldn't let me have my licence back just then. Yet there was no practical reason why I couldn't fly an aeroplane – sheer incompetence apart.

This was all in 1953. Early in the May I was approached by my young one-time friend, Mad Martin (not his real name, of course. I use it only to protect myself from solicitors' letters).

"They're holding a breakfast patrol at Panshanger on Sunday the ..." (whatever the date was, late that May), says he. "I'm thinking of booking a Maggie to go up there. Would you like to share?"

"Yes, I would."

At that time of year, with the season waking up, it was necessary to book well in advance if you wanted to be sure of getting an aeroplane at a weekend. So Mad Martin booked. I dare say you're ahead of me by now. That's right! Sod's Law. On the Thursday I got a card from the hospital. Would I report in at 10 a.m. on Sunday? *The* Sunday. Hell! Fat chance of Panshanger, breakfast, and back in time to make Smallfield Hospital by then. I told them I'd be pleased to accept the appointment, but ...

They were as nice as pie about it. If I could be there and settled in bed by lunchtime, that would be fine. Great! So it was on!

Sunday morning wasn't all that fine, though. It was a chill, grey dawn with a sullen overcast. But the overcast was plenty high enough for our purpose and the met men had said that it would stay that way all day. That was important as we were both strictly VFR merchants – none of this staring intently at the gauges and "Bloody hell! Who put that hill there?" We had to look where we were going and try to avoid solid objects.

So there we were at Redhill aerodrome preparing for the off. Mad Martin – in appearance somewhere between Errol Flynn and Omar Sharif – was strutting about stroking his moustache like he was about to win the Battle of Britain single-handed. And then (oh! dear God) he actually started sounding off about "The jolly old Battle of Britain, there" and making zooming movements with his hands ... "Neeowwwww. Ta-ta-ta-ta-ta-ta-ta ..."

I began to tremble slightly and to doubt the wisdom of the whole venture. Tentatively I tried a few remarks about the murky look of the sky, what would it be like north of London? And I wouldn't mind a bit if he wanted to call it off. All very diplomatic stuff. I didn't want to display my cowardice. It was there, all right. I just didn't want to display it.

But there was no stopping Mad Martin now. The 'Battle of Britain' was to be fought and he was going to fight it, come murk or hell-fire. These chaps jolly well had to be shown, and he was just the kiddie to ... etc. etc. Fearless, handsome and full to the neck with self-esteem was Mad Martin. Just a pity about the empty skull.

It'd been agreed that I should fly the aeroplane up there, while Mad Martin did the map-reading in the front office. We'd swop roles for the return journey. This did strike me as a slightly back-to-front arrangement in view of his bubbling enthusiasm for the flight.

But no matter.

Away we went, doing it all by the book, out west of London and keeping well clear of anything we should have kept well clear of. Eventually Panshanger hove in sight. I found it a little surprising since, with Mad Martin in charge of the map, I'd rather expected it to be Filton or Waddington or who-could-tell-where? But no, it was Panshanger, sure enough. 'Thar she blew!'

Simultaneously we spotted some early defenders milling about in the distance. On the instant I was assailed by an ear-splitting yell of "Tally-ho!"

"No, no," I corrected him in a fatherly manner, being some years his senior; "*we're* the raiders. *They're* the defenders. *They're* supposed to do the 'Tally-ho!' bit, not us."

Talk to the sky, boy, talk to the sky! "I'll take it," came shrieking through the Gosport as the stick was snatched from my palsied grasp (so I was going to fly up there, was I?). The mad one then set about hurling the Maggie round the sky in a virtuoso display of hysterical futility.

Silently I blessed the stress people who'd worked at Woodley all those years ago. They must've got it about right and then added on a bit for luck, because by my reckoning the aeroplane should already have shed several major components under this sort of treatment. But she hung magnificently together.

And all the display was entirely without purpose. There wasn't a defender within possible spitting distance of us. I'd had my eyes open; no one had sneaked in underneath us, no one was bearing down from astern. We were in clear space. All the great mad prawn was achieving was to make us far more conspicuous that we need have been. Miraculously, though, no one did come to investigate the rampant Hawk. But don't applaud yet!

Afterwards, in the clubhouse, when we looked at the 'casualty' list of those intercepted, there indeed were our letters. Methinks mayhap there had been gnomes and goblins with spy-glasses lurking in ye merrie hedgerow withal! Still, the mood was very much one of 'look happy and pay for breakfast.' Nobody cared a jot either way. It was all fun – wasn't it?

Ah, now, breakfast! Some long-haired poet once wrote, "How things that we have seen have been enchanted by the hour they kept" – or in plain English, almost anything can seem nice in the right situation. We were in such a situation. The chill and greasy collation of bacon, egg and fried bread, which might normally have set one retching and reaching for a basin, here looked and smelt and tasted gorgeous. We were all jolly flyers together and we wolfed it down with great glee. We followed it down with something which might have been tepid coffee, or it might have been time-expired hydraulic fluid. Hard to say. But to us at the time it was as a banquet fit for aces. Compliments to the chef!

So homewards. Remembering our plan to swop roles on the way back, I prepared to get into the front seat.

"I want to go in the front," Mad Martin said, sounding as if he might fling himself to the ground and drum his heels if thwarted.

"But I thought . . ."

"I'm the skipper, and I want to go in the front."

"Okay, Skip!"

We took off and proceeded in a more or less south-westerly direction to retrace our route in. But before very long a distinctly disenchanted Mad Martin came on the Gosport. "Either we're getting higher or this cloud base is getting lower."

I looked at my altimeter and confirmed to him that *my* bit of the aeroplane wasn't getting any higher. I couldn't speak for *his* bit. At last, with my brains and his good looks we worked it out between us. The cloud base *was* getting lower! It certainly looked uninviting up ahead. Damn the met men! We were already breaking V.F.R., being almost in cloud.

Mad Martin eased the throttle. Maggie sighed gratefully and sank a little. At least we now had some pretence of clear air above us, even though it meant having less than we should underneath us. In all reason we ought to have turned back to Panshanger . . . What? With Mad Martin at the wheel and me trying to keep a hospital appointment? Joke! By this stage I was as nearly certifiable as Mad Martin had been all along.

"We'll never make Redhill before that lot clamps right in if we go out round west," quoth the Head Lunatic. "Give me a direct course for Redhill."

One doesn't need a degree in geography to realize that a straight line from Panshanger to Redhill passes right across central – but *central* London: right across the thick bit. I gave him the benefit of my opinion on this. He said he didn't give a monkey's. He wanted a direct course for Redhill. What was the heading?

It was only then we remembered we'd left the map in the front cockpit. And I was in the back.

"Not to worry!" I chirped helpfully. "I'll fly the aeroplane for a bit while you sort out the course you want. Then I'll hand back."

No good. I'd flown it up there. He was flying it now. It was my turn to have the map.

"But look," I said, "there's not a lot of point in map-reading now. Just aim generally southwards. We're bound to find London. It's big enough. And when we've found London we can find the

Thames. And when we've found the Thames we can find Victoria Station. After that it's simply Clapham Junction, East Croydon, Purley, Coulsdon South, Merstham, Redhill, Earlswood and bingo!"

He wasn't amused. Bradshaw *out!* He wanted a course for Redhill and it was my turn to have the map.

I don't know if you've ever undone the harness and tried to stand up in the back of a Magister in full flight, reaching forward over the windscreen. If not, take my advice and don't. It introduces a certain element of anxiety into one's life – like, how much longer can it last at this rate? I did give a passing thought to the idea of jumping out, anyway. Without a parachute? Yes, even without a parachute. Anything to escape from the deteriorating situation. The only certainty was that I'd be going into hospital that morning – either hobbling into Smallfield under my own steam, as planned, or carried into somewhere else in little pieces in a cardboard box. I didn't much care which just then.

But the map! How about that? I'd succeeded in getting the map! Triumphantly I sat down and re-fixed my harness, only to have Mad Martin say he agreed with me (at last) about not really needing it now. Thanks a bunch!

The cloud base continued to get lower. And so did we. Thus we maintained the illusion of V.F.R. Visibility below cloud was good. Cramped, but good. To be sure, straight downwards it was rather frighteningly good. From that little height in a single-engined aeroplane Central London came sharply into focus as a very unfriendly place.

I called Mad Martin. "Is that Edgware Road coming up on the nose?"

"Damned if I know. All looks alike. Could be anything."

"There's the river, anyway."

Like two Prunes in a pod we plodded onwards regardless . . . Ah! A landmark even we could recognise to give us an east-west fix. The Big Ben clock tower at Westminster.

It'd be stretching a line-shoot too far to say Mad Martin missed it by inches. But, by God, he didn't miss it by much. It passed just below and to starboard. I checked my watch by it. Fine! Time enough to make it to Smallfield for lunch if our luck held.

If our luck held. In spite of myself I couldn't help thinking repeatedly about the official instruction to be at all times in a position to glide to open country 'should the means of propulsion fail.' We'd have been lucky to glide further than the next street of terraced houses. A poor outlook for us. A poor outlook for them. Mercifully our 'means of propulsion' was a Gipsy Major. Hurrah for that! Swing low, sweet chariot.

69

We must have been a sitting duck for any keen-eyed citizen with a malicious flair for noting registration letters. That's when I became most glad that it was Mad Martin who'd signed for the aeroplane. I was just an innocent passenger – "Not my fault, sir!" I guess a fairly weighty book could have been thrown at someone for this caper. But apparently there were no 'spotters' at large that Sunday morning.

We swung gently starboard and picked up the railway south of the river. Clapham Junction, East Croydon, Purley … Oh, joy! substantial green spaces below us now. Then we scraped over Nutfield Ridge and sort of fell onto Redhill Aerodrome.

Boy! Was I happy? Was I relieved? No, not really! The worst bit was yet to come, and I knew it: a trip on the pillion of Mad Martin's motorbike – which he rode rather more crazily than he flew an aeroplane.

Back to my digs in Horley to pick up my pre-packed duffle bag, then straight on to Smallfield Hospital.

I opened my eyes again only when I heard him say, "Okay, I'll dump you off here in the car park."

He wished me "Good luck" and roared away on some other, doubtless nefarious, business.

I made my way to the ward in the 'dot-and-carry' step which my rigid ankle dictated. There the kindly Sister smiled at me and regarded my pale, trembling state.

"It's only a very minor operation you're in for," she said gently. "There's no need at all to worry."

It was too complicated to explain to the dear lady that the operation was the very last thing on my mind just then. It wasn't what was going to happen next Tuesday which concerned me, it was what had just happened this Sunday.

So I undressed, slid in between those beautiful clean sheets, lay back and waited for lunch to be brought to me on a tray. And that, believe me, was pure luxury. Sheer bliss!

CHAPTER 8

TOM HAYHOW: RECORD BREAKER EXTRAORDINAIRE

Edited by

PETER G. CAMPBELL

[This chapter has been compiled mainly from information reported in the following issues of 'FLIGHT' magazine from 1952 & 1953: 11th April 1952, 18th April 1952, 25th April 1952, 30th May 1952, 13th June 1952, 8th August 1952, 15th August 1952 & 5th June 1953. This is reproduced by kind permission of the Editor of 'FLIGHT INTERNATIONAL.'

I have tried to piece things together in chronological order to show how determined – and indeed indefatigable – a man Tom Hayhow must have been. In prewar times he used to race cars and motor cycles, and in the early fifties, he was a familiar figure on the air racing scene, especially in his Auster Aiglet G-AMIH, in which he came second in the 1951 'Daily Express' South Coast Air Race. It is said that some colleagues in the Royal Aero Club bet him he couldn't set up a series of point-to-point speed records, whereupon he took up the challenge forthwith!

I did have the privilege of meeting him, but only the once; it was during the summer of 1952, while he was at Fair Oaks preparing his orange Auster Aiglet Trainer G-AMOS for yet another record-breaking attempt. As a fifteen-year-old schoolboy, I was rather shy at asking him if I could take a photograph, but I had heard of his exploits earlier in the year and my enthusiasm must have come through, because he was happy to stop what he was doing for a few minutes and pose for me in front of his aircraft 'Liege Lady.'

After his untimely death in April 1953 I wrote to his widow expressing my condolences, and received a very friendly letter back almost immediately. He was quite a man, as these excerpts will show . . .

The first is reproduced from the 25th April 1952 issue.

SIX-CITY RECORDS: THE STORY OF T.W. HAYHOW'S
ACHIEVEMENT IN AN AUSTER AIGLET

Tom Hayhow successfully completed on Easter Monday *[21st April 1952 – Ed.]* the series of flights by which he captured (subject to confirmation) 18 new light-aeroplane records for Great Britain. On each of six sorties in his Auster Aiglet Trainer, G-AMOS, named *'Liege Lady,'* he set up three point-to-point records in Class C.1b. Powered with a 130 h.p. de Havilland Gipsy Major 1 engine, the Aiglet had an overload fuel tank fitted in place of the rear seats, giving 61 gallons in all; an Arrow-type (small wheel) undercarriage; simplified strut-bracing; and various detail modifications.

The attempts were under the control of the Royal Aero Club, and Frank Dismore, DFC, manager of the Air Touring Department at Londonderry House, acted as official observer.

At Elstree on the Good Friday morning a met. forecast was obtained from Northolt, the flight plan was telephoned to Bovingdon for passing to Air Traffic Control at Uxbridge, official identification seals were attached to the Aiglet, and Customs formalities at Elstree (where special arrangements had been made) were completed. Then Hayhow left for the first flight, with Paris as the goal.

The Fédération Aéronautique Internationale recognises an outward record, a return record and an out-and-return record. In the third case the entire elapsed time from start to finish is included in the record time, so that any period which the Aiglet spent on the ground at Paris, while not affecting the one-way speeds, would have reduced the average speed over the round trip. Hayhow consequently planned non-stop out-and-home flights both to Paris and to the cities which were to be his destinations on the following days. In each case the aircraft was to be observed, as it made a circuit of the airport, by officials of the national club concerned.

After taking off from Elstree, Hayhow turned back for a flying start over the runway, where Philip Mayne, the RAeC official timekeeper, was waiting to time him. Over the Channel the Aiglet ran into heavy rain, low cloud and some icing, and came down to 400 ft, but presently Uxbridge passed on the news that it had reached Paris (Toussus-le-Noble airfield). Having crossed the line there, Hayhow returned over it to be timed for the homeward flight.

About an hour after landing at Elstree he was off again, this time for The Hague. This flight was made in better weather, and on the way back he was helped by a tail-wind, so that he reached Elstree 20 minutes ahead of schedule. His first words on opening the cabin door were in appreciation of the Decca Navigator: the

Aiglet carried a Mk.VI airborne receiver operated throughout by the British Chain of stations (the 'master' at Puckeridge, and the green, red and purple 'slaves' at Lewes, Norwich and Worm Leighton respectively), working on a very short aerial running from the cabin to the tail-fin. The set weighs just under 50lb. Charles Bovill, manager of the aviation department of the Decca Navigator Co. Ltd., was at Elstree to advise and assist generally. A de Havilland engine-servicing team, too, under George Blanchard, was on hand throughout the whole of the period of flights, with ready help.

The Saturday's records – to Brussels in the morning and Luxembourg in the afternoon – went off strictly according to plan, although some bad weather was met over the Ardennes on the latter flight which, totalling about 640 miles there and back, was the longest of the six.

The fifth flight of the weekend (on the Sunday) was to Dublin and back. For this attempt Hayhow took off from Croydon. FAI regulations decree that on a point-to-point record the distance flown between the two airfields must be greater than the official distance between the two cities, while the course of the flight must pass within 30 km of the city-centres at start and finish. Croydon was selected so that the necessary distance would be flown. Hayhow made a flying start over the control tower, where the R.Ae.C. observers were stationed, and headed north-west for Collinstown. As he approached the Irish sea he found the Welsh mountains hidden, but he broke cloud precisely on track, with Dublin dead ahead, and after circling headed back to Croydon.

Again, to provide the necessary distance, the Amsterdam (Schipol) flight on Easter Monday was timed from Denham. The weather was perfect, and on this flight Hayhow recorded his highest speeds. After returning to Denham to cross the line he flew back to Elstree.

Over the whole series of flights he flew nearly 3,000 miles, and his total flying time was 23½ hours. Both the Auster and the Gipsy engine have become so firmly established that their records do not perhaps have the significance they would have had some years ago, but the important thing about them is that Hayhow was able to get into a light aircraft on six separate occasions within 72 hours, fly precisely to a destination outside this country, and return as arranged. His main object, apart from the personal satisfaction of doing just what he meant to do, was to give a boost to British private flying, and he has now set up a formidable list of records which may encourage other enterprising pilots to try to better. He probably establishes an unofficial record in gaining more records at one go than has any other pilot.

[Route	Time hr min sec	Av. speed m.p.h.
London-Paris	1:56:32	110.88
Paris-London	1:50:36	116.83
London-Paris-London	3:48:02	113.33
London-The Hague	1:25:42.2	141.29
The Hague-London	1:43:22	117.15
London-The Hague-London	3:10:07.4	127.38
London-Brussels	1:54:22.1	109.9
Brussels-London	1:30:37.5	138.76
London-Brussels-London	3:25:47.6	122.2
London-Luxembourg	2:35:48.2	122.73
Luxembourg-London	2:19:10.4	137.4
London-Luxembourg-London	4:55:16.6	129.52
London-Dublin	2:20:15	126.1
Dublin-London	2:21:25	125.26
London-Dublin-London	4:12:51.2	125.26
London-Amsterdam	1:54:55	123.78
Amsterdam-London	1:34:59.8	145.83
London-Amsterdam-London	3:27:37.4	133.45]

*   *   *

Subject to confirmation, five more point-to-point records – his Easter batch of 18 were confirmed last weekend – now stand to the credit of T.W. Hayhow and his modified Auster Aiglet Trainer, G-AMOS (D.H. 130 h.p. Gipsy Major 1).

On Saturday last, June 7th, he took off from Fair Oaks at 6.45 a.m. and was clocked out as he flew over RAeC time-keepers at Brooklands. He then set course to Berne, where he landed at Belp airfield after 3 hr 21 min, a speed of 141.11 m.p.h. for the 472 miles. After 28 minutes on the ground he returned in 4 hr 15 min 28.8 sec (110.03 m.p.h.). His time for the round trip was 8 hr 4 min 46 sec (117.02 m.p.h.).

A little over a week before – on Friday, May 30th – he had left Fair Oaks with Copenhagen-Kastrup, 617 miles distant, as his objective, flying at a take-off weight of 2,202 lb. The outward trip was made in 5 hr 13 min 24.2 sec (118.115 m.p.h.). After 28 minutes on the ground he returned, against strong head-winds, in 6 hr 14 min 49 sec, representing a speed of 98.86 m.p.h. – just too low to rank for a record. The round-trip time, however, was admissable at 11 hr 56 min 28.8 sec (103.33 m.p.h.).

The Auster carried the same equipment as during the Easter attempts. . . . The only modification was the reversion to a tailwheel in place of the skid originally fitted in the hope of a slight reduction in drag; Hayhow found that that the skid wore away disconcertingly fast.

*   *   *

Instead of adding three more capital-to-capital records last week-end *[8th August 1952 – Ed.]* Tom Hayhow acquired only one. Saturday's weather, with strong head-winds, was primarily to blame. He took off from Denham at 0544 hr 17.6 sec . . . with Madrid (790 miles) as his goal.

His flight-plan envisaged a refuelling stop at Jersey, but as he neared the island he judged that he had sufficient fuel in hand, and decided to carry on. The head-winds, however, increased and when – owing to an inadequate map – he lost his way somewhere south of Madrid, he found that his 64 gallons were almost exhausted, while oil shortage was causing his engine temperature to rise ominously.

He accordingly put down, and quite successfully, on a cart-track, only to find that there was no fuel or oil in the district. Spurning Spanish hospitality in the shape of a glass of wine and two raw eggs, he took off again, and eventually made another road landing, this time near Cuidad Real, 100 miles south of Madrid. He here obtained seven bucketfuls of low-grade fuel, and strained it through a handkerchief. He then carried on to Madrid, landing at Cuatro Vientos at about 1630 hr BST.

As the stops had brought the Aiglet's average speed well below the qualifying 100 m.p.h. minimum, no London-Madrid record had been established; the out-and-home record, likewise, was now impossible of achievement. There was, however, nothing to prevent the irrepressible Hayhow trying for a Madrid-London record next day, Sunday. He accordingly took off at about 0714 hr BST . . . and, after an uneventful journey (though the Aiglet was forced by cloud to over 11,000 ft in the area of the Pyrenees) he reached Denham at 1406 hr 43.8 sec. If, as expected, the take-off data from Madrid results in a speed of about 115 m.p.h., the flight will, subject to confirmation, rank for record.

Tom Hayhow – who, incidentally, is 46 years of age – now holds 23 confirmed point-to-point records. When his three Stockholm records of the previous week-end are homologated, plus the Madrid-London flight, he will have no fewer than 27 to his credit.

*   *   *

Last Saturday, August 9th, was a very full flying day for Tom Hayhow. In the light of dawn and Croydon's floodlights he took off . . . at 5 a.m. and set course for Bromma, Stockholm, 895 miles

75

away. Aided by a strong tailwind, he made a direct North Sea crossing at between 5,000 and 10,000 ft, beating (subject to confirmation) Capt. Jan Christie's record for the journey: his time was but 6 hr 37 min 45.9 sec, equivalent to a ground speed of 134.46 m.p.h. . . .

The wind was now a severe handicap, and Hayhow followed a more coastal track; and, as fuel was more critical on this return journey, he had to put down at Leeuwarden, Holland, to take on additional petrol. This resulted in a return figure of 8 hr 43 min 18.6 sec, equal to 102.19 m.p.h., and a Croydon-Bromma-Croydon result of 15 hr 45 min 8.5 sec, or 113.17 m.p.h. . . .

[During Marshal Tito's visit to England early in 1953 Tom Hayhow wrote to him asking for permission to attempt a London-Belgrade record (1,051 miles). Permission was given, and the attempt was made on April 10th. He left Denham at 6.05 am heading for Munich, where he landed to refuel at 11.29 GMT. He took off at 12.08, intending to reach Zemun (Belgrade's airport) but nothing more was heard of the Auster, although it carried radio. It was several weeks later that reports came through from Vienna that his aircraft had been sighted by skiers on the 25th May on Rabenstein mountain, twenty miles south of Salzberg. Apparently it had crash-landed and overturned, but did not seem to be much damaged. The exact position was in a hollow at 6,000 ft between the Grosser and Kleiner Breitstein peaks. 'FLIGHT' of the 5th June reported as follows:]

Shortly afterwards, news reached London of the finding – by American Army and Austrian skiers – of the pilot's body, some 600 yards from the aircraft. He had suffered only minor injuries, and it was assumed that he had died from exposure in the deep snow whilst trying to make his way down the mountainside. Other evidence pointed to the fact that he had reached the Klagenfurt area, turned back towards Salzburg owing to bad weather, and eventually run out of fuel. He had been approximately on track.

Thus passes a good sportsman who during the past few years has consistently supported air racing and who, within the last twelve months, had made a unique series of 28 solo record flights between London and various European capitals. Forty-six years of age, he was a director of engineering and automobile businesses and of a small air-charter firm; he leaves a widow.

From Nat Somers, writing on behalf of his fellow-members of the 'Throttle Benders,' comes this tribute: "It is hard to realize that the jovial personality of Tom will no longer be with us. He was always wisecracking and was the life and soul of our air-racing parties."

CHAPTER 9

HOW TO BE A
TOTAL AVIATION PERSON

by

TIMOTHY R.V. FOSTER

My first flight ever was in an Auster Autocrat, G-AIZZ, a single-engine high-wing taildragger owned by Air Kruise (Kent) Ltd. It was August the 7th 1947, just before my ninth birthday. What we used to call a 'ten bob flip.' The pilot was Hugh Kennard and the airfield was Lympne. My flight lasted about fifteen minutes, during which time we flew to Folkestone, where my family was on holiday, did a turn over the harbour and cruised back to Lympne. It was a lovely sunny day. I can still vividly remember the experience, 48 years later. I noticed at the end of the flight I had not worn my seat belt and I asked the pilot why he hadn't made sure it was on.

"It makes first-time passengers nervous, so we don't usually mention it!"

I mean, really! I ask you!

At eight, I had gone to Barfield School, conveniently located just off the Hog's Back, on the downwind leg of Farnborough, home of the Royal Aircraft Establishment. My chief memory of those early days was seeing the Armstrong-Whitworth A.W.52 flying wing meandering about.

The father of one of my school chums, John Hockey, was a Group Captain of the same name, who had a senior position at RAE Farnborough. One day the RAE held an open house for special friends, and Barfield was invited to send a coachload of boys. Seeing an opportunity to incentivise the students, T.L. Griffith, the headmaster, announced that the top twenty boys in overall marks would get to go. Scores were calculated daily. On the morning of the big day, I was at position twenty-one. Ladies and gentlemen, I am here to tell you of the power of prayer. Nobody has ever prayed as hard as this ten-year-old to go on that trip. One hour before departure it was found that one of the day-boys had not brought his permission slip, signed by his parent, so he couldn't go. We boarders were under some kind of blanket permission, so at the last minute, I was admitted. What a day, touring this top-secret air base.

In my last term at Barfield, in 1951, I managed to get the school to start a Boy Scout troop. My sole objective in this was to get my aviation badge, which I did, courtesy of G/C Hockey, who acted as my examiner when I had to do the oral test on aviation knowledge. I can still remember him saying "Stick meets aileron!" in determining if the aileron controls are working properly.

In addition to my first flight, in Auster G-AIZZ, I also flew in other Austers during the fifties (G-AHSN, G-AHSO & G-AJEO). One of these flights (in 'HSO) took place at Fair Oaks, near Chobham, Surrey. We were doing the preflight walkaround, in front of the hangar, and a Tiger Moth took off toward us. As it got overhead, the noise of the engine at full take-off power suddenly died to nothing, with the Tiger about 400 feet above us. An engine failure?!! Everybody looked up, their hearts in their mouths, and a faint voice yelled down from the Tiger, "CHANGE THE TEE!" Then the power went back to full and the Tiger continued on its climb-out. No radio in Tigers! The T-shape marker on the ground, which shows aircraft which way to land, was pointing out the wrong runway, since the wind had recently changed direction. Nerve-wracking but effective communications.

Another favourite hangout of those days was the Farnborough Air Show put on by the SBAC (Society of British Aircraft Constructors). It was then intended as Britain's aeronautical shop window. Now anyone can display there, it seems.

Farnborough was where I saw, over the years, the Hawker Hunter piloted by Neville Duke break the sound barrier, the enormous eight-engined Bristol Brabazon with Bill Pegg at the controls, the appealingly ugly Saro Princess flying boat, the Avro Vulcan escorted by three little mini-Vulcans (Avro 707s), the D.H. Comet airliner flown by John Cunningham, and Ranald Porteous doing strange things with an Auster Aiglet Trainer.

One particularly memorable display was that put on by Jan Zurakowski, Gloster's chief test pilot and a wartime Polish fighter pilot in the RAF, doing something called 'Zurabatics.' He would take a Meteor, which had a jet engine on each wing, climb it vertically, then throttle back one engine while going to full power on the other. The Meteor rotated like a Catherine wheel about its vertical axis. Most impressive.

I was offered the choice of two schools after Barfield, Repton or Lancing. To this day, I have no knowledge of where Repton is, but even at the age of twelve I knew that Lancing College was situated on the South Downs, overlooking Shoreham Airport. So that's where I wanted to go.

It was from here that I saw my first ever Beechcraft Bonanza. My school chum Peter Campbell, who avers that I turned him on to spotting aeroplanes, tells me that our first sortie together was on the 22nd June 1952; only a fortnight later, on the 2nd July, this Swiss-registered Bonanza HB-EGB visited Shoreham.

One of my teachers, dear old E.B. Gordon, who even then seemed to be about eighty and had been teaching at Lancing since before it was built, or thereabouts, had taken pity on me and loaned me his First World War 20-power field glasses, officers for the use of, so that I could monitor aeronautical activity in those moments when I was not trying to understand calculus or the table of elements.

You have to understand about me and Bonanzas. It was, at the time, my most favourite aircraft. It was all-metal (in an era when most private 'planes were still fabric-covered, or made of plywood), had a low wing, four seats, retractable tricycle landing gear, and a V-tail (sometimes called a butterfly tail), making it unique in small private 'planes, then and ever since.

I was so turned on to this machine in those days that I actually wrote a fan letter to Beech Aircraft, asking for photos and stuff. They sent me a colour brochure for the bird (I still have it) and some nice air-to-air pictures. The day that thick package, in its distinctive yellowish-brown American envelope with all the stamps on it, arrived and was delivered to me at my Lancing breakfast bench was one I shall never forget.

Somehow, Peter and I managed to talk Mr Wigg, our Physics teacher, into driving us down to the airport to see the Bonanza close up. The pilot was there and he let us look inside. He was very proud of the fact that it had a Lear Orienter 'radio compass,' what we modern pilots call an ADF (Automatic Direction Finder).

Peter and I again had an involvement with a Bonanza on July 31st 1955. That day, a sunny summer Sunday, I had started flying lessons at Croydon with the Experimental Flying Group (see later). After an initial flight with Rex Nicholls in the Maggie G-AITN, he invited me to ride along to the Fair Oaks Aero Club where they were having a 'Tea Patrol.' Jolly good show, chaps! The idea was, you flew to Fair Oaks and tried to land without your registration being spotted by one of the defending aircraft launched by the local club. Succeed, and tea is free. Get logged, and pay up for the scones and cuppa.

Rex flew us there in a Proctor 4, G-ANYC, a lovely aeroplane.

He got quite excited when, diving swiftly to evade a defending Auster, he realised the needle had gone twice round the clock, and was, in fact, reading very high! There's an inner scale for the higher speeds, and that's where we were. Actually, I was a little more excited than him, because I'd never been in a Proctor before. But stand by, folks. Isn't there a Bonanza in this story? Yea, verily: G-AOAM, the only Bonanza then on the British register, and there it was, on the line at Fair Oaks. It belonged to a Mr L.R. Snook. I met up with Peter, who lived nearby and had cycled over, and we stood there drooling over the Beechcraft. I don't know how I did it; I was not yet seventeen, but somehow I managed to persuade Mr Snook to take Peter and me up for a flip, there and then. So now, not only had I seen a Bonanza, I had actually flown in one!

I had had my first flying lesson on June 15th 1954, at the age of fifteen, in Miles Magister G-AFBS, from Denham, a small grass airfield just north-west of London. (That actual Maggie is now on display at the Imperial War Museum, Duxford. However, there is no little blue plaque denoting its moment in history! One day, perhaps.)

I had flown in other types, too. My first encounter with a Hornet Moth, G-ADNB, had been a ten shilling joyride at White Waltham when I was barely a teenager. The pilot was Joan Hughes, a former Air Transport Auxiliary pilot during the war. My next encounter with a Hornet Moth was when I decided to go for broke and really start learning to fly. It was December 28th 1954. I was sixteen. 'FLIGHT' magazine always had an ad offering 'trial lessons' for thirty shillings at Stapleford Tawney, Essex. This was the day. I made a booking and took the tube out to the right-hand side of the Central line and hitch-hiked to the airfield. A Mr A.J. McMahon took me up for an hour in G-ADOT. It was very exciting. He climbed us up through the thin cloud (what, no clearance, Clarence? No radio, either. I guess this was not legal, but what did I know?) and we waltzed around in the blue sky above the low overcast. We dived back through the cloud, found our way back and landed at 4 p.m., so it must have been getting dark.

I was now working for a living. I was making about £6 a week as a clerk for a travel agency. Somehow or other I managed to scrounge together a few pounds to start flying lessons, joining the Home Counties Flying Group, which operated a Tipsy Trainer G-AFWT out of Denham.

The Tipsy had a unique cockpit arrangement. To keep the width down and yet still be able to accommodate a brace of broad-shouldered pilots side by side, the right seat was set back a few inches from the left. The aircraft had what could politely be described as dual controls. Both throttles were on the left – the one for the right-seat pilot (usually the instructor) being just behind the back of the left seat. So to operate the throttle, the instructor had to put his or her arm lovingly behind the student in a semi-hugging posture. This gave the student a strong feeling of protection! How to take flying lessons without becoming emotionally involved, etc. The stick was mounted in the floor between the pilot's legs and then had a right-angle extension at the top, pointing diagonally backwards and to the right, to present a knob for the instructor to use, in stick-like fashion, as required.

My introduction to the Tipsy was provided by Freydis Leaf, another wartime ATA pilot. She gave me a lesson on January 30th 1955, which involved a trip from Denham to Elstree to Bovingdon and back. We did not land at the other airfields and I logged the time as 48 minutes. Freydis was a keen air racer, and in fact became British Air Racing champion in 1954, flying the Tipsy. I remember taking an overnight bus from London to Swansea to support her at the air races there.

I could only afford a lesson about once a month. I had five lessons with HCFG instructor Dave Gurney (4 hours) and managed to get quite a bit of passenger flying with various group members. My logs of these flights have been lost, but I remember several flights with Ian Leno, a successful plumbing-supplies entrepreneur, including one to Shoreham on the 2nd April 1955; also with Ron Prizeman, who went on to design the Thruxton Jackaroo, and with Nigel Pritchett, who got killed several years later in the crash of a Cessna 182 G-ARAA on the Isle of Wight.

Nigel unintentionally gave me my first experience of a ground loop, a sudden and high speed course-reversal on the ground that can occur after a careless landing. I had gone to the Coventry Air Races at Baginton. Transportation was in a BEA Viscount G-AMOG to Birmingham (my first flight in an airliner!) and then by bus to Coventry. Nigel met me there and we mounted the Tipsy to fly back to Denham after the races. We decided to stop at Leicester East on the way, I can't think why. The landing on the grass there was where the poor little Tipsy decided to reverse course with dispatch immediately after landing. Nigel and I exchanged alarmed glances. But all was well. No damage, except to our egos. The trouble is, you have to talk to people who have just watched you do it when you go in and sign the airport register. It's time to look sheepish.

Denham became an awkward airport for me. I was now living south of the Thames and Croydon was much more convenient. So I recced the place and concluded I should switch to the Experimental Flying Group to continue my lessons. This was much more of a going concern than HCFG. There were two Maggies, two instructors and a cadre of 'Groupies' who spent all their weekends at Croydon. A presence in other words. The office was a table in the coffee shop. One could always join the Croydon Airport Club, which had a bar and a snooker table, as well as armchairs – somewhere to spend rainy days.

So every weekend I rode my bicycle from home to the airport, fifteen miles each way, both Saturday and Sunday – 60 miles every week. Well, it kept me fit. There was a tremendous 'Group spirit'. In those times of economic hardship, if you were involved in renting aeroplanes, you could afford little else. So all weekend spare time was spent at the airport. When you weren't flying, which, of course, was most of the time, there was always something to do. Move an aeroplane out of a hangar (if it was at the back, you might have to move six or seven others first). Swing a prop (no electric starters). Help wash a 'plane. Talk to each other about technique, dreams, gossip, always hangar flying.

As well as Rex Nicholls, I had another instructor, Ken Sirett. Looking back at my log, I see I had four lessons with Ken and twelve with Rex before soloing.

SUNDAY, OCTOBER 2, 1955. 1700 HOURS, British Summer Time. Location: Croydon Airport, at the holding point for runway 24.

"Would you like to try one on your own now?"

"Yes, please."

"All right, take it around nice and easy and bring her back in one piece. Just do one circuit."

Rex, my flying instructor, disconnected the intercom, clambered out of the front seat of the Maggie and secured the harness so it wouldn't snag the controls. I sat in the rear, brakes on, stick back, my heart thumping with anticipation at this, my first solo flight. Rex jumped off the wing and gave me a thumbs up.

"All right?" he shouted.

"Right!" I yelled back.

He walked away and, after making sure he was safely clear, I carried out the pre-take-off checklist. TTMFFGHH. I still use the mnemonic, some 4,000 flying hours and forty-odd years later. Throttle tension nut tight, trim set, mixture rich, fuel on and sufficient, flaps up, gyros and instruments checked, harness tight, hatches closed.

I made a right turn towards the control tower. I had no radio. Any other aircraft coming in or taking off? Nothing in sight. The tower gave me a steady green light. Cleared for take off! Brakes released, I opened the throttle enough to get her moving and taxied out to the centre of the runway. All runways at Croydon were grass, but this one had a tarmac apron at the beginning. I lined up on the tall chimney away on the horizon and set the directional gyro to 240. Then I gradually opened the throttle, holding the stick back for the first few seconds. I eased forward on the left rudder to counteract the tendency to turn right caused by the prop torque and brought the stick forward. The tail rose as we accelerated. Airspeed at about 50 knots, the Maggie leapt into the air. With only one on board, the aircraft performed as I'd never seen before. I climbed out at 65 knots. This was it! Solo at last! I felt terrific. I was absolutely determined to solo that day.

On Saturday I had done a 40-minute session in the same aircraft, G-AITN. Four spins and a forced-landing practice. Today I started in the other Maggie, G-ALIO, a 35-minute flight, three landings, back on the ground at 11.15. We had to return then because someone else had the aircraft booked. My total experience in Magisters was now 10 hours 45 minutes. At 1.15, Rex and I went out in 'LIO again. Four landings and one overshoot – an aborted landing due to a poor approach. Part of the training was knowing enough to go around if you could see it wasn't working. 50 more minutes and still no solo!

Later 'ITN became available, so Rex and I sallied forth into the sky once again. Three landings and another overshoot. 40 minutes on the clock.

Then the magic words: "Would you like to . . . ?"

I had completed exactly 40 landings in the Maggie up to that point. Total time in type 12 hours 15 minutes. I was 17 years old. That 41st landing was fine, after one gentle circuit: climb out on runway heading, throttle back half an inch at 500 feet agl (above ground level), continue climb out to 800 feet, look around, turn left 90 degrees, fly crosswind, level off at 1,000 feet, throttle back to 1,900 r.p.m., retrim for 90 knots, look around, turn left downwind on to a heading of 060 (adjusting for any crosswind). There's the runway, passing by under the left wing. Look out for other aircraft. Monitor the tower for light signals. Pre-landing check: BMFFHT. Brakes off, mixture rich, fuel on and sufficient, flaps up, harness tight, throttle tension nut loosened. As the trailing edge of the left wing goes by the runway threshold, throttle back and retrim for 65 knots and start descent. After about a minute, depending on wind, look around, turn left 90 degrees onto base leg and continue descent. At about 500 feet, turn left onto final approach to line up with the runway. Flaps down. The nose drops when you do that, so retrim again and continue approach at 65 knots. There's the steady green light from the tower. Cleared to land. Rock the wings to acknowledge. Check windsock and crab the aircraft to compensate for any crosswind, keeping it lined up. Watch the runway and monitor the approach. The bit that doesn't move is where you'll land – it just gets larger. If you're undershooting, add power. If you're overshooting, reduce power, or sideslip a little. Looking good. As you approach the ground, throttle right back, ease back on the stick. The aircraft stalls a few inches above the ground and settles gently to a smooth three-pointer. No overshoot required. Total solo time, 10 minutes.

Fortunately, fellow Experimental Flying Group member Peter Oake took a photograph of my approach, so I have it in my log book.

By this time I had decided to emigrate to Canada, and in the last few weeks before I left England I stayed with my sister in Hove, which gave me an opportunity to fly out of Shoreham. I was checked out in their Maggie on September 12th 1956 by none other than Cecil Pashley, a ten-minute flight in G-AIZK. The last 'plane I flew in England before crossing the Atlantic was a D.H. Puss Moth G-AHLO, later exported to Canada as CF-PEI. This was out of Croydon, with two landings, on October 7th 1956.

I finally said goodbye to England when I sailed to Canada aboard the Empress of France on October 12th 1956 with $70 in my pocket and high hopes for the future. Some day I'll tell you what happened after that.

[Hopefully it will not be too long now, as this chapter consists of extracts from Tim's forthcoming book 'AEROQUEST.'

In Canada he went on to acquire an Airline Transport Pilot's Licence and developed the extremely successful Fostair Instrument Course, which became the basis for 10,000 Canadians obtaining their instrument ratings. Later he became the author of six aviation textbooks, including the best-seller, 'THE AIRCRAFT OWNER'S HANDBOOK,' published in the USA in 1976 by Van Nostrand Reinhold, and he was also an Instrument Flight Instructor. He was the owner of a Piper Comanche 250, N8251P, from 1976 until 1983, and finally returned to the U.K. in 1986 – Ed.]

CHAPTER 10

MAINLY FARNBOROUGH

by

JOHN BAGLEY

[NOTES ON THE AUTHOR: John Bagley is one of the founder members of Air-Britain; for many years he worked at the Royal Aircraft Establishment at Farnborough, and in his spare time was one of the leading lights in the RAE Aero Club, which during the fifties operated Tiger Moths, first G-AMCM and then G-AJHS. Incidentally, this Club is still very much a thriving concern in the nineties, and indeed lays claim to being the oldest Flying Club in the UK, having been founded in the mid-twenties. The following extracts are reproduced by kind permission of Air-Britain (Historians) Ltd. and John Bagley himself, and, apart from two, all concern that most magnetic of aerodromes, RAE Farnborough.]

OCTOBER 6TH, 1951: THE RAE AERO CLUB, FARNBOROUGH

The RAE Aero Club operates only one Tiger Moth G-AMCM (at the moment it is suffering from a hangover following a heavy landing), but has another under overhaul. This latter started life with serial T6274, but the fuselage was not repairable and that of T5635 has been substituted. T5635 also supplies spare wings for G-AMCM and will probably suffer complete cannibalisation.

Three other Tigers, T5595, T5701 and T6098 (bought recently for 50/- each complete with engines) *[£2.50 in today's money, almost unbelievable now! – Ed.]* will probably be combined in due course to form a third club machine.

Also being repaired is Eon Primary BGA 589 (ex-G-ALMN), bought from the Army Gliding Club at Lasham.

Privately owned by members of the club are Proctor 1 G-AHAB of C.E. Berens, Auster 5 G-ALYB of L.R. Vandome and Aeronca 100 G-AEWU, property of J. Colbourne. This last machine was bought in October last, and after the owner had put in a total of 700 hours work on it, a new C. of A. was issued on August 22nd, and several hours flying have already been done in it. These the writer has been lucky enough to share, and G-AEWU seems already destined to rival the Kitten in the pages of this journal! *[The Kitten, G-AEXT, was operated by A.J. Jackson, then editor of 'British Civil Register News,' and was a regular sight at fly-ins – Ed.]* Some parts have been derived from the Ely 700 G-AFLU, whose wings may be seen in the club hangar in company with a decrepit Proctor 3, LZ598, which supplies spares for G-AHAB.

Also under repair by a club member is Comper Swift G-ABTC, but it needs much work on it to make it airworthy. Another member, J. Wilmot, owns Aeronca C.3 G-ADYS at present in store at Bedford, but hopes to bring it to Farnborough in October.

Three gliders housed with the Club are Gull 2 BGA 664, Gull 4 BGA 612 (which is ex-G-ALTH) and an anonymous Olympia.

*   *   *

JUNE 14th, 1952: THE GOODYEAR TROPHY MEETING

The Wolverhampton Club laid on its usual excellent weather on May 17th in honour of this event, and several interesting machines turned up.

The meeting opened with formation aerobatics by three pilots from 25 RFS, flying Tiger Moths DE955 '15', NM185 '19' and R5123 '14'. This was followed by some T.A. types who leapt from a balloon (with the aid of parachutes) after which F/Lt. Radley did a hedge-hopping stunt with the RAE's last Fieseler Storch VP546. This was followed by the production Balliol T.2 WF989 flown by Boulton-Paul's test pilot. Ranald Porteous then did the 'usual' with a newly-registered Aiglet Trainer G-AMMS, and a Wyvern T.4 VW882 was flown across from Bitteswell and demonstrated by an Armstrong Siddeley test pilot.

The race itself began at 15.00 hrs when the Piper Cub G-AIYU was flagged off. There were twenty starters; Comper Swift G-ABUS and Hawk Trainer 3 coupé G-AKRV did not turn up. There were no spectacular excitements, but a satisfactorily close finish showed up neat handicapping. Pat Fillingham was first in Chipmunk G-AKDN, hotly pursued by Hawk Trainer 3 G-AJJI which overtook Autocar G-AJYY on the aerodrome boundary. After this the two Messengers G-AJOE and G-AJYZ together with Fred Dunkerley's Gemini G-AKKB came across in close formation. After a longish pause the rest of the field came in in the following order: Gemini 3 G-AKDC, Hawk Speed Six G-ADGP, Falcon G-AECC, Proctor 5 G-AHWR, Chilton G-AFSV, Plus D G-AHGZ, Hawk Trainer 3 G-AKPE, Aiglet

Trainer Special G-AMOS, Falcon G-ADTD, Autocrat G-AIGH, Moth Minor G-AFPN and Globe Swift G-AHUU.

The Avro 621 Tutor G-AHSA *'Waltzing Matilda'* and the Cub G-AIYU both retired, but both landed back at Wolverhampton with no visible faults. The only non-standard mods observed were Hawk Trainer 3 G-AKPE and Moth Minor G-AFPN, both having the rear cockpit faired in. The Hayhow Aiglet G-AMOS was still crammed with extra tanks, Decca Navigators and similar impediments, named *'Liege Lady.'*

After the race the Storch towed an all-blue Olympia of the RAF Gliding and Soaring Association (RAE Flight) for an aerobatic display by F/Lt. Radley. This machine carries its constructor's number 'EON 086' on the fuselage sides, and appears to be a frustrated export – all the cockpit notices are in Spanish.

Individual displays were then given by Tiger Moth R5237 '21' of 25 RFS, and a Meteor T.7 which closed the show with a magnificent inverted loop.

* * *

[In the Editor's humble opinion, no book about the fifties would be complete without a report on at least one of the SBAC Shows at Farnborough. I have chosen John's report on the 1952 event – Ed.]

SEPTEMBER 13th, 1952: THE 1952 SBAC SHOW REPORT

For the first time for some years the Show includes two new major designs for the civil market – the Bristol 175 Britannia and the Saunders-Roe Princess. The Britannia with four Bristol Proteus propeller turbines is in full BOAC colours with white top and fin and the registration G-ALBO. The Princess carries her civil registration G-ALUN, but has no markings other than a Union Jack as there has been no decision on who is to operate the aircraft.

Another very interesting new civil aircraft is the Bristol 173 twin-engine twin-rotor helicopter. This prototype has its civil registration letters G-ALBN and a white top for passenger comfort but as yet has no seating or other internal furnishings.

Austers provide the fourth new one with the first public appearance of the Model J/5G Cirrus Autocar. As the name implies, this is a standard Autocar but fitted with a Cirrus Major engine. The example shown is fitted up by Pest Control Ltd. for crop spraying with a huge tank beside the pilot and spray-booms under the wings. It is doped in a violent shade of yellow, with scarlet letters G-AMPA and an enormous Union Jack all over the rudder. (It is understood that Pest Control have denied the suggestion that the colour scheme is intended to demoralise the insect before it is chemically attacked!)

Saunders-Roe also have a multi-coloured exhibit in the Skeeter 5 G-AMTZ, shown for the first time since Cierva's were taken over. It has a Cirrus Bombardier motor, as has the Royal Navy version WF112 shown in the flying display.

In the large transport section the Viscount 710 G-ALWE, flagship of BEA's 'Discovery' class is shown in full BEA colours. Apart from the registration it only differs from the 700 G-AMAV in having rearward extensions to the pilot's windows. The Comet prototype G-ALVG is still in BOAC livery, but is actually being used by the manufacturers for the testing of Sprite rocket motors. CF-CUM, the other Comet displayed, is the prototype of the Series 1A version with water injection for boosting take-off performance. This machine is for Canadian Pacific Airlines and carries the fleet number 421 on the fin.

Among the medium transports the de Havilland Heron is decorated with large Japanese characters and has the legend 'Japan Air Lines' over the door. In actual fact it is the prototype G-ALZL, shown last year in BEA colours. A Dove with a U.S. flag on the fin and trademarks of Hunkin Conkey Construction Co. of Cleveland, Ohio is another old-timer and is in fact G-AJLW shown at the 1947 Show and since used by the manufacturer as an executive transport (or 'hack' in English!). The Percival Prince G-AMMB, on the other hand, really is G-AMMB this year – we assume PP-NBG has gone to Brazil with its correct letters. The true G-AMMB is equipped as a VIP six-passenger transport with four rearward-facing seats and two orthodox ones. In the flying display is G-AMKY, last of three of the Series 3B machines ordered by the M.C.A. for its Radio Flight. The other Prince on show has no civil connections, being WM735 c/n P.57/49, first of the new batch of T.Mk.1s for the Navy. The Marathon T.Mk.11 XA250 shown by Handley-Page (Reading) is an outcast from the civil register, but even a detailed investigation failed to identify it.

The inevitable Bristol 171 G-ALSX flies alongside the new 173, and apart from a new coat of paint is in the same condition as last year. Another old one is the Prestwick Pioneer G-AKDF appearing in its fifth SBAC Show. The lion on the fin has changed from red to blue since last year. This presumably has no significance – probably just the result of old age. Austers show the now familiar demonstration Aiglet Trainer G-AMMS flown by Porteous, and on the ground the Model B.4 Ambulance/Freighter. This has now acquired a ventral fin extension. The civil letters G-AMKL are back again but the machine still shows traces of its military service during a few recent months when it was flown by the Army and at Boscombe Down as XA177.

Complete list of all aircraft exhibited:

Meteor N.F.11	WM166	Canberra T.4	WN467
J/5F Aiglet Tr.	G-AMMS	Canberra B.5	VX185
J/5G Cirrus Autocar	G-AMPA	Firefly Mk.7	WJ149
B/4 Ambulance	G-AMKL	Gannet Mk.1	WE488
Shackleton Mk.2	WG531	pilotless delta rocket	nil
Vulcan prototype	VX770	Meteor T.7	WL453
Avro 707A	WD280	Javelin Mk.1	WD808
Avro 707B	VX790	Marathon T.11	XA250
Universal Freighter	WF320	Sea Hawk Mk.1	WF147
Freighter 31	NZ5906	Hunter Mk.1	WB195
Sycamore Mk.1	VL958	Prince 3B	G-AMKY
Sycamore Mk.3	G-ALSX	Prince 2 (mod.)	G-AMMB
Bristol 173	G-ALBN	Sea Prince T.Mk.1	WM735
Britannia	G-ALBO	Provost T.Mk.1	WE522
Dove 2	G-AJLW	Princess	G-ALUN
Comet 1 (Sprites)	G-ALVG	Skeeter 3B	WF112
Comet 1A	CF-CUM	Skeeter 5	G-AMTZ
D.H.110	WG236	Pioneer 2	G-AKBF
Venom F.B.Mk.1	WE281	Sealand 1H	G-AIVX
Venom F.B.Mk.1	VV612	Attacker F.B.Mk.2	WK388
Venom N.F.Mk.2	WL808	Supermarine 508	VX136
Sea Venom N.F.Mk.20	WK385	Swift	WJ965
Heron 1	G-ALZL	Swift	WK194
Vampire Tr. Mk.11	WZ429	Varsity T.Mk.1	WF429
Chipmunk T.Mk.10	WP838	Viscount 701	G-ALWE
Avon Canberra	WD943	Valiant B.Mk.1	WB215
Sapphire Canberra	WD933	Wyvern T.F.Mk.4	VZ570
Olympus Canberra	WD952	Dragonfly H.R.Mk.3	WG707

*   *   *

JULY 30th, 1955: FARNBOROUGH NOTES

The highlight of the RAE's Golden Jubilee Exhibition on July 7th-9th to the civilian enthusiast was undoubtedly the appearance of the Kay Gyroplane G-ACVA. This is believed to be the first time it has left its hangar at Perth for about five years, and the first time it has been 'south of the border' since the Royal Aeronautical Society Garden Party of 1938. It still seems to be in first-class condition, the Pobjoy engine being particularly beautifully-kept.

Most of the well-known vintage aircraft were present; noteworthy were the Fulmar G-AIBE, Spitfire AB910 which now also carries its civil registration G-AISU painted below the tailplane, and the D.H.60 Moth G-EBLV which has been repainted blue and silver. The inevitable Tiger Moth G-AMCM was also on show, having been repainted in honour of the occasion; it is now all-silver, with blue cowling and flashes.

Near the Britannia tank test site were some relics of the RAE's Comet investigation; G-ALYS (used for pressure refuelling experiments) is apparently intact; and G-ANAV (used for the flight trials) is now reduced to a bare fuselage. It has recently been announced that six further Comet fuselages are to be tested in the water-tank, so the fate of the remaining Comet 1s is clearly fixed . . .

Highlights of the flying display were a wonderful 'falling leaf' by Neville Duke in the Tomtit G-AFTA on Thursday, and an 'impossible' formation by the Tomtit, Hart, Hurricane and Rapide G-AHGC on the final day.

*   *   *

JULY 14th, 1956: FARNBOROUGH NEWS

Some notes on the present position of the RAE Aero Club may be of interest . . . The well-worn Tiger G-AMCM was badly mauled by a five-barred gate down in Somerset last September, and although we dragged the body back again, its chances of resurrection are very slender. Then the Auster G-ALYB was sold by its owner to Old Warden, and the other Auster G-AHXE went to Thruxton in May (where the Wiltshire School of Flying completed in three weeks a C. of A. overhaul which has lingered for three years!).

The Aeronca 100 G-AEWU had been badly damaged by a hangar collapse, and its bones, together with those of G-AETG, were sold to some enthusiasts at Fair Oaks who are now rebuilding. . . . Thanks to the eagle eye of the ARB, the overhauled machine will probably be registered G-AETG (much to the owner's annoyance!). With the Proctor G-AHAB not much nearer a C. of A. renewal (it expired in June 1953) the local light aviation scene was rather barren.

Things are now looking up again, though. After many hours and months of hard labour, the Club's Tiger Moth G-AJHS is serviceable again, and should be representing BCAN at some of the season's meetings shortly. Latest news is that our tenders for two Chipmunks have been accepted, and WB563 for the Club and WB588 for a private owner should appear on the Register very soon. Even G-AHAB might appear, one day!

*   *   *

MARCH 23rd, 1957: TOAST TO THE TIGER
(written in conjunction with Denis Fox)

A sudden spell of spring on March 3rd was cunningly contrived by Mr Nepean Bishop to coincide with the twenty-fifth anniversary of the Tiger Moth's first C. of A., celebrated by an informal rally for Tigers at Fair Oaks. A good number of visitors turned up, and in due course there were over thirty Tiger Moths and a dozen lesser breeds to be seen on the field.

Air-Britain was represented among the visiting Tiger Moths by G-AJHS from Farnborough and G-ANEW from Croydon, being flown by Peter Keating probably for the last time, as the Airways Club intends to sell all its Tigers immediately. Winner of the arrival competition was one of the Norman Jones fleet from Croydon, G-ANZZ; the oldest civil machine was G-ADWO from Christchurch, which was supported by G-AHVY, G-ANPL and G-AOJJ. Most of the Jones stable of Tigers was present, including the stripped racing machines, Mr Bishop's 'own' G-ANSH with engine modifications to permit inverted flying, and the new taxi-plane version, G-AOXS. This has an elegant canopy over the front cockpit which stretches back to the rear windscreen. The front cockpit is plush-lined, and with the controls deleted has reasonable space for luggage. Colour is silver, with buff letters outlined in blue, and the machine looks most attractive.

Other visiting Tiger Moths were G-AHMN, 'MNN, 'NKY, 'NLB, 'NPI, 'NUE, 'NUH, 'OAA, 'OCX, 'ODR, 'ORY and 'OXJ, while resident machines on the field were 'HRM, 'IJA, 'KGF, 'NDV, 'NOM, 'NPB, 'NUD, 'OAC, 'ODS and 'ODU.

Among the other visitors the Hornet Moth G-AHBL looked very smart, and the Chipmunks G-AOSY and G-AOTT gave a foretaste of the future.

CHAPTER 11

UNDER FIFTEEN BRIDGES

by

MAJOR CHRISTOPHER DRAPER

[Reproduced from the International Auster Club News, Vol. 5, No. 2, 1982, by kind permission of the Club, after originally appearing in 'RAF FLYING REVIEW', May 1958.]

Let me say right away that this flight of mine from Waterloo to Kew under 15 bridges is not the sort of thing to be done on the spur of the moment just because you feel like it. If you pause to think you may remember the tragedy that befell the pilot of a jet who killed himself under the Clifton Suspension Bridge. I myself made two previous attempts at the Thames bridges before my last effort five years ago *[in 1953 – Ed.]*.

It was in Dundee in 1915, when I was at the Seaplane Station of the RNAS, that I first acquired a 'taste' for bridges. The Tay bridge across the Firth of Tay has no less than 29 arches and it was quite good fun flying our large, heavy seaplanes (when we could get off the water) backwards and forwards through these arches. The difficulty, with so many to choose from, was keeping your eye on one particular arch.

My next bridge effort was at the old motor racing track at Brooklands. Just behind the old Sopwith hangars was a small footbridge, and in 1916 when I was stationed with No.3 Wing of the RNAS at Manston I was sent many times to Brooklands to take delivery of the Sopwith 1½ Strutter, which had a 110 h.p. Clerget engine. After a short test flight it was rather fun, by way of waving a farewell, to dive down under the footbridge. It needed a calm day because the slope up and the turn of the track at that point made it a little bit more tricky than any straightforward bridge. As far as I know, the late Harry Hawker, who was then the Sopwith test pilot, was the only other man to fly under the bridge, and he used to do it in a tiny single-seat Scout, whereas the Strutter was a large two-seater. Hawker was, of course, furious with me. How dare this unknown Service chap treat it all so casually and wave goodbye to us as he flew away! He never spoke to me again!

It was September 1931 when I made a first attempt at the Thames bridges. This was in a D.H. Puss Moth with George Hill, an ex-sergeant gunner of the old Royal Flying Corps, as my passenger. We had borrowed a Newman Sinclair Auto-Kine camera, which unfortunately jammed so we did not get a foot of film (someone had left a halfpenny in the works), but it did not matter because the conditions were very bad. It was extremely bumpy and rough, so much so that after flying through the Tower Bridge I abandoned the rest. However, the law had been broken and I duly appeared at the Guildhall Magistrates' Court with two summonses – one for flying to the danger of the public and one for flying without a licence. On this occasion I was bound over a hundred pounds not to do it again for twelve months; the only cost – to sign my name over a four shilling stamp.

It was 27 years later, on the fifth day of the fifth month, 1953, that I finally succeeded. We had actually made an attempt two days previously, but after getting halfway down to the river there seemed far too much wind. I can assure everyone that the Thames can be very tricky indeed if there is even half a knot. I had learned the importance of the most careful preparations, and was nearly 18 months planning and waiting for the right day. I made nine trips up and down the river on a pleasure steamer.

It may not be generally realised that there is a difference in the time of low water between London Bridge and Kew of no less than 2 hours 45 minutes – it is nearly 12 miles. Low water gives an extra ten feet, besides reducing river traffic to a few light craft.

It was, of course, very important that no one should know what I was up to, especially those at the Herts and Essex club where I did my practice flying, otherwise it would have been impossible to hire a machine. A further difficulty was finding someone to come with me. It was important to have a man who could use a cine-camera, nor was it easy to get the loan of a camera – people were afraid of the risks and their insurance. On top of these worries was the big one of finance to enable me to keep up appearances and the big bluff at the club.

My passenger on this last occasion was Joe Matthews, a free-lance photographer, who, incidentally, does not like flying. His difficulty was to hold the camera out of the window in a 90-knot slipstream, which meant it could not be properly sighted. The resulting film, however, turned out to be quite entertaining – though at times there seems to be rather more water than bridges. Joe says I should have held the nose of the machine up a bit more!

It was only a little Auster, a bit underpowered, and my attention was more or less taken up with the job of getting through the 18 bridges from Waterloo to Kew.

The most agonising moment of the whole escapade was arriving over the river at 1.30 p.m., circling around at 4,000 feet, waiting for 1.45, the time I had fixed to begin. Joe told me afterwards that from that height the bridges looked like the eyes of a needle and quite impossible, and he was convinced I was really mad! I remember I did say to him that I did not like the look of the acute turn of the river at Charing Cross Bridge and might go over it, but he turned his head away and would not speak.

We came down low over Blackfriars Bridge to about ten feet or less over the water, and found the conditions as nearly perfect as they are ever likely to be, not a bump in the air nor a ripple on the water. We started at Waterloo because the previous summons was by the City Police, whereas Waterloo is in the Metropolitan Area, and I did not want to antagonise the City Police a second time. I did not know that nowadays the whole river comes under the jurisdiction of the River Police.

Waterloo was easy, with its wide sweeping arches, but Hungerford looked too dangerous, so I slipped over the top. Then to Westminster, in the shadow of Big Ben. Here were the narrowest arches on the river, and they gave me an anxious moment. But there was ample clearance.

I was getting into my stride now and went through Lambeth and Vauxhall without a qualm. But then I came to the severest test of the lot; Victoria railway bridge with, immediately after it, Chelsea. The two are so close together that they both have to be taken at one stride. Once under Victoria, I was committed to Chelsea, too; there was no room for second thoughts.

But it was all too easy! Apart from another railway bridge farther up, and the bridge at Kew, where the river on the other side seemed congested with an island and small craft, I went through them all according to plan.

We landed back at Broxbourne at 2.30, and I went as usual to the flight office to sign in and ask how much I owed for the time up. Buster Frogley was sitting there alone and was very angry. The River Police had been remarkably quick – my registration number, G-AGYD, had been spotted and they had been on the phone to the club. Buster asked what I had done.

After telling him, I said: "Don't worry. I don't suppose I will ever fly again," and he said: "You bloody well won't from this club."

We got back to my flat at about 4.30 to find the street outside more or less in a traffic jam. It seemed the whole of Fleet Street had turned up with one very young constable in uniform, who said his chief, Inspector Morley of the River Police, had sent him to tell me he would like to see me. The whole grisly process of the law was set in motion again.

The next move came from the Ministry of Civil Aviation – my licence was suspended, pending the result of 'certain proceedings in another place,' and shortly after this I was served with FOUR summonses, TWO charges on each! The maximum penalty for each charge could be six months and/or £200. It was therefore possible to be fined £1,600 and go to prison for four years.

There was no alternative to a plea of guilty, but the magistrate, Frank Milton, bless him, discharged me conditionally on payment of ten guineas costs, the condition being that I commit no further offence for twelve months. He pointed out, in no uncertain manner, and as a warning to others, what he could have done to me.

It took eight months to get my licence restored; I was very glad about this, because, as far as I have been able to ascertain, there is now only one other pilot left who was flying in 1913, 45 years ago, who has a pilot's licence today.

WHY DID I DO IT? This question has been put to me many times. The answer is simple and straightforward. It was to prove that because a man is over 45 he is not necessarily ready for a wheelchair. I was 61 at the time and quite desperate for a job. As a member of the Over-45s Association, it was appalling to know that many, who though in full possession of all their faculties, simply could not get work. Perhaps my little gesture may have contributed something towards the appointment of a Home Office Committee to inquire into the whole question. And, at any rate, it proved there's life in the old dog yet!

CHAPTER 12

SCHOOLDAYS AND SHOREHAM

by

PETER G. CAMPBELL

After my first-ever flight, at the age of thirteen, in a D.H. Dominie in driving rain at the 1950 Lee-on-Solent Air Display, I was well and truly bitten by the aeroplane bug. But it was not until June 1952 that I was persuaded by my school friend Tim Foster (himself a contributor to this book) to take an interest in individual aircraft by noting their registrations or serials. Thanks, Tim, for sparking off a lifetime's interest! At this time, we were at school at Lancing College, which sits on the South Downs conveniently overlooking Shoreham Airport.

I have a note that the resident aircraft at Shoreham on the 22nd June 1952 were as follows:

G-AITS & G-AIZK Hawk Trainer 3, G-AMDJ Aries, G-AKHF Aerovan 6 (with Lycoming engines), G-AHBI Proctor 5, G-AHVR Taylorcraft Plus D, G-AFHS B.A. Swallow 2 and G-AFSV Chilton DW.1.

On this day, as on most other weekends, there were many visiting aircraft, and a couple of weeks later, on the 6th July, the rare Dart Kitten G-AEXT paid an unexpected visit. American-built visitors included the Piper Cubs that they flew from Gatwick in those days, and the Aeronca Champion N79854 which later became G-AOEH (and is still airworthy).

Larger aircraft such as various Doves and a Prince were fairly regular visitors, along with the Dragon Rapides of East Anglian Flying Services and also those of Don Everall Aviation and Marshall's of Cambridge, who used to fly in jockeys for the horse-racing at Brighton. By 1954 we had the occasional visiting DC-3, along with more exotic types such as the Provost, Balliol, Firefly and even Varsity.

Other highlights during the early fifties included Summer Camps with swarms of Army Austers from Kenley, the development flying of the Sparrowjet G-ADNL, and a weekend visit in March

1954 by the Hurel-Dubois HD-31. This was unusual to say the least; it had an enormous wingspan for its weight, and had been designed to investigate the phenomenon of decreased drag at low cruising speeds when using a very high aspect ratio wing. The official photograph from 'THE AEROPLANE' has a special significance for me as I appear in the background!

Much of our spare-time spotting on weekdays took place on the balcony of the school chapel, where we could get quite a good view of the aerodrome, although we needed more than ordinary binoculars to make any positive identifications. Fortunately my father had lent me his ex-World War One telescope with 30-times magnification, but being made of brass this was very heavy and needed to be supported by the parapet of the balcony to keep it steady.

Sundays were special to us, as after morning chapel we were free for much of the day! Whenever a Sunday was fine enough for flying (and there seemed to be a lot more of them in those days) I and a fellow enthusiast (often Tim Foster) would install ourselves on the long bank near the Sussex Pad Hotel on the north side of the A27 overlooking the whole of the aerodrome. Sadly this superb vantage point is no longer in existence as it was bulldozed away some years ago when the road was widened to a dual carriageway.

We normally arrived at about half past eleven and were able to stay until just before half past five, so managed to witness most of the activities of the day. The snacks and drinks that we had brought with us were very welcome during our vigil, especially in the colder months, when we even had a Primus stove with us for brewing up hot drinks. Summer Sundays were enlivened by the regular arrival at about three o'clock of the Alpine Ices van, whose driver grew used to our appearing out of the shrubbery and flagging him down; his orange ice-cream 'brickettes,' sandwiched between two wafers, were a taste experience which I have never forgotten!

Apart from the aircraft which actually landed at Shoreham, many others, such as the Chipmunks and Austers of Air Service Training at Hamble, used the airfield as a turning point. Many Service aircraft also overflew the area, some of them quite unusual, such as US Navy R4D-8s and Albatrosses, probably from Manston. However the majority of types were from RNAS Ford, near Bognor Regis, and these included Attackers, Avengers, Fireflies, Sea Balliols, Sea Furies, Sea Hawks, Vampire Trainers & Wyverns. Others, such as Meteors and Varsities, came from Tangmere and Thorney Island, and even RAE Farnborough provided the occasional *rara avis*, such as the all-red Lincoln WD125, the Derwent-Lincoln SX971, the Varsity prototype VX828, the Eland-Varsity

VX835 and the deflected-jet testbed Meteor 4 RA490.

In May of 1953 the quiet of mid-week afternoons was frequently disturbed by the roar of dozens upon dozens of Merlin engines as formations of Lincoln bombers flew east along the coast at low altitude; this occurred almost daily during the fortnight immediately prior to the Coronation on the 2nd June 1953, as they rehearsed for the official flypast. As the fuselages were black with enormous white serial numbers, identification was easy using the telescope.

On the more leisurely side, advertising by banner-towing was quite common, and I well remember one day seeing the message 'Right Monkey' being borne over our heads in huge red letters behind the Auster 5 G-AJAK, and wondering what it could be advertising as it made no sense to me! It was only later that I discovered that the comedian Al Read, whose catchphrase this was, was doing his summer show in Brighton.

By this time I was a member of the school's Air Training Corps, and was duly sent off to Camp at RAF Cranwell at the end of July 1953. I have found in my diary the list of things which we were told to take with us: kitbag, groundsheet, emergency ration card, Service Record book, extra pair of shoes, extra pair of trousers, coat, towel, soap, toothbrush, toilet paper, change of underclothing, pair of gym-shoes, swimming trunks, running vest, running shorts, knife, fork, spoon and drinking mug. I cannot remember what we were intended to carry all of this in: perhaps it did all fit in one suitcase but it sounds unlikely! In accordance with standard forces procedure we were ordered to salute any officer we should pass, and after a confusing incident one afternoon shortly after leaving the NAAFI mess I had to remember that in future I should be sure to hold my cutlery and mug in my *left* hand!

On the second day of the Camp, there was some very important event taking place at the College, which on reflection must have been the annual Passing Out Parade, made even more of a special occasion because it was Coronation Year: I am fairly sure that the Queen was present.

An enormous selection of Service aircraft arrived for the occasion (including 15 Ansons, 8 Devons, 8 Meteors, 4 Valettas, 4 Harvards, 3 Shackletons and 2 Dakotas), and to my delight we were allowed to wander unmolested around them all during the afternoon. I remember discovering hidden amongst the larger aircraft the Autocrat G-AJIE and the Nighthawk G-AGWT (flown by a Wing Commander).

A month or so later I was on my way to the Isle of Wight for a few days holiday; my parents had friends in Seaview who provided

Bed & Breakfast accomodation, and whilst staying there I was lent a bicycle so that I could tour the three local aerodromes (Ryde, Bembridge and Sandown). The sole aircraft at Ryde was the green Autocrat G-AGYM, but at Bembridge a Bristol Freighter (G-AIFV) was engaged in loading cars, the first time I had seen this fascinating operation. When I got back to Ryde Pier the Saunders Roe Princess G-ALUN obligingly flew over sufficiently low for me to photograph it.

In 1954 I enjoyed a rather unusual flight: this was as the result of a competition in the *'Evening Standard'* newspaper, which during 1953-5 operated a bright red Westland-Sikorsky S.51 helicopter G-ANAL (a registration that was changed to G-ANZL in March 1955, presumably because it was considered that some people might find it offensive). I entered the competition without any expectation of being adjudged a winner, writing an essay on the theme provided, appropriately entitled "Why I Would Like to Fly in the Evening Standard Helicopter"; I was very surprised indeed to be picked as one of the twenty-five lucky winners. On Sunday the 18th July time away from school was granted for me to make the flight from Croydon, and although it lasted for only eight minutes I had now flown in a helicopter, a rare privilege in those days for a schoolboy. I was in eager anticipation shortly before the flight as I had discovered that one of my fellow passengers was called Jean Simmons (my favourite 'heart-throb' of the time), but alas a meeting with the great star was not to be!

As members of the ATC we were given several opportunities to fly, because once or twice a term an Anson from RAF Kenley would arrive at Shoreham to give Air Experience flights to some of us. Kenley's Ansons could always be recognised by their yellow spinners, and three examples in which I flew were MH117, PH528 & PH606. Normally there was a telephone call earlier in the day to warn us that an aircraft was coming, but one Friday afternoon we were busy assembling the school's primary glider (of which more in a moment) when I noticed a yellow-spinnered Anson flying low down the valley, obviously intent on landing at Shoreham. Fortunately I had sufficient credentials as a 'spotter' to be able to convince our instructor, Bill Dovell, that it had come for *us*, and we hastily left everything just as it was and ran (or 'sweated' might be a more appropriate word) in our uniforms to the aerodrome a mile or more away; it was just as well for me that on this occasion I happened to be right!

In June 1955, I took my 'A' Level exams, and after they were over there was a still a good month go before the end of term. It was usual for pupils then to be found some sort of work experience for a few weeks, which naturally had to be approved by teachers and parents alike. As for me, I had already made up my mind earlier in the year that I wanted to spend this time working for F.G. Miles Ltd. at Shoreham Airport, despite strong opposition from both my father and the Headmaster, who seemed to consider my interest in such things as aeroplanes to be a great waste of time. However I am pleased to say that common sense finally prevailed and it was eventually agreed by everyone concerned that I *would* be allowed to work at the aerodrome after all. And so, for three weeks beginning the 4th July 1955, I was employed by F.G. Miles Ltd on work experience; I must say that these weeks were probably the busiest and most enjoyable in my life, and I have never regretted one moment of them.

George Miles, who was a great deal more understanding of my interests than were my parents and teachers (as I suppose one might expect), ensured that I first had a whole week in Air Traffic Control under the watchful eye of a vivacious red-haired lady controller called Yvonne, who was very patient with her young and enthusiastic charge. It was a great privilege in those days for an eighteen-year-old to be able to file Flight Plans, meet the visiting pilots and book them in and out. I can remember an instructor from Croydon, 'Tiny' Marshall, a heavily-built man made to look several sizes larger still by being encased in the Sidcot flying suit obligatory for Tiger Moth operation throughout the year; he was having great problems with his hay fever that day. And then there was the pilot of a Dragon Rapide who, before he set off on a return solo flight to Newcastle, mentioned that he was not feeling too well; we heard later that he had made a forced landing at RAF Dishforth and had immediately collapsed at the controls, so he was fortunate to be alive. One fine afternoon the Spartan Arrow G-ABWP arrived from Denham, piloted by a Mr Dennison, and I persuaded him to let me take a photograph of him and his lady passenger in front of it.

Other memorable happenings during those three weeks included the first recorded visits of an Auster AOP9 (WZ 666) and a Beaver (G-AMVU), four Ansons arriving in formation, and the delivery by road of Meteor FR.9 VZ608 for modifications by F.G. Miles Ltd. At the time I was obviously not aware of the nature of this work, which of course was top secret, but in 1989, after I had met George Miles once again, he explained it in a personal letter to me as follows:

"The work on the Meteor originated with a contract from Rolls Royce who required a flying test bed for the RB.108 engines which could cover the transitional flight range between vertical take-off

and level flight with the lift engines shut down. The two RB.108s were installed on trunnions behind the cockpit with controls which provided several degrees of tilt in either direction from the vertical position.

Flight testing took place at Hucknall and provided data for the design of the Short SC.1."

So this must have been the very beginning of the project that was to culminate in the Harrier jump-jet many years later. This particular Meteor is still in existence and is currently being refurbished at the Newark Air Museum.

During the second and third weeks I worked in the assembly hangars on the Miles Aries G-AOGA, and amongst other basic skills I was taught how to drill and shape some metal brackets (which were to be used for attaching something important to the engines – I forget what!). At the end of the three weeks, I was called in to see George Miles, who thanked me for my contribution and insisted that I accepted a 'gift' of £6 as payment for the time I had been there; this was totally unexpected and a very generous gesture, as it was not an unreasonable sum of money for a teenager in those days (I estimate the current equivalent to be nearly £200).

During the summer holidays, I had a memorable flight from Croydon on the 20th September 1955. This was classified as an Air Experience Flight, and to be eligible I had to be wearing my ATC uniform; I was then entitled, at Her Majesty's expense, to about an hour and a half of flying at no cost to myself. A Mr Hibberson of the Surrey Flying Group, who had volunteered his services as pilot for the afternoon, met me at the airport and asked if there was anywhere I would particularly like to go; as it was a warm late summer day without a cloud in the sky, what else could I say but "How about Shoreham?" So we enjoyed an idyllic flight down to the coast in the blue & yellow Hornet Moth G-AELO.

During my last term at school in the autumn of 1955, there was still plenty going on at Shoreham, including the first visits of a Skeeter and a Twin Pioneer, and the first flight of the new Aries on which I had worked, which I remember had a phenomenal rate of climb. Several foreign-registered aircraft were noted, including Messenger 2A EI-AHL, Navion F-BESH, Auster 4 D-ELIT and TF-OSK, a Proctor 4; the Proctor was particularly interesting as it had been converted at Croydon directly from a demobbed RAF machine (NP278) and never carried a U.K. registration; it was intended for export to Iceland, but this never happened, and after a period at Croydon in early 1956 it was exported to Sweden instead.

Earlier in the year I had been made Flight Sergeant in the ATC, and now every fine Friday afternoon I was put in charge of assembling WZ796, the school's Slingsby Grasshopper primary glider (Ah! Grasshopper), in one of the playing fields. The opportunity of a free though short solo flight was something that we all learned to wait for patiently week after week until, at last, it was our turn; being of senior rank, it was my duty to wait until all the other cadets had flown, but my turn eventually came at last on the 18th of November when I made my only solo flight – fortunately without incident.

For those readers who may not have experienced the dubious joys of operating this type of aircraft, the Grasshopper had an almost two-dimensional fuselage framework of spruce, with a plywood seat bolted on in front of a pylon which supported the wings along with bracing wires. Both the wings and tail unit were fabric-covered and fairly conventional. Before each flying session the glider had to be fully assembled, and then afterwards it had to be dismantled again, as we stored it in a prefabricated concrete garage nearby.

When all pre-flight checks were complete, the aircraft was then attached to a stout peg firmly driven into the ground. Then a thick V-shaped rubber bungee was fixed by a ring to the nose, and this was stretched to its extreme by two teams of 'volunteers.' I could visualise two teams of boys unable to withstand the pull of this stretched bungee and hurtling out of control back towards the glider at an ever-increasing rate, but in practice the launch was always uneventful. When a toggle was pulled by the pilot to release the glider from the peg, the acceleration was generally sufficient for it to leave the ground for ten or twenty yards; this was quite an experience to remember although it hardly compared with the first flight of the Wright Brothers. Our only recorded mishap occurred when the Instructor, our science master Bill Dovell, made a heavier than usual landing and his backside went right through the plywood seat!

I have recently learned that our glider WZ796 is still in existence in Gloucestershire, owned by Peter Mallinson; I would love to sit in it again. There are few remaining examples now, but at the time Grasshoppers were standard issue to all schools with ATC Forces.

And so on the 18th December 1955 I finally said goodbye to Lancing College and Shoreham Airport. However, as later events were to prove, it was not really 'goodbye' but very much 'au revoir,' as I must have been back to Shoreham Airport almost every year since!

I can remember one such visit particularly well. On the 24th of

102

July 1957, less than three months after my great friend David Timmis had got his licence at Fair Oaks under the Flying Scholarship scheme, we decided to embark on a cross-country flight to Shoreham; the aircraft was Tiger Moth G-ANUD (in which he had had his first lesson, coincidentally). About ten minutes or so after passing Guildford, we spotted ahead the tell-tale plume of smoke from the cement works just south of Steyning (sadly no longer there to act as a giant warning 'windsock' to visiting pilots), and within a few minutes landed at Shoreham, just after half past three local time. We had a cup of tea and then examined the visiting and resident aircraft, which included the HDM.105 Aerovan-based development, G-AHDM, and the Miles Student still in its Class 'B' markings as G-35-4.

Within about an hour we took off for Fair Oaks. The weather that afternoon was beginning to deteriorate from the south-west; the sun had gone in and the cloud, although still fairly high, was developing a lower layer which could only bring rain in time. There was not much communication between us (those Gosport tubes were not intended for casual chat), but after about twenty minutes I realised that, whereas we should have been somewhere near Guildford, I was unable to recognise any of the terrain beneath us. I was not made to feel any more confident when I shouted as much to David and he, too, admitted that he didn't recognise where we were either!

So here we were, two inexperienced teenage aviators, in charge of one of the Club's Tiger Moths, without radio, in rapidly worsening weather conditions, and without being too sure of just how much fuel there was left (this was not uncommon in a Tiger). Ours was not a unique situation by any means but it is not one that I can recommend in any way; in fact, I think that if it was to happen to me now it would prove to be a real 'white-knuckle' experience. But oh! for the innocence and optimism of youth! At the time we had probably never tasted real danger before, so I'm sure that we didn't recognise the true potential of the situation. Quite undaunted, we decided to press on, hoping to identify some feature or other, and it was not too long before we came upon a railway line (inevitable in those days, fortunately). We followed it northwards until we spotted a station, and then with one of David's famous side-slips we quickly lost enough height for me to be able to recognise it as Haselmere (on the main line from Waterloo to Portsmouth and about halfway between Fair Oaks and Portsmouth); we were at least 25 miles further to the south-west than we should have been! All I can think of is that David must have set up the compass incorrectly before we left Shoreham, but we certainly appreciated the opportunity to fly by 'Bradshaw' that day, and reached Fair Oaks without further incident in another twenty minutes or so. We were closely followed in by J.R. Johnston's Hawk Trainer Coupé G-AJRT which, so it turned out, had left Shoreham three-quarters of an hour later than us!

It has come to my mind more than once since then that perhaps it was that particular experience which made David realise that he had a lot to learn in the navigation department: he certainly made up for it later, first in the Tiger Club and then as a kingpin of the British Precision Flying Team, before he regrettably lost his life in a freak accident in 1990.

For me, the most recent high point relating to Shoreham was on the 15th June 1996, when I was present to witness the results of my efforts at organising a special Vintage Fly-In at the Airport, as part of the 60th Anniversary celebrations of the Terminal Building. I am fortunate enough to possess the official Shoreham Movements Books for most of the 1950s, and so earlier in the year I had been able to send out special invitations to owners of aircraft which had actually visited Shoreham (or had been based there) during the late forties and the fifties. Probably not too many of those attending the event by road realised that over fifty of the visiting aircraft had specific associations with the airfield of one sort or another.

On that day I couldn't help noticing that the huge clock which has always graced the north face of the Terminal Building was missing its hands; although the prosaic reason for this was undoubtedly that it was out of order and awaiting repairs, I was reminded in some perverse way that the appeal of Shoreham is indeed timeless!

CHAPTER 13

OF HUMMING, DRONES AND GIPSY QUEENS

by

TED GOULD

(as told to

PETER G. CAMPBELL)

[NOTES ON THE AUTHOR: When Ted Gould came out of the Air Force, he bought the Broadway Garage in Bournemouth, which, although it provided him a living from repairing motor cars until he sold it in 1966, was also the scene of a number of aircraft restorations over the years; these were his hobby at that time, and indeed he is still very active in light aircraft building and restoration. It is perhaps significant that almost all the aircraft he had a hand in restoring or owning are still in existence today.

Although many of his achievements have been chronicled in an excellent article by Jack Meaden (Air-Britain Digest, Vol. 46, No. 3, Autumn 1994), the following experiences have not been published before: this applies also to the later chapter entitled 'Christchurch Chronicles'.]

TAYLORCRAFT PLUS D G-AHUM

My friend Tommy Marshall and I bought 'HUM from Exeter, and ferried her back to Thruxton on the 27th November 1949. I was still learning to fly and hadn't yet got my 'A' licence although Tommy had his. I did quite a bit of flying in 'HUM to build up hours, along with Bert Hawkins, who was the instructor then at Thruxton.

On the 22nd of December, only a month or so later, I had taken off in 'HUM and the engine then cut out at 150 feet; I couldn't make it to line up with the runway, so I did a partial circuit but had to land in a field adjacent to the end of the runway. Of course the aircraft tended to float a bit, not having flaps, and I overran into the hedge at the end; I got a bump on my head and damaged the prop and the undercarriage.

What had happened was that the throttle arm had fallen off; it had not been locked because of a missing split-pin, and so the revs had gone back to tick-over.

After the repairs were done, I finally qualified for my 'A' licence on the 27th April 1950, and later that year did a lot of flying with Roger Mann, including quite an historic flight down to Lympne in Kent and all around the coast in that area. That was as a prelude to the *'Daily Express'* South Coast Air Race. Tommy Marshall and I had just bought the D.H. Moth G-AAWO which we entered for the race; it was flown by Roger and he did very well, actually. But I still did a lot of flying in the Taylorcraft; it was a very good aircraft.

[By 1952 'HUM was part of the Club fleet at Christchurch, and was repainted in the distinctive colours of an olive green fuselage with silver registration, and silver wings and fin with olive green letters. It was a regular sight along the south coast during 1953 & 1954, and was then sold to D.G.S. Cotter at Gatwick. Its C. of A. expired on the 16th June 1955, and it was later rebuilt in about 1961, incorporating sufficient components from other aircraft for it to be re-registered G-ARRK. It was then sold abroad to Ireland as EI-AMF and is last reported being rebuilt at Abbeyshrule in 1993 – Ed.]

DRAGON RAPIDE G-AIYR

In the October of 1955 Viv Bellamy took myself and my wife and a few more people from the Eastleigh Aero Club down to Tangier. This was the aircraft that he had converted with variable-pitch props; I think the Gipsy Queen engines may have been from Proctors. It had a very good rate of climb, could reach a greater altitude, and gave a slightly better cruising speed than the standard Rapide.

We had pretty marginal weather most of the way to Bordeaux, and from there we were intending to go down to Biarritz. The weather report, which Viv was very careful to get, because I saw it, was pretty marginal, but it was quite acceptable. The conditions at Bordeaux were perfectly all right for flying, but as we went along the coast, which was quite a long way, gradually the cloud base got lower and lower, and when we got to Biarritz you could just about see the lighthouse. Of course these were early days, and we called up Biarritz and there were some hysterical screams in French: it was no good, it was hopeless, they couldn't accept us, they hadn't got any aids. It was really quite grim! Anyway, Viv made two or three tries to find the airfield; we went over the town, with several chimneys poking up alongside the wings, which was quite frightening to all of us, and in and out of low cloud. But we couldn't find the field, so he turned round and climbed back into the cloud and went back along the coast, which we could find because it was a little bit clearer there. We then came down to fly northwards along the beach, so that we could get to the next aerodrome, the only one being Bordeaux, which was quite a long way away.

However, before we could get there the weather had become very very poor, and darkness was falling, which made it very difficult to cut inland to get to Bordeaux. So Viv elected to land on the beach; he had said he was going to ditch, and everyone was prepared for that, but he landed beautifully, a most fantastic landing on the beach between all the boats at Arcachon. We thankfully got out of the aircraft, after having had quite a long time to have thoughts of the next world! Amazingly there was no damage to the aircraft itself, although one wing had just touched a boat which was so rotten that the whole bow section had then fallen off! I think we paid compensation, probably far more than the boat was worth.

We spent that night in a local hotel, and the next morning we managed to get some fuel for Viv, and he took off from the beach solo and flew the aircraft up to Bordeaux. The rest of us went by car, and when we met up at the airport the authorities seemed very niggly that we'd landed on the beach. I'm afraid I went very strongly at the Commandant, who said he didn't understand English, but I'm sure he did; he understood my language well enough, anyway! I said it was disgraceful that they had issued a report which suggested that the weather was quite acceptable for our proposed flight, but was obviously not right because by the time we got to Biarritz it was dreadful. However, we decided not to press the point!

By the next day the weather had improved a lot, and we took off and climbed easily over the Pyrenees to get down into Madrid, where we stayed the night; the next day we went on to Tangier, a really lovely trip.

[The Dragon Rapide G-AIYR is currently owned by Clacton Aero Club and is used for pleasure flying at Clacton and Duxford – Ed.]

KRONFELD DRONE G-AEKV

I have always been interested in 'minimal' aircraft, and when the Drone came up for sale early in 1956, I took the opportunity to acquire it from John Fricker at Broxbourne, and brought it back by road to Christchurch aerodrome.

It was more or less airworthy, although the Authorization to Fly had expired on the 11th June 1954, and it wasn't long before I was experiencing several of its unique flying characteristics.

One was the nature of the water cooling system for the Carden Ford 32 h.p. engine. The rate of climb was abysmal in any case, but if you managed to get the nose up a bit more, most of the water (and there wasn't much of it) started to boil, causing the engine to become overheated very quickly.

Another was the enormous amount of noise it made, which was the main reason I eventually sold it, but more of that later.

I can remember my flight on June 17th 1956 particularly well because I can admit to being frightened at various times! There was a Popular Flying Association Rally (probably one of the first) planned at Shoreham that weekend, with visitors from the continent expected, and I very much wanted to attend. The weather was not too good, with quite a stiff breeze blowing, but undaunted I left Christchurch for Shoreham (helped quite a bit by the wind behind me), accompanied by the Auster Autocrat G-AJAC, flown by Adam Fisher with Jack Harris as passenger.

I managed a few hundred feet of height over the New Forest, and passed by the Sway tower at the same level as the top of it. I then had to fly over the Solent. The Auster, in order to keep back with me as my 'shadow,' had to fly almost continual circuits around me with one or two degrees of flap down! It took us about three quarters of an hour to reach Portsmouth, where we stopped for a drink. By the time we took off the visibility was getting worse, but I flew so low that it didn't really matter that much! I followed the railway line to Chichester, where I went round, rather than over, the cathedral. Anyway, we both reached Shoreham without any real problems just before eleven o'clock.

By the time I took off from Shoreham at about half past two the wind had increased considerably, and of course to make things more difficult I now had a headwind. It took me about an hour and a half to make Portsmouth, just over 30 miles away! By that time I needed a break, and had a quick drink and chat with Harry Mitchell. When I took off again from Portsmouth, I managed to gain a little height (about 200 feet) over the harbour, and when I turned the nose towards Christchurch, I could see a destroyer down below. A few minutes later I had another look to gauge how much progress I was making, and was astonished to see that the destroyer was still in exactly the same position relative to the aircraft. At that point I realised that it was not just the ship that was stationary – so was the Drone! I could see all the details of the crew and the deck quite clearly.

The wind speed had by now obviously increased to be equivalent to my flying speed (which was about 40 m.p.h.), or perhaps slightly more. I obviously wasn't going to get home to Christchurch that evening, so the only thing to do was to turn round and try to get back to the aerodrome at Portsmouth again. As I did so and began the downwind leg, the aerodrome seemed to rush past me and I was afraid of leaving it a long way behind, but I managed to turn, and found that I was then more or less stationary over the hangars; finally I got down a little bit lower and managed to get into the lee of them, when the wind abated enough for me to get the Drone on the ground, at less than walking speed, I remember.

Harry was watching all of this, and when I had safely manoeuvred the Drone out of the worst of the wind passed the comment: "You're better off on the bloody bus, aren't you?", a sentiment with which I fully agreed at the time.

It later turned out that the Drone and the Auster had been the only two aircraft that attended the meeting that day, and I was quite annoyed to read in the P.F.A.'s write-up of the event (or rather non-event) that I 'slipped in through a gap in the clouds'; in actual fact I was flying so low that the clouds didn't make any difference! I was rather proud of that flight, and I think justifiably so; after all, nobody else apart from Adam Fisher in the Auster managed to get there on that day (Sunday), and the Drone was a pretty marginal aircraft at the best of times.

[Twelve French home-built machines had been expected on the Saturday but were not able to cross the channel, and the Tipsy G-AFSC had force-landed at Hastings en route. The only aircraft that did manage to struggle through the low cloud and heavy rain on the Saturday was Tiger Moth G-ANUE from Stapleford – Ed.]

The Drone actually handled pretty well in the air and was quite a delight to fly. But it was rather noisy, and in fact that was the main reason I finally sold it, because we started to get some of the local residents complaining about it. As there was no gearbox, the tiny propeller was driven directly off the engine, so the revs were very high, and consequently the tips of the prop were almost going supersonic (rather like the Harvard).

There's a historic story about the noise it made: I often used to fly into Hurn on a summer evening, and the controllers were very cooperative and pleased to see us. On one occasion I landed back at Christchurch, where there was no flying going on at the time, and as I taxied up, Tommy Marshall said, "I could hear that bloody thing start up at Hurn, and hear you all the way back!"

About three weeks after the Shoreham trip, on the 8th July, I

109

had to make a forced landing in the Drone. On this particular Sunday evening I had been flying around quite a bit locally. When taking off it was important to clear the aerodrome as quickly as possible, although on reflection this wasn't awfully clever because you had very little height at that stage. I had taken off and was flying down Dennison Avenue, which was just adjacent to the field and led down to the main road with Henley's Garage on the corner. As I got halfway down the avenue and had reached about 300 feet, the engine radically dropped revs as one plug cut out: I was losing power and couldn't keep the height up. There was the awful prospect of all the council houses in the estate on the other side of the road, but it would have been very stupid to have turned back and I thought I might just about clear the main road. So I kept it straight, and then I saw the local school and its tiny playing field, which was clear apart from the basketball posts in it. I managed to pop the Drone down there safely, but ran on and just touched the leading edge on one of these posts, which bent a bit.

I jumped out of the aircraft, and prepared to walk the half mile or so back to the aerodrome, and it was then that the caretaker rushed towards me shouting: "There's an aeroplane crashed, there's an aeroplane crashed!"

I looked at him and said: "Well, it didn't actually crash, old boy, it's a sort of forced landing."

As he skidded to a halt and looked round, there was the aeroplane standing in the field, and me in my flying jacket talking to him; I shall never forget the remarkable look on his face!

Then several people came over from the Club to find me, and we took the wings off there and then and carried the aircraft back to the airfield, as it was that close. I also remember that awful meeting with my wife and children when she tore up in the car and really chewed me up, accusing me of behaving dangerously, without considering her and the children. I was duly chastised: no, I mean chastened!

I rang up the headmaster the next day and apologised, and he said: "Well, it's all right, I shan't put in a report, but would you get someone to come along and bend my basketball post straight again, and then I'll forget all about it."

One day Viv Bellamy came down from Eastleigh; he was game to fly any sort of aircraft, and I persuaded him to jump in the Drone, which he did with a sort of mock horror on his face! He did fly it round, and very quickly encountered the poor rate of climb and the overheating problem.

When he came back down his comment was: "That's marvellous; I haven't been so frightened for a long time!" After a short pause he added: "You don't want to sell it, do you?"

I said cautiously: "Well, everything's for sale."

He then asked: "What sort of price do you want for it?"

So I said: "Oh, about a hundred pounds, I suppose."

His reaction to that was: "Well, things are a bit tight at the moment; there's nothing we can do a deal on, is there?"

If I recall correctly, he had two Gloster Gladiators at Eastleigh; one of them he had rebuilt to flying condition, but the other one was pretty well complete except for a few bits that he had taken off to help with the restoration of the first one.

He said: "Well, you can have the Gladiator if you like, that's about the only thing."

"What would I want a heap of old rubbish like that for?" I retorted.

How stupid can you be?

[Ted finally sold the Drone after about eighteen months because of the complaints about the noise it made; it went up to Vigors Aviation at Kidlington, and after eighteen months there it was delivered on the 25th January 1959 by Tim Vigors himself to a new owner at Shoreham, of all places, where it remained as a resident for several months before going briefly to another owner in Hertfordshire, and then to Elwyn McAully at Little Snoring in Norfolk. Currently it is owned by Mike Beach and is kept at the Brooklands Museum in excellent condition, although it has not flown since 1960 – Ed.]

CHAPTER 14

THE CAMBRIDGE FLYING GROUP

by

BILL ISON

[The major part of this article was first published in 'Vintage Aircraft' No.20, April – June 1981, and it has recently been brought up to date by Bill Ison himself – Ed.]

At the end of 1953, as the RAFVR was thinning out, I was approached by John Peak to join with him and his associates in forming No.22 Flying Group under the auspices of the Popular Flying Association. I was at that time instructing with No.22 Reserve Flying School on Chipmunk aircraft but the writing on the wall said that this was to end and it was with some trepidation that I agreed to the proposition. I had certain misgivings because I have always had a great respect for the 'bull' of the Service and little time for the slapdash of some private owner operations. Now that I am responsible for civilian aircraft I have tried to adopt and preserve some of the discipline which I am sure is the backbone of safety and the reliable operation of aircraft.

John Peak was operating Gemini G-AKHV in those days and I was flung in at the deep end by giving dual instruction to would-be twin pilots on this very pleasant aircraft. The Cirrus Minor engines were never the most reliable, as I found out on the day when I chopped one for a student to carry out a forced landing. On base leg we were treated to a loud bang and the live engine packed up, having pushed out a cylinder. Oh, the joys of civilian aircraft! For that matter, it had happened to me a year before when flying an Oxford at 8,000 feet in cloud over Yarmouth, but on that occasion we were all wearing parachutes and it had not seemed so bad!

During this period the other member owners of No.22 Flying Group were operating a Proctor and a Chrislea Ace, G-AKVB, neither of which were suitable for *ab initio* training. By forming themselves into a Group they availed themselves of a rebate payable by the Government on hours flown. However, I was interested in the basic training aspect and the committee enlisted the aid of Mr Reg Marsh who loaned his Taylorcraft Plus C/2, G-AFWM, for this purpose. I viewed this little aircraft with some disdain – not only was it lacking in paint, but it was powered by another bloody Cirrus engine. In all fairness it proved most reliable and after a respray looked and flew quite well. The fuel tap fell off during one flight but since the cock was in the 'ON' position at that moment, the flight proved uneventful.

We commenced a training programme and I enlisted an RAFVR pal of mine who had joined with me back in 1946, one Jimmy Taylor. I think he shared my views that were instilled into the gang of cowboys calling themselves No.22 Private Flying Group. Jim had flown Stirlings with No.7 Squadron until a Luftwaffe night-fighter brought him down on the way back from Stuttgart and he had ended his RAF flying in Stalag Luft III. Jimmy proved a great help with instruction, and we became busy enough to look for better things.

My idea was to obtain an aerobatic and spinnable machine and after looking at a very smooth Magister (with canopy) my adrenalin speeded up quite a bit. Unfortunately this aircraft, nice as it was, was very cramped because of the canopy, and we looked further afield. Joy of joys – a Tiger Moth, G-ANLG, as new, nil-hour engine, price with full C. of A. £275, and off I went to Panshanger to collect. This was a real ex-Service machine and it was put to good use on its immediate return to Cambridge.

More students appeared (we called them 'pupils' in those days) and I was delighted to get more help from Den Cash, another ex-RAFVR pal who had joined at about the same time as Jimmy Taylor and myself.

It was obvious that as things were going well, we needed more aircraft. Marshall's, our hosts at Cambridge, did all our servicing and, since they also operated Tigers, spares were readily available. I opted for another Tiger, and in January 1956 we bought G-AHIZ from Panshanger – the price, I think, was £325, and the aircraft was finished in the London Aero Club colours of silver and yellow. We liked the colour scheme and adopted it as our standard since the London Aero Club had ceased to exist as such. She remains with us today and has proved to be a delightful aircraft for aerobatics.

It was a sad day for us when poor old 'NLG ended its days on a hangar roof at Luton in May 1958; a badly judged 'touch and go' with considerable swing caused it to sink with a sigh onto the roof. Fortunately, no casualties, although my blood pressure suffered for some time.

We had been looking for another Tiger to replace 'NLG and I found one dismantled at Old Warden which emerged in July 1958 as G-AOEI, priced at £700. This machine had a history: she had been in service with No.81 Squadron B.E.F. in France during 1940 and was a genuine Hatfield-built Tiger. She is still with us today and going well, having been written off twice and rebuilt since those early days.

Looking back over those years we enjoyed the use of many types at the Cambridge Flying Group. One of these, owned by Mr D. Jackson, was Miles Monarch G-AFJU. This was a good aircraft – a three-seater behind a Gipsy Major 1 at 115 m.p.h., what have we today to better this? Not much. We also flew for a time the little Zaunkoenig, G-ALUA, with a Zundapp engine; great fun – 'chicken' if you used the airfield, as you could land it in the dispersal area. We flew a Messenger, G-ALAI, known as 'The Skyhook,' but the owner left Cambridgeshire and took this aircraft out of the local scene. We had the use of an Auster G-ANIO, a lively old brute, but oh! dear, no self-starter, and if you went on a cross-country with this little beauty you were lucky to get back the same day!

One of our trained pilots bought a Piper Cub, G-AKAA, and several members flew this; we also tried out an Ercoupe, G-AKFC, owned by Stan Parkin, who let us amaze ourselves with this little machine. One of the most interesting types was a Magister, G-AKKR, which was flown in by one of our members, and we managed a solo or two with it. This particular Maggie now resides in the Manchester Museum of Science and Industry.

When John Peak sold his Gemini he bought a Rapide, G-AHEB, and, fool that I am, I introduced several people to the gentle art of twin-engined flying on this machine. Those who have rolled down the field whilst standing behind the trainee pilot, with little opportunity to grab the pole and none at all in checking the swing with rudder, will share my view that there is an easier way to spend your leisure time.

After the Rapide was sold, John purchased a remarkable aircraft, the Percival Q.6 prototype G-AEYE. This particular aircraft was demonstrated at Cambridge when the present airfield opened in 1937 or thereabouts. Since Mr Peak was a friend I was glad when he got rid of this aircraft, which, although ahead of its time, was not a placid aeroplane and would bite rather hard unless you came in like a jet.

*   *   *

POSTSCRIPT

What of our Group today? We continue to operate G-AHIZ and G-AOEI. I have reason to believe that we are the only organisation in the world still training to P.P.L. standard on Tiger Moths, although the major part of our training is conversion from tricycles to taildraggers. Students today tend to find the Tiger very demanding, which it probably is when compared to a Cherokee 140 or Cessna 150, but it is still, in my opinion, one of the best basic trainers ever built. Let us remember that in the early days we took off at Cambridge into wind, today we are obliged to use our grass strips which are not necessarily into wind. Cope with your Tiger out of wind on take-off and then landing and you are beginning to learn something about cross-wind components. And, my friend, you have no brakes, so don't taxi so bloody fast, especially crosswind. Back in 1981 when this article was first written, we were experiencing problems resulting from the loss of 80 octane fuel. Since then we enjoyed the use of it again for a while with better performance and less in the way of running problems as a result. Regrettably, we are now back to square one in 1997 – 80 octane has again been withdrawn as uneconomical to produce by the fuel companies.

However, both our aircraft G-AHIZ and G-AOEI are now sporting Gipsy Major 1C engines with aluminium cylinder heads and sodium-filled exhaust valves and running on 100LL fuel. We are now on Public Transport Category maintenance and have a strict programme in that respect.

Betty Willink, one of our first lady members to qualify on Tigers (and additionally to get a night rating), became operations manager and is now Mrs Ison!

One of the problems today is to find instructors for the Tiger Moth aircraft, and anyone wishing to do this is very thoroughly checked in all exercises. It is hard basic flying and the aircraft, although easy to fly, are difficult to fly *accurately. Any* instructor will not do – he/she has to endure limited instruments, cold cockpits *and* be prepared to get oil on the hands *and* watch out for cross-winds – the Tiger does not let you get away with it!

CHAPTER 15

THE EXPERIMENTAL
FLYING GROUP

by

REX NICHOLLS

Having spent about two years being flown around Southern England and the Continent by a friend in Piper Cubs (J/3 and J/4), Tiger Moths and a Fairchild Argus, I decided to learn to fly. My training commenced in August 1950 on G-AFOZ, a D.H. Moth Minor operated by the Experimental Flying Group (EFG) of the Ultra Light Aircraft Association at Redhill Aerodrome. The sole instructor was Miss Jean Bird, a former ATA ferry pilot. The flying was simple, there being just a few items in the take-off checks and even fewer in the pre-landing checks. Circuits were always left-hand with the altimeter set to aerodrome elevation. We knew nothing of QFE and had no scope for learning its value when visiting other aerodromes for we flew without radio. We just added 1,000 ft to an aerodrome's elevation for circuit height.

All the lessons were short, rarely more than half an hour at a time. My first solo came as a complete surprise after little more than seven hours instruction. Such an event was rarely if ever discussed among the handful of members under training and I was about 300 ft on the climb-out before the enormity of the situation hit me. As I didn't drive I was, for the first time in my life, not only flying alone but in charge of powered machinery!

My qualifying solo cross-country was to Woodley, near Reading, and to Somerton near Cowes on the Isle of Wight. These two aerodromes were among the first of so many to be closed down over the ensuing years. When I obtained my Private Pilot's Licence I carried two 'bodies' as my first-ever passengers. This was in the two-seat Moth Minor and was achieved by installing Jean Bird in the rear cockpit and her black Labrador, Jet, in the rear baggage locker behind, which was open to the cockpit. Jet didn't mind this as he was used to flying in the Oxfords and Ansons with Jean when

116

she flew these on fighter affiliation exercises with Redhill's No.15 Reserve Flying School in the RAFVR.

Having done all my training on 'FOZ I was pleased to compare it with G-AFPR, a Moth Minor purchased by Jean. She attached it to the EFG and in due course I carried out a tour of France in it, routeing via Lille, Epernay, Toussus, Orléans, Tours, Deauville and Le Touquet. This was in 1952 but by that time the writing was on the wall for the Moth Minors due to spares problems. Only on one day were 'FOZ and 'FPR both airworthy. Thereafter 'FOZ was robbed of components to keep 'FPR flying and then 'FPR was cannibalised for a while to provide spares to renew 'FOZ's C. of A. This was clearly a ludicrous situation, so 'FOZ was traded in for a Miles Hawk Trainer G-AMBM. I had always wanted to fly the 'Maggie,' as they were called from their RAF name Magister, and I found it a most agreeable aeroplane. I commenced an Assistant Instructor's Rating on 'MBM, which included learning aerobatics. It also included instrument flying under the hood, which could be pulled over the rear cockpit to shut out the world outside. The instruments were simply an airspeed indicator, altimeter, turn-and-slip and a rev counter: what is known today as a 'limited panel.' Recovery from spins under the hood using so few aids was quite an experience!

Very soon 'FPR was disposed of and another Maggie purchased: this was G-ALIO, which came from the Royal Engineers' Flying Club at Rochester. We named her 'Pongo'!

By the summer of 1953 I was yearning for a more ambitious foreign tour, and decided on landing at Lille, Mézières, Nancy, Basle, Zurich, Berne, Lausanne, Geneva, Lyon, Nevers and Toussus-le-Noble. The Maggie was a much better tourer than the Moth Minor, with its greater speed and endurance. However, it had the same three navigation aids – a compass, a map and a pair of eyeballs – or rather two pairs, but my companion, Peter Amos, had just started to learn to fly and had yet to develop navigational skills. It was a wonderful flight and we received much help at each of the aerodromes visited, particularly with transport to and from hotels for overnight stops.

The Maggies were soon earning their keep on *ab initio* training and the Group's membership increased. One summer afternoon we watched Jean conducting a session of circuits and bumps and we had a feeling that the pupil was coming up for his first solo. Sure enough, we saw Jean clamber out of the Maggie after a tidy landing and off went the student on his own. After a few minutes we watched for the final approach and landing, paying great attention, for there would be much banter afterwards if there was the slightest hint of a bounce. But there was no pupil, no Maggie, nothing! Jean, strolling towards the Clubhouse, was looking over her shoulder with increasing frequency as she realised her charge was nowhere to be seen. Ten minutes went by, twenty and then thirty. There was nothing anyone could do about this except wait, there being no radio. At last the Maggie appeared and made an immaculate landing. Jean was livid about all this and stormed up to the Maggie as soon as the pupil had stopped the engine.

"What the hell do you think you've been up to?" she demanded.

He replied quite casually: "Well, when you got out, you said 'Off you go' so I did – down to the South Coast and back."

Jean had to admit that she hadn't been precise about the solo flight, which should have been just one circuit, while I made a mental note that when I reached the required instructional qualification to send pupils on their first solos I would spell out exactly what was expected!

Some time later one of the instructors in the Redhill Flying Club sent one of his students to practice solo circuits and bumps. The student's first approach was a high-speed run down the runway with a pull-up at the end. The second circuit produced a similar result, as did the third and fourth. As with Jean's student, there was nothing to be done as the Maggie had no radio. However, one of the Redhill Club's members owned a radio-equipped Gemini, so he and the instructor set off in this with the intention of flying close to the student to try and encourage him to get down safely. This seemed like a complete waste of time and in any case the Maggie was not to be seen; like Jean's student earlier, this one also had flown away from the circuit. Eventually he reappeared and recommenced the series of fast low runs. Then quite suddenly he set up a normal approach, lowered the flaps and carried out an immaculate landing. He taxied up to the Clubhouse, jumped out, and found himself face to face with his irate instructor, now landed and deplaned from the Gemini. Asked what he thought he'd been doing, the student simply grinned from ear to ear and said: "Oh! I was just enjoying myself!"

When the Fair Oaks flying club organised a Tea Patrol one Sunday I asked Jean if she would let me take the Maggie G-AMBM. It had to be that one, not G-ALIO. I had hit upon the idea of trying to get into the Fair Oaks circuit without having my registration noted by 'defending' aircraft, knowing that one of those defenders would be G-AMBN, 'MBM's sister ship and otherwise identically marked. Sure enough, no defenders approached 'MBM; they sheered off and we duly landed, confident that our ruse had worked. Taxiing in, a marshalling crew were directing visiting aircraft to one parking area and the based aircraft elsewhere. We were directed to the latter so the scheme worked even on the ground! There was a certain amount of muttering about this but it was taken in good part, and we enjoyed our free tea!

I was beginning to do more and more flying at Croydon, having another Moth Minor available, G-AFNI, owned by the fellow who had got me into flying. This had a very smart red and cream colour scheme, and heads would turn when we arrived at Breakfast and Tea Patrols in such a trim aeroplane.

It was early in January 1954 that I was invited to join five other pilots in ferrying the first of a batch of eighty or so Tiger Moths that were being offered for tender now that the RAF had finished with them. Many of them were stored at Aston Down aerodrome, so I was conveyed there with two others in Messenger G-AJWB; the other three followed in Proctor G-AIHG. There were several rows of Tigers in the hangar; we checked out our six and I was handed the Permit to Fly for G-ANJZ. The letters were crudely daubed on the fuselage sides in black, while similar daubings partially obliterated the RAF serial number and roundels on the wings. The flight to Croydon was via Gatwick, and that winter flight in the notoriously draughty rear cockpit of the Tiger was the coldest I ever made.

I began instructing my first student to solo standard on G-ALOX, the Vendair Flying Club's Croydon-based Tiger Moth. In addition, I helped out with the Croydon Flying Club's two Taylorcraft Plus Ds, G-AHHX and G-AHVR. The closure of Redhill aerodrome in May 1954 saw the EFG decamp to Croydon, which suited me nicely because the airport was but a 15-minute cycle ride from my home. By similar means of transport Redhill was at least an hour's ride away. Their two Maggies also wanted an instructor to keep them busy, so there was a small fleet for me to utilise.

During the summer of 1954 our Maggie 'MBM was damaged beyond repair in France, but before long we obtained another one, G-AITN, which we named 'Speedy Gonzalez,' though not because of any surprising performance on its part; we bought it for £210.

The fleet was added to by a most enjoyable aeroplane attached to the EFG for about five months; this was the one and only Hirtenberg HS.9A, a Gipsy Major-powered Austrian design. It began life registered as OE-DJH, the letters derived from the owner's name, J.H. Davies. The 1938 *Anschluss* saw it wearing D-EDJH and then it duly fled to England where it became G-AGAK. The aeroplane had a parasol folding wing above open cockpits and by the addition of a wing tank to starboard of the main centre-section tank the HS.9A could carry fuel for six hours flying plus an hour's reserve. The aeroplane was semi-aerobatic and before entering a spin it would give a sort of curtsey before it rolled over into the manoeuvre, something I've never met on any other type of comparable size.

Ferry-flying increased, and next came two Auster 5s from St. Athan to Newcastle; these were G-ANHX and G-ANHZ, their markings daubed on less crudely than on the Tiger Moths. Several refuelling stops were necessary on this flight, for, in contrast to the Hirtenberg, an hour's reserve fuel gave just about 90 minutes flight time (or about 120 miles in still air) from the remainder of the tankful. This was the reason why many civil Austers were fitted with belly tanks.

Ferry flights always seemed to crop up in the winter, and an attempt to collect another Tiger from Aston Down and to retrieve one from Blackpool where it had diverted on its way south from Kilbride were frustrated by the weather. In the latter case three of us flew to Squires Gate in a Proctor, only to have that stranded there as well. We returned home by train!

In 1955 a Tiger needed ferrying to France and was one of a sizeable batch sold to that country. It looked smart in its new coat of silver dope, with F-BHIF on the fuselage and wings in black. It had been overhauled at Thruxton but the pilot who brought it to Croydon wished to proceed no further. So I was in luck, and – via Le Touquet – delivered it to Les Mureaux, accompanied by two others. In all fifty Tigers went to France but some took the sea route in packing crates, never to fly again: they were wanted for spares. Incidentally, the smart silver finish was referred to by wags as a 'C. of Spray,' meaning that that was all that was done to the aircraft to issue it with a C. of A.

A number of pre-war types added to the variety in my log books, and these included the D.H.60 Moth G-ABJJ and the Puss Moth G-AHLO, both based at Croydon. An odd type was the Slingsby Motor Tutor G-AKJD I flew at Lasham; this was the nearest I ever got to a glider, it being a Tutor fitted with a 36 h.p. JAP engine. A new type in at Croydon was the Jodel D.11, the first time we had set eyes on that now well-known cranked wing configuration. In the late fifties I was also able to fly the Turbulent single-seater G-APKZ; this was a practical ultralight, in contrast to so many barely effective efforts. In 1952 I had also flown the Dart Kitten G-AEXT at Shoreham, which, although slightly larger that the Turbulent, seemed to me an excellent design, also using the 36 h.p. JAP.

When the RAFVR was closed down in 1954 the disposal of surplus Tiger Moths was followed by a similar exercise with Chipmunks. Everyone said what a delightful aeroplane it was, but I hadn't had the chance to fly one. Then the opportunity came: four

The unique Miles Aerovan 6, Lycoming-powered G-AKHF, seen at Shoreham in 1953 (P.G. Campbell)

The 'Evening Standard' WS.51 helicopter, showing its 'unfortunate' registration, at Croydon on July 18th 1954 (P.G. Campbell)

Len Snook's Bonanza G-AOAM, seen at Fair Oaks on July 31st 1955
(P.G. Campbell)

Vivian Bellamy stands by his Dragon Rapide G-AIYR at Eastleigh
(E.H. Gould)

'Adam' Fisher (founder of Christchurch Airport), Tommy Marshall (secretary of the Flying Club) and Ted Gould (a founder member) (via E.H. Gould)

Taylorcraft Plus D G-AHUM in a steep bank (E.H. Gould)

BAC Drone G-AEKV is returned to Christchurch by road after a forced landing nearby (E.H. Gould)

The newly-painted Auster 5D G-AGLK awaits collection at Tarrant Rushton in August 1957, beside a Gemini G-AKDJ (E.H. Gould)

The Cambridge Flying Group's Tiger Moths G-AHIZ & G-AOEI (W. Ison)

Mr J.W. Tomkins brings in Messenger G-AKIR onto his farm strip at Apethorpe; the tractor driver is seemingly used to this sort of close encounter! (via C. Tomkins)

April 1947: Aerovan G-AILF is loaded up ready for sowing wheat (via C. Tomkins)

April 1947: Aerovan G-AILF sowing wheat at Apethorpe, with
Mr Tomkins' Tiger Moth G-AHME on the strip below (via C. Tomkins)

had been purchased by an Irishman who had based them at Weston Aerodrome, Dublin, while awaiting civil conversion. These had a variation on the 'daubed marks' routine – they wore EI- marks. The owner had then fatally crashed aerobatting a Tiger Moth, so the Chipmunks came up for sale again. Two had commenced a ferry flight to Croydon via Belfast and Carlisle, where they had been stranded due to the weather. Two of us were asked to go and fetch them, and we took a night sleeper to Carlisle. We flew EI-AHT and 'AHV south to Sherburn, then Cambridge and finally to Croydon. The aeroplane lived up to all I'd heard about it and the type remains a favourite.

A few days later I was asked to go to Weston to fetch another Chipmunk back. The outward trip was by Aer Lingus Viscount from Heathrow to Collinstown, my first flight in an airliner. The most dangerous part of the trip was the journey through country lanes in a car driven at hectic speed around sharp bends: fortunately nobody came the other way. Weston was really just a farm, with barns and outbuildings stuffed mostly with dismantled aeroplanes. Mud abounded, and the only thing that was clean and bright was a solitary yellow and white fuel pump. A strong wind blew and there was a low cloudbase. The trip looked doubtful but having gone all that way I decided to fly EI-AHY to see if it was serviceable. This I did and was very pleased to see a shaft of sunlight illuminating Collinstown Airport just a short distance away. This signalled the approach of a cold front, so a landing, followed by a phone call to ATC Collinstown, got me permission to land there non-radio. A quick refuel and then off to Liverpool, via Valley, for onward clearance into the Manchester Zone. That howling wind came in handy for I shot across the Irish Sea in a very short time. Valley gave me a green light to proceed. Time was of the essence, for it was December and the daylight was at its shortest. Then it was Liverpool to Stapleford for clearance by telephone into Croydon, using the N.E. Free Lane through the London Zone and a touchdown a minute or two before official night. It was just as well I was home and safe by this time, as the Chipmunk's navigation lights did not work – the aircraft's batteries had been removed.

To give some meaning to the 'Experimental' in the Group's title it was decided to modify our Maggies. There was a lot of space outboard of each centre section 11 gallon fuel tank, so we removed the tank, sawed off the outer end, inserted a strip about six inches wide and had the end of the strip rewelded; the result was a 14 gallon tank, the two thus modified providing a further hour's endurance. When in 1960 I flew G-AKAS as far as Trondheim, Norway and back via Stockholm and Frankfurt, that extra fuel meant a lot. Some legs on that wonderful flight would have been impossible otherwise.

The Maggies had powerful flaps, and overshoots with flaps down were a bit dicey when climbing out over the mature trees on Croydon's south-west boundary. So we disconnected the outer panels of the five-segment flap array and the rate of climb with the remaining three down was much improved. However, to one's surprise the marked nose-down trim change when all the flaps were lowered became a nose-up change with the reduced amount of flap. We also changed the side engine cowlings, which needed a screwdriver to operate the Dzus fasteners, for a two-piece arrangement hinged on the centre line and using the type of fasteners common to the Tiger Moth. All these mods were approved by the Air Registration Board and at least one other Maggie had the flap change incorporated.

The 1957 Popular Flying Association Rally at Sywell found an Australian companion and myself representing the EFG. We flew G-ALIO to Sywell, leaving Croydon early to land at Shoreham, Bembridge, Thruxton, Fair Oaks, Luton and Cambridge. This complex route was in order to win points for the most landings at aerodromes at least 50 km apart. At Cambridge we were given details of objects to be seen on the ground en route to Sywell, where we had to cross a line at a precise time given to each competitor. We won hands down and were awarded £5, which equated to the cost of about two hours flying time at EFG rates. The win was easy, none of the other 'aviation enthusiasts' making much effort to score points.

A further ferry flight of ex-RAF equipment was organised by a man who appeared at Croydon operating a Maggie. He asked me if I would like to fly a Prentice. Needless to say the thought delighted me, so a few days later he turned up at Croydon in Gemini G-AKDD. This I boarded, and we flew to High Ercall in Shropshire. There Prentice G-AOPY had been readied, but first it was intended that the other passenger in the Gemini, described as a photographer, would photograph the Gemini air-to-air from the Prentice. I was to fly the Gemini for this purpose, so now I flew my first multi-engine type, and the first with retractable gear.

I was dismayed to see that the cameraman had the simplest of cameras, which need not have mattered but he rested it on the Prentice's window-sill. We landed, swapped over aircraft and I flew the Prentice towards its destination, Southend. The Gemini formated and the cameraman again rested his camera on the window-sill. The results were as I expected – competely blurred. Never mind, it had been a throughly enjoyable day's flying and I learned what a delightful aeroplane the Gemini was. I intended doing some aerobatics in the allegedly cumbersome Prentice before reaching Southend, but was thwarted by a cloudbase down to 700 ft over Essex. G-AOPY was the last of 150 Prentices ferried to either Stansted or Southend, and was one of all but two dozen which were broken up for scrap. It was sad in a way to think of that perfectly airworthy machine having made its last flight.

Next, a batch of fifteen Proctor 4s needed ferrying from Cosford to Panshanger. On separate days I flew two of them, G-AOAR and 'OAZ. Here again flyable equipment was then broken up in fourteen out of the fifteen cases so that they would yield engines for Dragon Rapides which would then become Mark 4s with the Gipsy Queen 2s. Only G-AOAR survived for a number of years as a civil aircraft. This ended the ferrying of ex-RAF equipment as far as I was concerned. It had been a most interesting era, one unlikely ever to be repeated on such a scale.

All the ex-military equipment had a certain smell about it, particularly the cabin types. This had something to do with anti-corrosion precautions, and engines etc. would be protected while in store with a compound known as 'sozzle.' It was therefore something of a novelty to fly an aeroplane that not only *smelled* new but *was* new. Lord Kemsley, through his Kemsley Newspapers, encouraged private flying, arranging a Trust whereby loans at very low interest rates could be negotiated by flying clubs, gliding clubs and suchlike for the purchase of aircraft, club buildings and so on.

One of his papers, the 'Daily Sketch,' ran a series of competitions, giving away prizes such as a house, an expensive car, a racehorse and others. We all sat up and took notice when an aeroplane was offered. It had to be a British product, of course, but there was little risk of anything foreign being given, least of all American, because in the post-war games which came under the general heading of Annual Financial Crisis, nobody could buy aircraft for dollars (except BOAC). Thus it was that a brand-new Auster was chosen and this was a new variant called the Alpha 5. It was in fact based on the military Mark 5 airframe with its Lycoming 0-290-3 130 h.p. engine. It differed in having cabin glazing on the lines of the J/1 Autocrat but with two bulges in the perspex roof over the rear bench seat, for the Alpha 5 was a four-seater. The instrument panel was downgraded from the Mark 5's full panel to the Autocrat's limited panel. A reasonable amount of upholstery was fitted in the cabin and, most important, a silencer was fitted to each of the two exhaust pipes. An unsilenced ex-military Mark 4 or 5 was the most noisy by far of all the light aircraft I have flown. The silencers brought the decibels down to reasonable levels.

A somewhat puerile competition was run in various issues of the *'Daily Sketch,'* in which it was intended that your brain would be stretched by thinking up captions to a series of cartoons. At that time the Alpha 5 in question, G-APBE, was based at Denham (where, on one occasion, it was parked and draped with an assortment of 'Windmill Girls' for publicity purposes); it then came to Croydon, its pilot Alan Stocks being the former owner of the Hirtenberg. The winner would receive not only the aeroplane but flying lessons to PPL standard, a year's fuel, hangarage and maintenance, and a trip to Switzerland in the Alpha 5 to the 1957 Rallye de la Montre Suisse. When Alan, the appointed pilot, was suddenly sent away by his employers there was a hunt for someone to take over. I was available and had no hesitation in volunteering for what was to be something of a second prize, for my entry in the competition had not been successful.

On the appointed day I flew the Alpha 5 from Croydon to Lympne and there met the winner, Edward Holt. A retired Lieutenant-Colonel and a batchelor, aged 53, he was undoubtedly a wise choice. He was also an excellent travelling companion, as was another passenger, the *'Daily Sketch'* man, who was to see that all arrangements went well. We were to fly to Bienne in Switzerland and the route I chose was to Beauvais, Epernay, Nancy and Basle, where we stopped overnight. This put us in a good position to fly into Bienne the next morning, to arrive by flying over a white line painted across the single grass strip at the precise time notified to us by the organisers on our Rallye papers. The frequent stops on the journey again emphasised the abysmally limited endurance of the Mark 5 Austers.

We flew over the line at Bienne as near the time as I could judge but I could not tell what the judges' watches read compared with mine. We didn't win the arrival competition, but the following day a Dutch competitor asked me how we had fared. I explained that my watch may not have been accurate.

"Ho, ho!" he said, "I suppose it's a bloody Swiss watch!", and went on his way.

In those days, of course, the Swiss thought they were the only nation who knew how to make watches. The Japanese had yet to get in on the act.

The Rallye was a great success, the banqueting out of this world, the weather perfect. It was so hot in the valley that most pilots and their passengers spurned the copious quantities of wine in favour of bottles of iced water. I know I did! The return flight to the U.K. was by way of the refuelling stops we had used on the outbound trip.

The winner went on to gain his PPL on an Auster based at

Southend, leaving his own aeroplane at Croydon, where I and others took him on occasional flights. When his Licence was issued he was able to fly it solo, but rarely did, preferring more experienced pilots to accompany him. When, after a year, he was on his own with the payments, he rapidly lost interest in the Auster, so when he finally decided to sell it, we in the EFG jumped at the chance to own it, for it had flown barely 50 hours. The Maggies were becoming difficult to maintain due to a shortage of spares, while this problem did not occur with the Auster, which was still in production. So in 1958 G-APBE joined the EFG. Eventually one Maggie, G-ALIO, damaged in a taxying accident on the 6th July, was broken up; it was replaced by G-AKAS. The other we had at the time, G-AITN, was later sold to the comedian Dick Emery and was then based at Fair Oaks. Thus ended the days of open-cockpit flying, the last Maggie flights taking place in 1960 and G-AKAS being broken up for spares.

It was during 1958 that rumours of the imminent closing of Croydon grew stronger. After a time we were told that when this happened Biggin Hill would be available for civil use. Despite many protests, Croydon was clearly doomed and it was one gloomy day in November 1958 that I first set foot on the famous RAF base to look, with others, for future accommodation. A standard RAF wooden hut was selected and negotiations began. We got it for 10/- (50p) per week! A former 615 Sqdn. RAuxAF crew room, it was to be EFG's headquarters for many years.

We were told that from the 1st January 1959 circuit training would have to cease at Croydon. Biggin Hill would be available instead, so on Saturday the 3rd January that year I determined to be the first into 'civil' Biggin. When booking out at Croydon I was dismayed to hear one of Airways Aero Association's Aiglet Trainers also being booked out for Biggin. The pilot had two advantages over me: there was radio in his aeroplane, and he had but 100 yards to walk to where it awaited him. My Maggie, G-AKAS, had no radio and was about half a mile away in 'D' hangar. However, with Frankie O'Kane, an Air Traffic Control assistant at Croydon, I got the Maggie ready and took off for Biggin via Croydon's N.E. Free Lane via Bromley. The weather was far from good but we found Biggin and landed on the grass alongside Runway 21, from which a solitary RAF Chipmunk was operating. A visit to the Tower found two RAF controllers, very 'bootfaced' about the invasion of their precious aerodrome by mere civilians. I enquired about the Aiglet Trainer: it had turned back to Croydon because of the weather. So we were first to fly from Biggin Hill now it had been declared available for civil use, although we returned to Croydon later that day.

On February 14th all the club aircraft were barred from Croydon except for maintenance, but by then we in EFG were ensconced in our new clubhouse at Biggin, outside which we could park our two Maggies and, soon after, the Auster 5 (the name Alpha 5 had been dropped). We had not had a clubhouse at Croydon so our new one at Biggin was a great advantage. Equally important, we were now outside the restrictions imposed by the London CTR, a much larger affair than now. My last flight from Croydon was as passenger in the SCAN 30 EI-ALE into Biggin on the 30th September, the last day for the airport.

Thus the final year of the fifties was spent settling into our new home. It was the final year too for the Maggies, apart from a few weeks in 1960. Another pre-war specimen came my way, and this was the B.A. Swallow G-AEMW which by this time had a canopy over its open cockpits. A visiting Tripacer SE-CEI gave me my first experience of modern American equipment. Soon the dollar restrictions would be lifted and an influx of American light aircraft begin. But that is a story for the 1960s.

CHAPTER 16

I SURE AM

by

CHRIS DEARDEN

It was a beautiful evening, that thirtieth of July, 1950. I can't swear to that, but I can say it with some confidence because I'd bicycled over to Gatwick with the intention of having a stooge round in one of the Piper Cubs. And I wouldn't have been squandering my scant pennies on a dull evening!

I dug the Club Secretary out of the bar, and he confirmed that 'LVR was available.

"Just for half an hour's stooge round," I explained.

To this very day I don't know how he did it, but suddenly I found I'd been conned into doing "a nice little cross-country to Shoreham" – where, surprise, surprise, he wanted to see some bloke or other on business.

"Don't mind if I come along with you, do you, old boy?"

"No, not at all," I said, by now too bamboozled to know what I was saying.

The rat! So there I was, paying the Club Secretary the flying rate for giving him a 'freebie' to Shoreham and back. How did he work that one on me? Ah, sweet mystery of life!

The relevance of this tale, and the bonus I got out of it, is that I had the pleasure of being introduced to the great Cecil Pashley that evening. He had little to say to me, but I was aware of being in the presence of a legend. I arrived back at Gatwick certainly gratified by the meeting but financially over twice as poor as I'd reckoned to be. Half an hour? Joke! Yes, how did he do that? Such was my first flying visit to Shoreham.

Nearly seven years passed before I flew there again, and that was on the 4th of May 1957 in Tiger 'MNN. At that time there was no fuel to be had at Redhill, where 'MNN lived, so there was a good excuse to fly to Shoreham to tank up. This was very nearly a memorable occasion.

It was a pleasantly uneventful flight down there – aim for the power station chimneys, then right hand down. I parked neatly enough near the south-east corner of the 'drome, checked in and enquired about fuel. No problem! Since it seemed a bit too far to man-handle the Tiger up to the pump, a kind soul wound the elastic for me so that I could taxy up there.

As any ace will tell you, a Tiger should not be taxied on a hard surface because it grinds away the pad on the tail-skid at a rate of knots. Therefore I kept to the grass until the last moment, when I swung left, then right, on to the hardstanding to line up with the pump. Bad move!

It was thus the first time I'd driven a Tiger on a hard surface and I forgot two things. Firstly, without the drag of the grass on the skid a Tiger rolls forward quite freely. And secondly, there are no brakes on a Tiger. In blissful inexperience I carried on until I felt that I was within easy man-handling distance from the pump. There I chopped the throttle. Nothing much happened. 'MNN rolled majestically on, the pump now dead ahead and growing harrowingly close.

At least I had the wit to cut the switches while I rammed my sweating feet frantically against the rudder pedals in a futile effort to find the brakes which weren't there. But fate and the prophets smiled. We stopped inches – and I mean very few inches – from impact.

The man in charge of the pump gave me a sort of "Oh, yeah" look, then said rather sarcastically: "That'll do you, squire. That's near enough."

I smirked as if I'd just judged it very nicely, and quietly went prematurely grey. What a bonfire party that might have been ... ! 'ARSON ATTACK ON SHOREHAM BY CRAZED AVIATOR. MINISTER TO REVIEW DOG LICENCES.'

But there were sweeter times to come that summer. My friends Len and Ron and I had a little game going (what? Three in a Tiger? No, not quite that – though it has been known. Quiet Trixie!). Len had a BSA 'Gold Flash' motorbike and sidecar and the game was to race to Shoreham. We'd rendezvous at Redhill and Ron would come with me in 'MNN while Len careered off on the 'Flash,' having been given about ten minutes start.

The cherry on the cake was that Len had a relative – an aunt, I believe – who lived just on the Lancing side of Shoreham. We'd leave 'MNN safely parked, all pile variously into and onto the bike, and shoot off to Auntie's for a leisurely tea. Then back to the 'drome for the return race, Len now with me in the Tiger and Ron on the bike, and all of us laughing our silly heads off.

I dare say today we'd be condemned as 'politically irresponsible'

128

or some such for even thinking of our game as a race – 'racist swines,' maybe! In those summer days, though, we saw it as harmless fun. Private flying was pleasure flying. This was the very spirit of it. And the staff at Shoreham made it even more so; always friendly and helpful, always conveying a wonderful air of laid-back hospitality. We were gloriously free of landing fees, radio chatter and other 'Charlie Romeo Alpha Papa.'

On subsequent visits they even remembered me by name (or were they remembering the petrol pump?). Yet a sour note was waiting to be played.

Maybe fittingly, it didn't come during a flying visit. I'd arranged to meet my sister and her two young sons there. The boys were interested in aeroplanes and Uncle knew all about them and could explain (ho, ho!). Anyway, there was a Tiger parked on the grass, by Southern Aero's hut, and the three of us were no more than wandering towards it when a window in the said hut flew open and a fire-breathing dragon thrust her great red face out.

"You!" she bawled in a tone which could have shattered glass as far away as Lancing College, "Get away from that aeroplane! Get off the aerodrome! Go on, right off! NOW!" – and that's no exaggeration, I recall it very clearly.

Had she been a mere Storm Trooper or an SS General I might have found the courage to have stood my ground and argued my case. But a female dragon commands instant compliance.

So I muttered a lame apology to my young nephews and tiptoed away, feeling about two inches tall.

Even now, some forty years on, my strictly ground-locked visits to Shoreham aerodrome are fraught with fear. I go furtively, on tiptoe, I keep glancing over my shoulder, I wince at shadows. They do say as there be dragons there, young master.

Am I still all that apprehensive, then? I SURE AM!

CHAPTER 17

CROYDON TO CAPRI
– AND BACK

by

TREVOR G. PRYTHERCH

(With a foreword by Eric Bell)

[This article first appeared in 'FLIGHT' magazine dated the 14th December & 21st December 1956, and is reproduced here by kind permission of the Editor of 'FLIGHT INTERNATIONAL.' Regrettably the author passed away not very long ago, but Eric Bell, one of the passengers on that flight, has very kindly supplied some original photos that were taken during the journey. The Messenger used, G-AILL, is still in existence, owned by the Miles Aircraft Collection, who have hopes of restoring it one day – Ed.]

FOREWORD: I was having a cup of tea with Trevor in the Croydon airport canteen when he asked me if I fancied a short trip to Switzerland and on into Italy, returning over the South of France. He explained that as a geography teacher he felt that he should visit these countries rather than just get the information from books. We would fly there but it had to be done on a shoe-string! I happily agreed to accompany him and that same day we contacted Surrey Flying Club, who agreed to let us have the well-used Miles Messenger G-AILL at a cut rate. We needed two more to make up the crew; I immediately thought of a colleague named Bill Lofting who worked with me at Vickers Armstrongs and had recently acquired his pilot's licence – he too was keen to come. Trevor asked a radio ham acquaintance of his called Norman, who was a keen photographer, and he agreed to accompany us in the hope of getting some good mountain shots, which he certainly did!

I planned the route and within a week everything was ready, but it was not until the night before take-off that we were told that our Messenger, which was a single-engined aircraft, had been fitted with Gemini wings which were somewhat heavier as they had been designed for a twin-engined aeroplane; this meant that we had to reduce the payload. Trevor, Bill and I turned up for the flight with not much more than our toothbrushes, but Norman, who had little experience of single-engined flying, arrived with three large suit-cases which he reluctantly had to reduce to a small hold-all. This was only the beginning of a holiday which turned out to be not quite what any of us expected . . .

*   *   *

D-Day plans could scarcely have been more thorough than those we made for our journey. An expenditure of two pounds ten shillings on maps was a prelude to a foolscap sheet full of place names, statute miles and magnetic courses. I had not flown further than Paris before, and the proposed trip Croydon–Reims–Zurich–Locarno–Venice–Rome–Naples–Pisa–Albenga–Cannes–Lyons–Le Touquet–Croydon seemed as formidable a task as breaking through the sound barrier.

I had enormous faith in the Miles Messenger that we hired, and a preliminary flight, four up, convinced me that it had almost a Proctor-like performance combined with take-off and landing characteristics all its own. With 36 gallons of fuel and a six-channel Plessey radio we felt prepared to face anything – though quite late in the arrangements we discovered that our Messenger had been rebuilt with Gemini wings, and the additional 300 lb reduced our luggage to the resemblance of a packed lunch each.

[After talking with Ron Paine, who was responsible for the modification of these wings, with ARB approval, it is now thought that the figure '300 lb' should really read '30 lb' – Ed.]

After days of indifferent weather August 8th dawned as one of this summer's few good days. After the usual paperwork our estimated ten o'clock take-off became eleven. We were off the ground after a ridiculously short run, and set course for Dungeness in brilliant sunshine. The Channel crossing at 5,000 ft from Dungeness to Le Touquet was uneventful, and we reset course over Le Touquet for Reims.

I held a cruising speed of 100 m.p.h., and after 2½ hours we landed at Reims to refuel. The next stage, to Zurich, was notable for the sensation of height conveyed by clearing the hills near Basle by 800 ft at 6,800 ft and then being projected, as it were, over a sheer drop into the valley beyond. My first view of the Alps was impressive. What I first dismissed as clouds in the sunshine resolved themselves into majestic snowy peaks which made mankind seem very puny indeed.

Four miles from Klöten, Zurich, I managed to make radio contact, if intermittently, and found it essential on such a busy international airport, where we landed after a Constellation and a Viscount. In deference to the big stuff I obtained radio permission to put down on the short grass strip being used by club aircraft. Radio instructions for taxying to the imposing airport building were most explicit, and we felt quite important as we lined up between a Constellation and a Viscount, watched by large crowds on the three-tier balconies. The landing fee was the equivalent of six shillings and hangarage cost 15/- a night.

With 5½ flying hours behind us we enjoyed a good meal in the glass-fronted palace with its background of a moonlit sky, and were oblivious to the cost, which far exceeded a pound sterling apiece. The taxi-driver recommended a good hotel, and at 16/- each for bed and breakfast we were satisfied. Our slumbers were cut short by a loud fire-alarm and some church bells at five o'clock. There followed the Continental breakfast of rolls, and then sightseeing and souvenir-hunting, capped by a ride on the funicular railway to a hill overlooking Lake Zurich.

Next morning we were to encounter our first snag. The club pilots at Zurich were most helpful, but few had flown in the Alps. Those who had done so favoured the crossing of the St. Gotthard Pass, over 9,000 ft up. At 11,000 or 12,000 ft they assured us, we should be all right. Then the met. man warned us off – the dreaded south wind in the St. Gotthard Pass, the Föhn, caused sensational downdraughts; and we were to see the wrecked engines of a Twin Navion caught out in this way, and a hair-raising photograph of a concertina-like Piper Cub. The way we fancied was down the lake to Chur, then via Disentis and the Lukmanier Pass. This pass is some 6,500 ft high and all we had to locate the turning-off point was a wooden bridge and a monastery.

The mixture control of the Messenger had been disconnected, and we deemed it a prudent move to have this restored immediately. Swiss engineers worked hard for over two hours and installed a neat cockpit control.

The weather man warned us that bad weather was coming in, and that if we did not go that afternoon we should face two or three days delay. Our midday take-off became 4.50 p.m., but at last we were off down the runway, loaded with all we could carry. I reached 9,000 ft at the easterly tip of the lake and gingerly entered the next valley. We were 100 ft below the sides and fairly filled the valley, leaving vision ahead and down each side of the nose. I was pondering on the futility of keeping to the right in the valleys when I spotted a Piper Cub over to our left, skimming the peaks. We joined another valley and almost immediately ran into thick haze. This suggested turning back, for the narrowness of the valley left no margin for error. However, we emerged again into clear weather and were now at 9,500 ft. We identified Chur, a town of reasonable size, boasting according to the *European Air Touring Guide* an airstrip.

My idea of a monastery is that it should resemble a church, so when we flew over what looked like an hotel with green-tiled roof and white walls, surrounded by houses, we went sailing on. Presently we spotted a lake which was not marked on the map (the half-million map is nigh-on hopeless for Alpine flying) and simultaneously we were confronted by a sheer rock face that towered above us. Large helpings of flap assisted us to turn on a sixpence and we started back towards Zurich, 100 miles away, feeling distinctly frustrated.

We had been so preoccupied in finding the way (in one place, where the map simplified it to three valleys we found seven, all looking alike) that not until the return did we notice that in the next valley to the west it was as black as night. Upon reaching Chur we were concerned to find that the valley ahead was enjoying a first-class thunderstorm; and although I had a reasonable petrol supply I could not have climbed above the storm to reach Zurich. High winds in a darkened valley lit by vivid lightning flashes made only one course possible. Since the *Air Touring Guide* listed Chur as having an airstrip, I turned round again to look for it. We lost height from 9,000 ft to 1,000 ft; but that strip was nowhere to be seen. Much of the ground was cultivated, and only small patches presented themselves as landing grounds, with no possibility of take-off.

Keeping a wary eye open for the many power cables, I waggled the wings in the vain hope that somebody could point out the airstrip. But no, we were on our own. I considered one long narrow strip, but it was ringed by tall trees. The next village had a field which, though cut in half by telephone wires, looked unbelievably long. I was mystified by its neglected look, and decided it must be marsh or swamp. Two dummy runs revealed that it was worth a try, so I approached over a power cable and some tall trees and, using brakes, stopped in 30 yards.We were down and in one piece, and in the fading light there even seemed room for a take-off, despite the presence of grass three feet tall.

We had scarcely come to a halt, near a main road, when people came from all directions and we were hard put to it to prevent damage to the aircraft. They were a well-meaning crowd, and a few spoke some English. The stopping cars caused chaos on the road,

133

but we saw no police at any time. I had the greatest thirst I had ever known, and our new friends soon brought us bottles of beer and sandwiches in profusion. In the now-failing light we spelled out, Braille-fashion, the name of the place on the beer bottle – CHUR! Our first positive fix! We were actually at Domat-Ems. We received our second surprise when it transpired that we were on a wartime emergency strip, unused since 1945 and in active course of being measured into plots with hefty stakes and stones like milestones – all invisible in the tall grass.

Of our new friends Rudy Schaffer, Jack Schneider and Otto Wurth were pilots, but they had little chance of flying for some time, because the club at Chur had closed down. Transport was provided and Norman Bennett and Bill Lofting were taken to seek accommodation in the local inn. I decided to stay with the aircraft, and Eric Bell and I settled down in splendid isolation in the all-covering darkness. At 11 p.m. we welcomed a cyclist who brought us more beer and sandwiches.

That night we were treated by the elements to a first-class thunderstorm. Lightning danced all around us and torrential rain fell. We pondered on the chances of being struck – the prop pointed upwards like two hands in prayer and we had the aerial sticking up behind us. The cockpit was watertight and we spent the night being rocked and rolled by the wind, with nothing on the clock but 2,000 ft on the altimeter. Quite early Bill arrived from the inn on a borrowed bicycle and took over guard duties, while Eric and I accompanied Norman to the inn by taxi for most welcome bacon and eggs.

There was a telephone at the inn, and Zurich Airport had been informed. I was pleased to learn that they themselves had experienced 'impossible' weather the previous evening, and that they had congratulated us on a wise alternative. The weather was still poor, with heavy rain and clouds low in the valley, and I enjoyed the opportunity to relax.

That afternoon we taxied the aircraft the length of the field to a sheltered place beside a large barn which would reduce its attraction for every passer-by, as its present place made it a magnet. The taxying process was most enlightening, for we found all the stakes and rocks, and resolved to have a thorough check-up before take-off. Our taxi-path was anything but straight.

Later we returned to the inn, a place with an old-world look outside, but up-to-the-minute electrically inside. We needed petrol, and Rudy offered to bring some in by train. Zurich, however, were alert and Shell telephoned us to ask the quantity of fuel necessary and to inform us that it would leave by road immediately. From 70 miles away it arrived only two hours later, and while I took on 20 gallons from a two-gallon measure through a chamois-leather filter, my three companions left for a motor ride to Chur with Otto Wurth. They were shown the airstrip there, but they expressed great doubt about its size; it certainly would not have been recognised from the air as a strip. Incidentally, our petrol consumption in the mountains had been phenomenal; we had been consuming ten gallons an hour instead of six.

Early that evening our kind friends came to inform us that they had locked the aircraft in the barn, so that we could sleep at the inn that night – a splendid achivement for which I felt more than grateful. In the evening we dined at Rudy's home with Jack Schneider, and Rudy's wife provided a magnificent dinner. We were supplied with excellent maps of our route, with photographs of prominent landmarks, and were given alternative routes which, unfortunately, we could not use because the safe altitudes were beyond our maximum.

The following morning, Sunday, we walked to the field. The clouds were still obscuring the upper valley, but with Rudy, who produced a bundle of home-made flags, we paced out the runway into wind, in the opposite direction to our landing and slightly uphill in places.

We had hardly finished when Norman arrived from the inn with Otto and Jack to say that we should get airborne as soon as possible, for there was good weather to the south. I taxied empty to our pre-arranged mark, loaded up, shook hands with all our friends, and, with the engine at full throttle, released the brakes. We bumped along to the first flag, then to the second, and lined up on the tree. Our rear passengers leaned forward, and within fifty yards of the boundary she came off suddenly and climbed like a lift over the trees and the power cables.

As planned, I turned left at first, then right to go over the town, and a tight climbing turn sent us back towards the field at 4,000 ft. I waved, and waggled the wings, to the small knot of people watching us on the field, and we continued the climb at full throttle to 9,200 ft. This time the monastery did not elude us, and we turned off to find that the one valley became two a few miles on. A quick consultation over the map sorted it out, and the compass heading of the valley proved a valuable check.

Our maximum altitude was now 8,200 ft, maintained by full power but reduced r.p.m. with a little flap and an airspeed of 70 m.p.h. When the valleys joined ours we encountered slight turbulence, but nothing comparable with the Föhn of the St. Gotthard Pass. After rugged peaks, and a glacier, and snow, we turned at right angles into another valley heading south past a rock-face that seemed to look down at us with a sphinx-like expression. I saw two lakes in the distance, and a conference with Eric, who was not expecting them, raised doubts; but uncertainty was soon dispelled by Bill in the rear seat, who at that moment caught sight of the beginning of Lake Maggiore. We were through. How reassuring was the sight of flat land at Locarno! Despite the cold we opened the side windows and indulged in a spate of photography. I lost surplus height by circling over the lake and then we landed in an oven-like Locarno.

Followed the paper work, a telephone call to Rudy back at Domat-Ems, refuelling, and the six-shilling landing fee, and we were ready to go on to Venice. A welcome Coca-Cola and then we all four invaded the wrong room before the difference between the words "Signore" and "Signora" on the respective doors dawned on us.

We took off towards the lake and climbed steadily. The mountain came right down to the water, leaving no possible landing space, and where there was the occasional village in near-impossible terrain I made for it. At 4,000 ft we flew along south of the mountains past Como, and Bergamo, and Lake Iseo. Now the ground below was a patchwork quilt of cultivated areas, and I felt pleased to see airfields. On a big military aerodrome near Brescia we counted upwards of fifty jets, apparently drawn up on parade. We flew north of Milan but could clearly identify it as a sizeable centre of population. As we crossed Lake Garda, between Brescia and Verona, we had a splendid opportunity to line up on the little finger of land sticking northwards into the lake.

Our complacency suffered somewhat soon afterwards, when we watched a cumulo-nimbus cloud come right down to the deck. We diverted northwards for ten miles and I succeeded in making contact with Venice San Nicolo Airport, whose controller provided us with QDMs in. At Locarno they had told us in an old-fashioned way that the airport officials at Venice were real gentlemen. Emerging from the murk to see the toy town that was Venice, with the airport on the Lido beyond, and with assuring voices giving QDMs, I was halfway to believing them.

Over the airport I watched fascinated as a Dakota landed, sending up clouds of dust, and taking every inch of the small runway. The wind there is always a beam wind, and the approach over tall buildings almost on the boundary roused in me a great admiration for the Dakota pilots who use the field. We bumped to a stop and back-tracked down the runway on radio instructions. And now I shared the reactions of a woman who encounters another

136

wearing an identical dress – for sitting on the tarmac was another Messenger. It was flown by Mr Woods of Perth Flying Club, who had avoided the Alps and was now returning via Milan.

After seeing Lima Lima lashed down we took the trolley-bus to the landing stage and caught the steamer to Venice, a 20 minute trip costing threepence! The hotel situation was desperate, but the manager of the Tres Rosa Hotel, a charming man who spoke perfect English, arranged for private people to take us in, two at one place, and the others elsewhere. For a spotlessly clean double room we paid a thousand lira each a night, about 12/-. Reveille was more or less determined by the deep-toned bells of St. Mark's.

With a Continental breakfast inside us and seven shillings the poorer, we admired the splendour of St. Mark's which in the glorious sunshine made an unforgettable sight. The English-speaking tour at eighteen shillings was value for money, for one finds that private-venture exploration involves an admission charge at every corner. We were fascinated by the last item on the tour, the glass-blowing factory, where we saw glass in every conceivable shape and colour; the temperature out-of-doors was near 90°F and the short visit to the ovens nearly finished us off.

We just had to make a gondola trip by night. Given excellent weather, a moon, the singing that characterises the canals, and a gondola at thirty shillings an hour, we had the requisite romantic set-up – even if the gondolier did demand two hours pay for one hour.

In readiness for an 11 a.m. departure we invaded the airport early next morning. Landing and take-off charges were 12/-, with an extra 12/- for customs. We were becoming used to manual petrol tankers, and before we finished we had all had a hand at the pumps. I found it essential to supervise refuelling, for one can be anything up to two gallons short; equally, it may be right over the top, with the attendant smell of petrol in the cabin.

We took off with our usual foolscap or map-sized weather-information chart. The weather so is wonderful there that they must feel fireproof in their forecasts. We left this delightful airport, with the built-in crosswind, whose runway finishes within two yards of the sea, and indulged in a climbing turn that gave us a last glimpse of Venice from 1,000 ft as we crossed St. Mark's Square.

"Please do not fly over Venice below 300 metres" was the airport's last word.

We flew on towards the Apennines at 4,000 ft and the sight of the range of mountains heralded the approach of Bologna. We were a good two miles off track and were tempted to think another town was Bologna, but we soon sorted it out, and admired the city's lovely airport. Once again we followed a valley, this time through the Apennines, and flew into very misty conditions. There were peaks that must have been 7,000 ft high, and we met the usual assortment of valleys galore. I climbed to 6,000 ft and pressed on, following a compass course that suffered when peaks appeared in our way. The land below occasionally showed signs of life, but there were many barren areas in which (so I have been told) bears and wolves still roam.

Now we were over a large town on low land, complete with a dome which at first sight suggested Florence, but on the friendly-looking airport the name PISTOIA was to be seen. Florence lay just beyond, and we feasted our eyes on this artistic gem of Italy, feeling sorry our time schedule would not permit a stop here. Eric, my navigator-in-chief, will not forget the question which seemed to be ever on my lips: "How high?" accompanied by a pointing finger. But the remainder of the trip to Rome was free of mountaineering, a welcome relief, and we noted with interest an occasional flying-boat base on the lakes over which we passed.

That Rome was near we could tell by the number of large aircraft converging on it. There are at least three aerodromes, and our flight plan was for Urbe, three miles north of the city. Bounded on three sides by the meandering river it looked very attractive, with grass runways clearly marked, but it also appeared completely deserted. I actually spotted a windsock, and it proclaimed that the runway was almost into wind. Approaching over high ground and power cables we found that near the ground the heat and the wind made it a "to me, to you" business; and when we touched down the ground was anything but level.

Our landing brought the place to life. Two jeeps cavorted around, doors and windows opened, and as we approached we were waved in by a good friend (as he turned out to be) who spoke some English following a sojourn in Manchester as a prisoner-of-war. He organised hangar space and transport and would not hear of taking a tip. Incidentally, the hangars were full of Italian and American aircraft, and two Consuls. I appreciated the hangar's light folding aluminium doors, which opened at a touch.

Formalities over, we sped to Rome, where, after a 'phone call, we met friend Peter, son of an English mother and a Swiss father. He spoke perfect English and promised a crowded itinerary on the following day. The first hotel was full, but the second, the Alicorni, fixed us up, and at 16/- a night was a marble palace which reminded me of the geological museum at South Kensington. Before dinner we visited St. Peter's, but not before we had been stopped in the street and offered Parker 51 pens at 15/- each.

After the promised day of sightseeing, the details of which must perforce be omitted from this mainly-aviation story, we had dinner in Peter's home, a most enjoyable experience. The flat had a verandah screened above and on each side by a wooden-framed structure lined with rushes, and since it was still very hot we welcomed the outdoor setting for the meal. After the usual preliminaries came a local dish of some fame, resembling a folded pancake and containing meat, fish and tomatoes. A local wine picturesquely named *Est, Est, Est* we found delicious. Our evening concluded with some coin-throwing in the well lately made famous in film and song.

Capri was now beckoning to us, and next morning we left the paperwork at our hotel in Rome, only to begin it again at the airport. The snag was that petrol at Urbe is brought to the airport from outside, and the man responsible was, with nearly everyone else, on a two-day fiesta of some religious significance. We had some fuel in hand, but not sufficient for any diversion, and I decided to go across to Ciampino Airport. At Urbe, hangarage, take-off and landing charges totalled two pounds for two days.

We had seen Ciampino when we first arrived, and after take-off I climbed to 2,000 ft for a better view of it. I nearly mistook for it another aerodrome which lay between the Urbe and Ciampino, a military field also with a single runway; but ten minutes' flying brought us over our target at 2,000 ft. Here the radio became intermittent, and being near such a busy airport I decided to remain aloft until contact was restored. This we achieved with the help of a radio expert on board, who removed the crystal cover and pressed the appropriate crystal. After seeing a Viscount, a Dakota and a Constellation land we put down in the fifteen-knot beam wind after some fluttering near the hot runway. Our landing run made me think the tailwheel had gone, but it turned out to be no worse than shimmy – a fortunate thing, for replacement of a tube or tyre would have gummed up the works in no uncertain manner. As we turned off the runway at an intersection we watched a USAF Globemaster land, marvelling at its size, and at its short run with reverse-pitch propellers.

Once again we were parked between DC-6s, Viscounts and Constellations by a 'follow-me' van which, its task fulfilled, left us as mysteriously as it had appeared. The petrol crew refuelling a DC-6 fixed us up with 80-octane, the transaction being achieved without difficulty although they spoke no English.

It took some time, and a long walk, to find out where to report. At first they wanted a pound for a landing fee, but, pleading a club aircraft, I found it promptly reduced to five shillings. Feeling wealthy, we partook of Coca-Cola all round.

All set to be on our way, we had to wait for some time for radio permission to taxi. The track was narrow and flanked by lights on stalks a foot high; many of them were broken. At the run-up point we were pursued by three other large aircraft. We had made out a flight plan from Urbe to Ciampino and to Naples, and now I had to make another, oral, flight plan, during which I had to transmit my name in the new phonetic alphabet – no mean feat, I assure you. We were then cleared to line up and take off immediately. The wind swung the tail sharply, and I could only keep on the runway by large helpings of brake.

The direct course to Naples would have taken us over mountains at 4,000 ft, so I diverted first to clear a forbidden stretch (which had been pointed out to me at Urbe) by flying inland, and then dodged some of the higher mountains. It is surprising how misleading the heights of mountains can be when one approaches over low ground, in contrast to being right among them. What at first appears to be 3,000 ft becomes 4,500 ft, and I found that the metres multiplied by 3½ or 4 gave a truer picture. If we checked mountain heights once we did it more times than I care to remember.

An hour and a quarter brought Naples into view; at 4,000 ft we were level with the crater of Vesuvius. According to our gen we had the frequency of Naples Capodichino but I called in vain; then I pressed on, sorting it out in two circuits. Our caution was not misplaced, for we spotted a jet in the circuit and waited to see him land. The eternal windsock was cleverly disguised, but in the absence of any show of pyrotechnics we landed gently. After we turned off the only runway a jeep came out to guide us, for miles it seemed, to the far end of the field and the control buildings. We had scarcely stopped the engine when the Shell representative appeared, tall, handsome and bronzed and speaking excellent English. He was invaluable, and assisted us in the most rapid refuelling we had experienced – by can and chamois-leather too – and arranged hangarage and transport to Naples to catch the last boat to Capri, all within half an hour of landing. As I left the hangar (in which were some Italian Air Force Mustangs) I was shaken as I hurried through the grass to see lizards slithering in all directions.

The coach driver made a real taxi run to town to enable us to catch the last boat to Capri. What I saw of Naples in our dash – it was a slow dash at crowded places – belied adverse opinions one had heard about. The fare to Capri was eight shillings return, and we enjoyed the hour and a quarter the journey occupied.

At Rome we were recommended to stay at Roberts' Pensione,

and as we entered harbour we felt almost there on seeing a Volkswagen Minibus with the name on it. Mr Roberts was there in a white suit and a broad-brimmed hat, a genial host who might have stepped straight out of a Somerset Maugham novel. We climbed the narrow steep roads at record speed, and were soon completing formalities in the hotel. The double room, plus a shower, plus breakfast and dinner came to twenty-five shillings a day – most reasonable, we thought, and proved shortly by one of the best dinners we had had.

At 11.30 p.m. we decided to turn in. Our host expressed his surprise. "But you must visit the Piazza," he said, "where the evening is just beginning."

We were there in five minutes. Imagine a village square floodlit until it resembled a film set, then pour in an orchestra, beautiful women in the most exotic clothes, and with all shops ablaze with light and life, and you have it. Incidentally, I was wearing my white shorts, and the combination of this and my lily-white skin really shook them. Everyone except us had a tan like mahogany. Until 1.30 a.m. we roamed in and out of the shops and bars, stopping for a celebration bottle of wine, for we had now completed our outward journey. We decided to call it a day at 1.45 a.m., and retreated to our room overlooking Gracie Fields' private beach and swimming pool.

Space does not permit a description of our visit to the famous Blue Grotto next day, or of the events leading up to a warm sea bathe, during which I swam out to a lovely white yacht anchored in the bay and flying the American flag. My intention was to rest there a few moments and swim back. Instead I was accorded a typical warm-hearted American welcome: "Say, come on board and have a drink." I found to my delight that this friendly character, who had chartered the yacht for a month, was a USAF flyer based at Capodichino. Presently I expressed concern for my friends ashore, who must have thought they had lost their pilot, so I was invited to fetch them in the yacht's dinghy. In a short time we were all on board and bound for a cruise around Capri in sunshine that, back home, seems impossible to believe. Hours later we dropped anchor in Capri harbour and bade Alan and Mickey and their two children not goodbye but *au revoir*, for we hoped to see them in London during Farnborough week. Another Piazza night rounded off a perfect day.

Saturday, the next day, we had an early breakfast brought to our rooms, then left at 7.30 to catch the 8 a.m. boat to Naples. Formalities completed, many willing hands from the Italian Air Force moved three heavy aircraft to get the Messenger out. The usual charges came to a pound. I had watched a Dakota land earlier, but they changed the runway for us after reference to a control tower midway down the runway. This time we had lamp signals galore, for their radio frequency was an unusual one, not one of our six, and not even that good old stand-by 119.7. My flight plan was for Pisa, with Florence as an alternative, and once airborne I circled to reach 2,000 ft over the airport and then set out to follow the coastline as far as possible. Three thousand feet kept us just below the four-eighths cloud-base and was sufficient except where we cut over headlands, sometimes flying at 4,000 ft and going round the clouds. After sighting Rome we enjoyed the three-and-a-half-hour flight to Pisa, where we established radio contact and made to land on their fine big runway. When we were about twenty feet up I was surprised to see that the wide runway was made very narrow by a double row of lights a foot high, which made it imperative to keep straight. After some "to me, to you" we touched down very nicely indeed and were met by the inevitable jeep, which led us some distance to the control buildings. They were very nice about it, but Pisa is a military aerodrome with quite a collection of twin-engined transports, some American; and although Shell was available on the carnet they advised us to fly to Florence or Albenga (west of Genoa) for Customs clearance.

To divert eastwards to Florence would have meant going out of our way for nearly a hundred miles, so I decided to make for Albenga although the weather men quoted a cloud-base of 1,500 ft, with the possibility of thunderstorms. After some light refreshment, and a word with the Americans, I paid the six-shilling landing fee and we were off again. The 140 miles to Albenga was, for me, the most unpleasant part of our flight to date. The cloud cover was pretty solid and the mountain-tops were lost to view. Following the coast necessitated continuous flying just out to sea with not a hope of a landing, except in the water, in an emergency. It is true that we sighted one airfield soon after leaving Pisa (and the leaning tower, of course) but at times we were forced down to 600 ft and I kept a wary eye on the compass in case the weather should close in on us. (I learned a valuable lesson last year, when hazy conditions off Littlehampton suddenly plunged me into sea mist right down to the water. I was following the coast and I made a mental note that in future I would always have a course to steer in emergency. After two stabs at it at Littlehampton I landed at Ford, where the weather forecast gave nothing below 1,500 ft – until twenty minutes later, when Shoreham gave 300 ft and 400 yd.)

Genoa was unmistakable, and since the mountains drop abruptly into the sea it was something to see a large town on such a narrow strip of land. Albenga is an easy place to find, for there is an island big enough to be marked, at the precise little valley leading to the small airport. Pisa had sent word to them and the Customs man was tearing out from the town by taxi. The field offered a very small, ill-kept runway or a deceptively flat-looking grass area. I chose the latter, and in view of the threatening sky above I felt relieved to be down before the storm.

The Customs man was determined to do a job to justify the taxi fare. He virtually went through our passports with a microscope, querying all blanks and alterations of address until we felt quite naked. This cost a pound. They had no petrol on carnet, but we had sufficient to reach my objective of Cannes if the weather did not deteriorate. They were most obliging, however, and the weather was apparently improving to the west. After handshakes all round we picked our way to the runway and were off after a bumpy ride.

Before setting out immediately over the water I deemed it wise to gain 1,000 ft over the airfield first, a course of action that called for steep turns in the basin-like setting. Presently, at 700 ft over the sea and a quarter of a mile out, we had a grandstand view of Monte Carlo, Nice and Cannes. Monaco presented the most enchanting view, although aerodynamically I approved of the fine runway at Nice. We could speak to Cannes Tower, and all was well until I heard that we were fourth to land. A little research pinpointed two aircraft, and further research brought to light a speck on long finals, and another just alighting on the short mesh landing strip. They have two runways, and also use the grass strips beside them. I chose the runway, and we had guidance in from the runway car. After six hours flying I felt satisfied.

Hotel accomodation in Cannes had reached the chaotic stage, where large numbers were sleeping on the beaches. Eventually a kind and energetic inhabitant, who spoke little English, took all four of us in his Citroën some six miles out of the town and billeted us in a new bungalow. Next morning, our host – a human dynamo in open-necked shirt and shorts – willingly agreed to drive us to the airport at least seven miles away. At a pound a head for two good meals, clean and comfortable accomodation and taxi I thought he had treated us handsomely. He took a great interest in our Messenger and particularly wanted to sit in it, a wish that was easily granted.

I made out a flight plan to Lyons with Toussus-le-Noble, near Paris, as an alternative. The landing fee took the usual five shillings, with an additional seven shillings for Customs, the latter payable to a dear old gentleman I was most pleased to see again, for the evening before he had cycled up to us in civilian clothes and had

143

pedalled off with the carnet; it all seemed a little 'Fred Karno.' The weather man had bad news. The Rhône Valley was upset by thunderstorms and low cloud, and I had to wait three quarters of an hour for a further met. report to arrive. The spare time was used in checking the aircraft. Eric looked over the airframe and Bill the instruments (I was most impressed to see him blow down the A.S.I. and to hear Eric record the passage of a high rate of knots in the cockpit). Norman fiddled with the radio, but I knew he was batting on a sticky wicket.

I had to chase up the petrol man, who had had many calls on his services. I found him refuelling a Cessna 195 and chatted with the pilot – a Frenchman who spoke no English – in my schoolboy French. His machine cruised at 160 m.p.h. and had a ceiling of near 20,000 ft. He proudly showed me the three radio sets and radio compass. His radios had a range of nearly eighty miles, and he was flying to Paris over the top, at 15,000 ft and in three hours. Nuff said! I trudged back to our faithful bird deep in thought.

The weather man now pointed out that had we gone two hours earlier it would have been O.K. We were to have a cloud base of 1,200 ft, with perhaps odd thunderstorms and five-eighths cloud. The runway car led us out, a service I thought particularly nice.

Our mobile lift carried us aloft into sunshine, and we had a pleasant flight to Marseilles at 2,000 ft, cutting off the corners where possible, and only once seeing more cloud than we wanted. There were two aerodromes there, and I called up one for a weather check. They were on the ball, and asked me to wait a moment while they obtained later information. Lyons was giving seven miles visibility and cloud at 1,700 ft. We forged on at 110 m.p.h., following the Rhône, and at times it seemed like standing still. I took great interest in passing over Avignon, complete with Pont. The huge hydro-electric schemes looked very fine, and some were still being constructed. This was the area for high-speed crack trains, which, I am told, can travel at a light aircraft speed of over a hundred miles an hour. I followed the path of one keenly, but it must have been the Sunday service. To the east we could see the peaks of the French Alps, and I felt grateful that our course from now on lay over smaller stuff.

We sighted one very good airfield early on; and now Bill, our back-seat wizard at spot-on ETAs, started us looking ahead for Lyons. The sharp bend in the river nearly fooled us. I first spotted a grass aerodrome with nine gliders floating above it; but we knew that Lyons had runways. With radio contact we dropped in after a three-hour flight and taxied to the imposing control building with its public balcony. To maintain our schedule and reach Croydon that evening it behoved us to press on. It was still very hot, and I felt better for a wash and drink before taking off in record time, with sandwiches to eat aloft. So far as weather was concerned our way to Le Touquet was quite good; but they painted a poor picture of London, with rain and eight-eighths cloud at below 1,000 ft.

To the north of Lyons lies a range of hills 4,000 ft high. They are so near the airport that to climb them on course was not a sporting proposition, and I had to resort to circling to reach 4,500 ft. The Rhône Valley is synonymous with the Mistral, which is a winter wind; but I was reminded of it because we had a cracking headwind all the way up. We cleared the tops safely and left the river for a course that would lead us over Nevers and Paris, for our next stop was Le Touquet. We identified two aerodromes en route, Cosne and Nevers. At the latter one we changed course to port, but therein lies a story. We knew we must be near Nevers, but we could not see anything resembling an aerodrome. I was becoming convinced that we must have overshot it, and that I should turn onto the new course right away. Imagine my feelings when, on looking immediately down past the front of the wing, I saw the edge of an aerodrome flitting past. I turned so that we could identify it, and from there on we had the mixture representative of many parts of France – few good landmarks for miles, chiefly open country scorned, except for aerodromes, by the half-million map.

We went boring on until the Eiffel Tower came into view; we seemed to fly for ages before it grew bigger. I diverted to the west to look for Toussus, and to look for Toussus with certainty one must find the Palace of Versailles; we did. Toussus informed us that conditions at Le Touquet were 'fair,' but after the Italian weather it looked grim, with clouds whipping past at 1,000 ft. The wind at Toussus was 18 kt, and 25 kt at Le Touquet. I knew the run from Toussus to the west, and it seemed like home. After Abbeville we were soon over our destination, where they informed us that the short runway was in use, and that the wind was gusting to over 30 kt. The Messenger fooled the wind by demonstrating its helicopter-like qualities over the runway, and before we touched down daintily much throttle had to be used.

Our problem now was one of daylight. We had less than an hour left, and our pecuniary embarrassment could not face another night away from home. I warned the lads to stay near the aircraft in anticipation of a scalded-cat performance if met. gave anything reasonable. They did, and we made record time in getting off again. We headed straight across the channel after circling to 2,000 ft – the cloud base – but the haze plus the setting sun made it difficult to see the compass, which in the Messenger lies in a little cubbyhole in the dashboard. Together with a fair-sized air bubble in the compass the needle seemed determined to swing, and I set the gyro-compass, only to find what I knew – after a very short time it revolved rapidly (Bell had pinpointed this early on, as a blockage in the pipelines). At this juncture we spied a Freighter overhead on course from Le Touquet to Dungeness, and it needed little deduction to figure out that it was going to Lydd. We crossed the 48 miles of sea in 25 minutes, and I was more than happy to see quite good visibility inland.

I contacted Croydon at five miles range to find that the wind was only 4 kt. We landed at 8.25 p.m. after a day of 8½ hours flying.

We had flown for a total of 29 hours in the twelve days, covering just over 3,000 miles. At five pounds an hour for flying time only, the cost was £36 each. In conclusion, given a reliable aeroplane with a good range and suitable maps – which, if the Alps are envisaged, must be four miles to the inch or less – no ordinary club pilot need feel chary about aiming at destinations beyond Paris.

CHAPTER 18

AIR RACING AND THE HAWK SPEED SIX

by

RON PAINE

[Reproduced from two articles originally published in 'VINTAGE AIRCRAFT' magazine, by courtesy of the aircraft's then owner, Ron Paine – Ed.]

I entered the Magister G-AHNU in the Tynwald Air Race at Ronaldsway on 26th May 1947. Ken Waller was flying the Miles Aerovan G-AILF, Tommy Rose was on the Speed Six G-ADGP, and Gp. Captain 'Bush' Bandidt flew a Sparrowhawk, G-AGDL. I learnt an awful lot in that race and will always remember my surprise as Tommy Rose swept past me on the finishing straight when I had not even known that he was there! I was quite pleased with my sixth place but resolved that I had to do better in future.

Following the Manx Air Derby I took the Magister, now somewhat cleaned up and with the rear cockpit faired over, to Rochford for the re-opening of Southend Municipal Airport on 9th August 1947. I was pleased to see that amongst the entrants for the Southend Cup Air Race were a number of pre-war machines including Tommy Rose's Speed Six, Ranald Porteous on the Chilton D.W.1A G-AFSV and R. Hartnall on the de Havilland T.K.2 G-ADNO. My efforts at cleaning up the Magister were rewarded when I won the trophy, the race having been held in two heats with a final over three laps of a 20.5 miles triangular course from Southend–Canvey Island–Shoeburyness–Southend. The winning speed was 134 m.p.h. and Tommy Rose came in second, to be awarded the Southend Air Speed Cup and a prize of £50 for putting up the fastest speed of 178 m.p.h. The handicappers were not amused with the sudden increase in speed over my Ronaldsway performance and took some convincing before all was well; from then on I kept a very careful eye on what they saw and what they did not – this being all the fun of the thing!

I took 'HNU to the Thruxton Air Races later in the year and was pleasantly surprised to see another very familiar pre-war personality in the form of Jim Mollison, who was racing a light blue G.A.L. Cygnet 2, G-AGAU. I well remember fighting it out with him from Thruxton down to Totland Bay and back; in the end I managed to leave him behind and I was most gratified to get back to Thruxton in the lead.

With the close of the 1947 racing season I was back and forth to Woodley quite a bit as we had the agency for the Messenger and Gemini up at Wolverhampton. As time went on it became apparent that sales were not as high as they might have been and, to our shock, we learned that Miles Aircraft Ltd would have to go into liquidation; it was then that I realised that I must not let the Speed Six out of my sight. I had followed its fortunes with keen interest since 1937, when it had been owned and raced by Luis Fontes, and I had been particularly impressed when I saw the work that George Miles put into it for the abortive 1939 King's Cup. This had included the installation of the blown perspex canopy – which gave them a lot of trouble in getting it optically perfect – and the fitting of a Sparrowhawk centre section to reduce the wingspan from 36 ft to 28 ft. It had been stored by Fontes throughout the war, dismantled in a London Mews off Wimpole Street, but Fontes was unfortunately killed and his aircraft was bought back by Miles Aircraft and restored to fly at Woodley, Tommy Rose making the first flight on 23rd August 1946. It was then used as a high speed Company taxi aircraft for Test Pilots Rose, Kendall and Waller, Tommy racing it with some success.

I made four or five trips to Woodley to see 'Bush' Bandidt, who was in charge on behalf of the Receiver, and Jack Angel, both of whom were very loath to let the aeroplane go. However, I finally managed to acquire it, together with three other Hawks and the M.18 Mk.2, G-AHKY. The Sparrowhawk, G-AGDL, which was also on the fleet at that time, went to Shipsides at Tollerton but it did not last long; on 19th June 1948 it was taken off with the petrol 'off,' stalled, and that was the end of a Sparrowhawk, leaving only G-ADNL with Geoffrey Alington at Birmingham. With my offer accepted the great day finally came for me to be dropped off at Woodley to fly 'DGP back to Wolverhampton: it was 6th February 1948. It was handed over with 44 gallons of 73 octane and 3 gallons of oil, and I was very proud as I flew home that day. Now I had to learn how to fly it and to do so as well as Tommy Rose had done.

It was obvious to the handicappers that the Speed Six had a very high top speed and it was therefore up to me to improve upon that, particularly as it had never been fast enough to catch a Mew Gull. In 1948 there were no Mews around but little did we know that Henshaw's 'EXF would reappear two years later in the hands of Hugh Scrope! With the first post-war King's Cup Air Race due to be held at Elmdon in 1949 I had to get cracking on the Speed Six if I was to be anywhere near the front three.

My first job was to get de Havillands to agree to my up-rating the engine to a Gipsy Six 1F. I then felt that I would have to modify the trousers as I had noticed that after take-off the wheels would protrude by eight or nine inches. I made up a cable arrangement which held the legs in compression at all times and that did the trick, the wheels only protruding about three and a half inches from then on. We then brought the fairings well over the wheels and generally tidied up the whole area, these modifications coming off extremely successfully. I then turned my attention to the wing root/fuselage fairing which was rather 'dirty'; this was cleaned up considerably before I started on the flap fairings and much balsa wood was consumed there before I was satisfied.

It was then that we discovered that all Hawks and Falcons had a large gap between the rear spar and the leading edge of the ailerons. We re-profiled the aileron and built up the spar to reduce the gap, at the same time taking the opportunity to remove the direct drive mechanism to the aileron rock shaft and fit Magister units to give us differential ailerons. The final point to be attended to was the aileron horn balances which were rather troublesome, so they were faired in too.

With the engine upgraded to 1F standard, the carburettors were overhauled by Hobsons, we reduced the undershield from three and a half to one and a half inches, fitted a finer pitch airscrew and we were ready to go. I was delighted with the performance and felt that I could go to Elmdon with some confidence of putting up an increased speed.

The 1949 National Air Races, organised by the Royal Aero Club from Friday 29th July to Monday 1st August, brought together most of the leading manufacturers with their new Service types. Competing pilots included John Cunningham on the Vampire F.3, VV190; Tom Brooke-Smith on the Sturgeon, RK791, and Sealand, G-AKLM; Neville Duke on the Hawker P.1040, VP401; John Derry on the D.H. 108 Swallow; and several pre-war pilots and types including Charles Hughesdon on a Proctor 3, G-AHGA. There was a new system of picking finalists for the King's Cup that year; they were selected from heats or complete eliminating rounds which were spaced out throughout the racing season. 'Bush' Bandit and 'Nat' Somers were there with the prototype Miles Gemini 3,

G-AKDC, which was powered by D.H. Gipsy Major 1C engines in place of the standard Cirrus Minors and, as it had not raced before, very few people knew of its performance. This was a dark horse which I knew I would have to watch.

The King's Cup was held on Saturday 30th July and was arranged in three heats so that 13 finalists from the 36 entrants would be selected to race over three laps of the 20.315 mile quadrilateral course. It was restricted to British pilots flying British-built aircraft with a maximum sea level speed of not less than 120 m.p.h. and a maximum sea level power of not more than 1,000 h.p. I had done very well in my heat so I was in; the Speed Six was performing very well but in the final I had some trouble catching Tony Cole's Niagara-engined Comper Swift G-ABUS which had been handicapped extremely well. We came up on the last pylon, which was about a mile from the final run in to the finish, and I remember that about eight of us arrived at it together. I elected to turn high and as I put the Speed Six on its wingtip I saw all these aeroplanes of varying shapes and sizes turning beneath me; I then had to straighten out and dive off my excess height to cross the line at maximum speed, and, as I looked ahead, I could plainly see the little Swift with Fred Dunkerley's Gemini, G-AKKB, right on his tail. I had to get past these two before we reached the runway intersection to win the race.

I steamed ahead and took Tony with about 200 yards to go to the finish; I felt home and dry, but to my astonishment I then saw 'Nat' Somers with the Gemini 3 well ahead of me and already over the line! I was second but not too disheartened as I had increased the Speed Six's speed to an average 184 m.p.h., 5 m.p.h. up on its previous best.

Following the 1949 Nationals I was appointed to the Committee of the Royal Aero Club and we decided, despite the high costs involved, to offer the opportunity of staging the King's Cup Air Race to leading clubs and aerodromes of the day. I was naturally pleased when I learned that the 1950 race was to be staged at my home field, Wolverhampton.

An excellent team had been created under Col. Preston and two new handicappers had appeared, Joe Lyons and W.J. Charnley. Col. Preston was anxious to get British types back into the record books and an application was made to the FAI to enter various aircraft for the 100 km record in their appropriate classes. I was asked whether I would be willing to enter the Speed Six but this meant that I would have to do even better. The Class C.1b record was then held by the Russians, but to break it was within the capabilities of the aircraft. I got to work once again and one of the first modifications

150

was the installation of 6:1 high-compression, oversized pistons in bored-out cylinders. The camshaft was exchanged for that of a Gipsy Queen 2 so that the bottom end closely approximated to that of a Gipsy Six Mk.II. These mods necessitated larger carburettor choke tubes, Hobsons coming to my rescue once again with their main factory situated only a few hundred yards off the aerodrome at Fordhouses. The power output was thus raised to that of a Six Srs.II but we managed to keep the weight down by retaining the fixed pitch airscrew.

The modification was highly successful and the revs went up. In conjunction with this I fitted a ram air intake in the nose cowl, took away the flame trap and made the installation almost the same as that which had been fitted to Henshaw's Mew Gull in 1938. The cowlings were tidied up by drawing them in by an inch all round before we turned our attention to the tail end where a smaller skid and shaft were fitted and faired in. We finally replaced some warped ply skin and put a great polish on the airframe, above and below, the test flights proving that we had done it again.

The 1950 King's Cup Air Race was held on 17th June; the weather was ideal and the 36 entrants included a number of very interesting types such as the blue and gold Hurricane II, G-AMAU, flown by Peter Townsend; the Spitfire T.8, G-AIDN, flown by P.G. Robarts; two Vega Gulls, G-AFBC and G-AFEA; Geoffrey Alington's Miles Sparrowhawk G-ADNL, and a Parnall Heck, G-AEGI. My main worry was to make sure that I did not put a foot wrong; if all went to plan I stood a good chance of winning the cup and breaking the speed record. In the event Edward Day, in the Miles Magister G-AKRV, was very well handicapped and won the race at 138.5 m.p.h.; Peter Townsend came second at 283 m.p.h. and Gp. Capt. A.H. Wheeler came third in the Auster 5C G-ALKI. I finished about fifth but at the end of the afternoon, when all the times and pylon judges had been checked, it was announced over the Tannoy that I had lapped the course at 192.83 m.p.h.. This was a new Class C.1b record and the fastest that the aircraft had flown up until that time. To the best of my knowledge the record still stands today and if I had to repeat the performance with the aircraft in its current state I would have no problem in raising the speed by at least another 8 m.p.h.

Having gained the Class C.1b record in 1950 I left the Speed Six in that configuration as there was little that I could do to improve upon its performance. The handicapping team were very good and provided I maintained my handicapped speed there was always a good chance of winning – especially if it was a rough day. Two events spring to mind in which the bumpy weather was of positive benefit to me. The first was the Bristol Air Race, held at the old Whitchurch aerodrome on 14th July 1951 over three laps of a 30 mile course. It was a very rough day and I can remember scrapping it out with 'Timber' Wood who was flying a very fast Proctor 1, G-AHVG, which he had from Blackburns. I managed to come in first at an average speed of 193 m.p.h. R.H. Bennet on a Tiger Moth, G-AMBK, was second and 'Timber' was third.

Another very rough day was 16th May 1953 when the weather really threw the slower aeroplanes around but I managed to come home first to win the Goodyear Trophy at Wolverhampton.

The years 1950 to 1952 were memorable for the three *"Daily Express"* air races along the south coast. The first was held on 16th September 1950 and 75 aircraft were entered for the race from Hurn to Herne Bay. 67 started and 61 finished, some of the more exotic entries being two Gipsy Moths, G-AAWO and G-ABJJ; the Hawker Tomtit, G-AFTA; Hawker Hurricane IIC, G-AMAU; Boulton Paul Balliol T.2, VR602; and a Handley Page Halifax C.VIII, G-AKEC! This race was significant as it marked the post-war reappearance of the historic Mew Gull, G-AEXF, which Hugh Scrope had re-discovered in France earlier in the year.

The second race was planned for 6th August 1951 but that summer's inclement weather conspired to postpone it until 22nd September. This time the course was of 186 miles from Shoreham to Brighton, Newhaven and Whitstable, and then along the coast via Hythe, Rye Harbour, Hastings, Eastbourne, Beachy Head and back to the finish over Brighton's West Pier. That year the race was won by Hugh Kendall in his tiny 32 h.p. Chilton DW.1 G-AFGI. He had spent many hours preparing for the race and his hand-carved propeller was superb.

It was in these races that I discovered that if I got the Speed Six down in the dead calm about 50 feet from the water it would really motor. After a number of test flights I fitted a boost gauge which enabled me to accurately fly at just the right height to give maximum boost. With a following wind I managed, for the first time, to record a speed of 207 m.p.h., winning my class and producing a nice surprise in the way of prize money.

The last of the three races was held on 2nd August 1952 over a course from Shoreham to Reculver and back round the coast to the West Pier at Brighton. 46 aircraft were entered and the winner was R.H. McIntosh in a Proctor 1, G-AHGA.

I continued to enter the Speed Six for the King's Cup and other events throughout the 1950s and 1960s but by now the handi-cappers had really got things sewn up and we were treated to some really excellent finishes. I particularly remember the long-running duel between J.N. 'Nat' Somers in his Gemini 3 and Fred Dunkerley in the cunningly cut-down Gemini 1A, G-AKKB.

I had been consistently in the top six finishers in the King's Cup and had been second at 189 m.p.h. in the 1959 event but it was in 1962 that I had high hopes. I came second to Johnny Spiller's very fast Proctor 3, G-AHFK, during the Air League Challenge Trophy, missing first place by less than 50 feet, and thus qualified for the King's Cup during the afternoon of 18th August. My luck was out again: Peter Clifford won in his Tipsy Nipper 2, G-ARDY, and I tied for second place with Dennis Hartas on the Tiger Moth G-ANZZ.

Over the years I had been putting up speeds that kept placing me in scratch position and I was winning the SBAC Trophy, which was awarded for the fastest speed in the King's Cup each year. By the early 1960s my traditional place was being challenged by newcomers, the most significant of which was the little Le Vier Cosmic Wind, G-ARUL. This won the 1964 King's Cup at 185 m.p.h. with Dennis Hartas at the controls but I came in second (again) at 187.5 m.p.h. I had now won the trophy five times, the last three years in succession, and the Society made a magnificent gesture in presenting me with the trophy for life.

By this time I had become very tied up with the airline business and could no longer afford to devote the time to racing most weekends throughout the season, so I parted with 'DGP to W.H. Todd of Halfpenny Green. Following a slight accident to the canopy it never put up such good performances as it had been doing with me and it was unplaced in both the 1965 and 1966 King's Cup races.

After two seasons at Halfpenny Green the aeroplane was bought by A.J. Osborne, who was then in the process of setting up the British Historic Aircraft Museum at Biggin Hill, and it was raced by him for the 1967 Manx Air Derby Challenge Trophy. After this event he decided, for some reason, to strip it down and make a different animal of it altogether. I saw the speeds that it was putting up and realised that it had regressed considerably.

After a period of storage at Stapleford Tawney the Speed Six, unbeknown to me, was put up for sale and my good friend John Blake, of the Royal Aero Club, mentioned this to David Hood who was, at that time, looking for a vintage aeroplane. David contacted me and we went to look it over at Elstree shortly after it had caught fire *[at the end of a flight from Shoreham, when a fuel line fractured – Ed.]*. Although damaged I decided that it was repairable but I would have to dismantle it and take it to my new base at Castle Donington where it would take the best part of a year to put it right. Once it had arrived I stripped it and replaced 50% of the covering, restoring it to its cream and red livery. But that was not all. When the time came for reassembly I took the opportunity to carry out some modifications which I had always wanted to do but which were not possible when the aircraft was all in one piece. From an external point of view the most obvious of these is the new canopy. I had a cooper build a mould which fitted over me when seated in the cockpit and from which we made a new, much lower, hood.

Just after I completed the work it so happened that the 50th anniversary King's Cup Air Race was due to be held at Booker on 15th July 1972. The Speed Six had not raced for some years and had not been competitive for even longer so this would be an interesting test of how well I had rebuilt it. The qualifying heat was run in the morning as the Aspenair Trophy Race; there was a very wide field, many of which were very different from the types that I had been used to racing against in the past. I came in second to a very fast Piper Twin Comanche and was encouraged to think that after the rebuild I could still get alongside it!

We were re-handicapped for the afternoon and off we went. Bearing in mind the large field I looked for a route that would get me back over the finish without being baulked by the twenty-odd back markers ahead of me. I noticed that the Forestry Commission had thoughtfully cut a gap in the wood which ran straight up the hill and onto the end of the runway so I took the Speed Six through it at a very low altitude and swept onto the airfield thinking "This is my day!" Then on my left I spotted a Victa Airtourer! I called the tower and they confirmed my worst suspicions – second again! Despite this disappointment I was delighted to learn later in the day that we had put up a speed of 196 m.p.h.

After the 1972 King's Cup I took the Speed Six to Shobdon, where we came in third, and then to Halfpenny Green for the Goodyear Trophy. Although I came in second place the day was tragically marred by the death of Prince William of Gloucester in the take-off crash of his Piper Cherokee Arrow, G-AYPW. This was the last time that the Speed Six completed a race as I pulled out of the 1973 King's Cup at Cranfield.

As most people now know, G-ADGP is retired from racing and is permanently based at Old Warden under the ownership of Mike Stow. [This was in the late seventies – Ed.] As with David before him I have an agreement with Mike that should it ever be offered for disposal it will revert to me and I am responsible for looking after it, renewing the C. of A. and all pre-flight preparations. Mike is absolutely delighted with the aeroplane and is now very accomplished at displaying it at Old Warden. We will still take the Speed Six to the occasional air show and if the Mew Gull is there people can see them flying together. I feel that this is the best way to keep it now.

[*Since this article was originally written, the Speed Six has had several other owners: first, Roger Reeves (to whom I sold an original oil painting of the aircraft in the mid-eighties), then an Irishman, D. McCarthy, who shipped it out to Florida where he hoped to sell it. But little interest was shown in an antique British aircraft and the Speed Six would probably have rotted away had it not been for Ron Souch, who alerted the American art dealer and aircraft enthusiast Tom Buffaloe to its plight; he set about rescuing it, and happily it finished up in the UK again with Ron Souch, who then started to restore it late in 1986.*

It was agreed that the rebuild should be more or less to the original prewar configuration, and, interestingly, when the aircraft was stripped down traces of the original black factory paint were found on the fuselage.

The Speed Six flew again on May 23rd 1989 at Lee-on-Solent in the hands of Martin Barraclough, and although still owned by Tom Buffaloe, it is now based at Old Warden, from where Ron Souch still makes the occasional sortie elsewhere. I was delighted – and almost overwhelmed – when Ron brought this, my favourite of all aeroplanes, to Shoreham Airport's 60th Anniversary celebrations on the 15th June 1996 – Ed.]

CHAPTER 19

AROUND FILTON
AND OTHER PLACES

by

EDWIN SHACKLETON

[NOTES ON THE AUTHOR: Edwin Shackleton has been mentioned in the "Guinness Book of Records" eight times since 1990 as 'most experienced passenger'; he has now flown in over 600 different types of aircraft.

After National Service, he came to Bristol in 1949 to work as a Technical Assistant in the Bristol Aeroplane Company's Structural Test Laboratory. He set up their Cold Test Facility (Altitude Chamber), and later worked on pressure testing, fail-safe structural development on Concorde and tank test work on the BAC.111 and BAe.146. He retired from British Aerospace in 1987.

He has been involved with the organisation of a number of Air Displays, including the International Air Tattoo at Greenham Common since 1973, and the Avon Air Days at Weston-super-Mare during the 1970s. He is a founder member of the PFA Wessex Strut, and commentates at all their Fly-In.]

It seems rather odd to be looking back to the fifties when life was so very different. Television was virtually non-existent, car ownership was really limited and public transport was the backbone to 'getting around.'

After two years National Service in the Royal Air Force, I had been employed for less than three months (of an eventual 38 years) in the Structural Test Laboratory of the Bristol Aeroplane Company at Filton by the start of the decade.

The Brabazon had flown one month before I arrived at Filton and the Britannia was well on the way to its first flight on 16th August 1952. The Type 170 Freighter was well established as the design was started during WW2 (first flight on the 2nd December 1945) and production was proceeding in batches of 10 machines.

The biggest customer was the Pakistan Air Force (e.g. 38 were built in under two years commencing late 1953). The Type 171 Sycamore, designed by the Austrian Raoul Hafner, had flown initially with P & W Wasp engines on the two Mk.1s, then with the availability of the Alvis Leonides the Mk.2 became the production prototype. A batch of 15 Mk.3s (many of which became Mks.11 to 13 military types) were being built when I arrived. Also the twin rotor Type 173 was being developed, albeit through quite troubled development, and it first flew just before the Britannia. The eventual result, though built by Westland at Weston-super-Mare, was the Belvedere for the Royal Air Force.

Looking back, the Britannia was quite a triumph for the Bristol airframe and engine companies, but sales were sadly affected by the 'jet age' Comet and Boeing 707. In January 1956, the airframe, engine and car production was split into three separate divisions, the first stepping-stone towards the current British Aerospace.

Filton airfield at that time was always very busy with company aircraft and visiting machines. The north side was occupied by the odd Meteor T.7 and the Vampires of No.501 Squadron, Royal Auxiliary Air Force, who were active at weekends. They quickly disappeared with the RAuxAF disbandment on the 10th March 1957.

No.12 Reserve Flying School, equipped with Tiger Moths and Ansons, operated from the old Bristol Flying School hangar adjacent to the A38 road, just north of the newly extended 'Brabazon' runway. But their days were numbered by Government policy when all the RF Schools were closed on 31st March 1953. It was from this hangar in pre-war days that the prototype Bombay troop carrier appeared. I remember Bert Clatworthy, Structural Research superintendent, telling me that the Bombay was built parallel to the doors because of the limited door width. Then it was rolled out sideways on rails. The historic hangar, which was eventually occupied by Rolls Royce, was finally flattened to make way for a huge Royal Mail sorting office for Bristol, Bath and Taunton, which opened this year.

While working in the test laboratory, my attention was diverted by a young lady, Irene Passmore, whom I married in June 1952. The previous year, we had a holiday in the Isle of Wight, journeying there on my Sunbeam S8 motor bike. Just by chance, we called at Bembridge Airport and took a trip in a joy-riding Autocrat G-AGVL. It was Irene's first aeroplane flight and was the first of my many Auster trips. Some years later, I mentioned the flight to my late friend Graham Blake, and he told me that this was the machine that was stolen by 18-year-old Borstal boy Brynley Fussel from Bembridge on 30th May 1949 and flown to near Newport, South

Wales. Apparently a year later he stole another Auster and crash-landed it in France.

Irene and I took a coach holiday to the Lake District in the summer of 1953 and we had a northbound lunch stop at Southport. I mentioned to Irene that there was a 15-inch gauge light railway and maybe also the Giro Aviation Fox Moth which operated from Southport Sands. The coach driver said that lunch was organised for 1 p.m. at a certain hotel and we *must not be late*. So we dashed off to the little railway, had our ride, then on to the sands. The pilot was stood by his machine so we paid the fee, took some quick photos and climbed into the Hansom-cab-style cabin; although it was difficult to swing-start we were finally off for a short trip over the town.

When we landed, we ran to the hotel, several minutes late, to a displeased coach driver who asked: "Where do you think you have been?"

I responded: "Well, just for a train and aeroplane ride."

That seemed to deflate him – so off we went for our lunch!

At the time I did not have any opportunity to ask the name of the pilot and quite often wondered about it. Then, in an issue of 'FLIGHT' 25 years later, there was an article by Ken Hartley who was reminiscing about flying the Fox Moth. I wrote to him, giving exact times (who could forget!) and three photos. The reply gave a definite response; the flying gear draped over the fuselage was the old overcoat which was the trade mark of Norman Giroux. Monsieur Giroux operated G-ACEJ from those sands from 1936 to WW2, then post-war until July 1964. The Fox Moth was bought by Norman Jones, then Tony Haig Thomas. It became a virtual write-off in 1982 when a Beech Musketeer crashed into it on the ground at Old Warden. The wreck was bought by Ben Cooper who spent 10 years restoring it to airworthy condition.

In 1954, BEA acquired two Bristol 171 Mk.3A Sycamores (the first examples with the bulged baggage hold behind the cabin) and announced that they were starting a helicopter service from Southampton to London (alternately Heathrow and Northolt). Thomas Cook booked us a couple of seats and we awaited our first helicopter flight. My parents stayed with us for a few days, then we all had a short tour of the south coast until the weekend. On Monday, Irene and I were at Eastleigh Airport, boarding the Sycamore G-AMWG as back-seat passengers, just us and the captain. Once airborne, I was attracted by the Decca Flight Log where a pen traced our route on the map which passed from drum to opposite drum. Large towns were not on our track but I was able to locate Odiham and see distant Meteor night-fighters taking off, then we flew really near to Windsor Castle. Soon we were landing amidst a collection of BEA Pionairs (Dakotas) and Vikings. My sister, Florence, met us and took us to lunch at her Ruislip home, thence by train to my parents at Ipswich.

In a fit of idiocy, I joined the Royal Observer Corps in 1954 and had a brief flight in an Anson 12, PH769, from Filton. But that was not my scene and I soon left, losing the opportunity to fly in a Hastings or Beverley!

Britannia test flying dominated the Filton scene in the mid-fifties and I was able to contrive a flight in the second production Britannia 102 G-ANBB which was my largest aircraft type up until then. We flew west along the Bristol Channel and off to St. David's Head, where we were asked to sit aft (actually on the step leading to the toilets) while stall testing took place. After much shuddering – both to the aircraft and to ourselves! – the ARB Chief Pilot Dave Davies flew us back to Filton. Two years later, I was selected to fly on a BOAC handling flight in the first long range Britannia G-AOVA, much more sedate with full catering crew. However we were disappointed not to fly over scenic Europe but over the north of England, criss-crossing in steady outside ambient conditions for some air-conditioning calibration work. We were airborne for 7.5 hours on that trip.

Just before the first Britannia flight I had joined an Air-Britain (Bristol Branch) coach trip to visit the D.H. Factory at Christchurch, where we were able to see Vampire Trainers, Venom and Sea Venom night-fighters all in production, but we were discreetly kept away from anything connected with the D.H.110, still very secret. Afterwards we visited the Christchurch Aero Club where various members enjoyed flights (at 5 or 10 shillings) in either their Autocrat G-AHAT, as I did, or a Tiger Moth. I persuaded the coach driver to drop me at Bristol Maternity Hospital on the way home so that I could see Irene and our newly arrived son, Michael.

Graham Blake and I started the Bristol Branch of Air-Britain in mid-1954, resulting in some very long friendships. Sadly that with Graham was not to be so, as he joined the RAF and lost his life in a Hastings crash near to Benson. Peter March, who later on was so very helpful in arranging some of my 'flights,' inveigled me to join the IAT team on its move to Greenham Common. I took on, for the early growing years, the task of Ground Exhibition Manager. Air-Britain friends Reg Bloomfield, Brian Lavers, Pete Elliott and Dave Molyneux later became my Photobus team of which Reg later took over the reins.

Another Air-Britain trip was by a 14-seat coach to the 1955 National Air Races and Aerobatic Contests at Coventry. The highlight was to see the Fokker S.14 Mach Trainer, SIPA Minijet and Focke Wulf Stieglitz (Argentinian-registered).

I went back to Coventry in 1958, this time on my own, taking my BSA Dandy 70 c.c. scooter on the train and staying locally. The Czech aerobatic team stole the scene with their single- and two-seat Zlin Treners. Their Aero 45 support aircraft, however, looked very sad with one engine completely stripped down. Next day, it was back together and, I thought, was just engine-running, but I quickly realised that it was about to taxi out. I managed to attract the pilot's attention and, through some improvised sign language, was soon aboard the Aero 45. We flew locally – then the port engine was cut, prop feathered and we were landing with fire cover on standby, but all was well. I didn't follow up that story!

One of my colleagues of that time, Roy Matthews, was working on the Britannia water tank fatigue test at Filton. He had gained his PPL and was building up hours for his CPL. Ian Davies and I joined with him for a one-hour flight in Auster J/1N Alpha G-AGVM of the Bristol and Wessex Aero Club from the old Bristol Airport at Whitchurch. This was one of the first Autocrat conversions with the Gipsy Major and bigger rudder. Roy left us to follow his flying career and I remember meeting him at an Agricultural Aircraft Show at Cranfield in September 1959 where we saw such rarities as the Czech Omnipol Brigadyr, Djinn helicopter and Auster Agricola in the flying display. Roy wrote later to say he was flying 'twins' in Africa. A couple of years ago, I heard the same name mentioned on the TV programme *"This Is Your Life"* connected with an African mercy flight – I wonder if that was the same Roy?

Apart from 'spotting' at Filton, I managed to get around quite a bit but the highlights were the RAeS Garden Parties and the SBAC Shows. A particularly good Garden Party was that at Wisley in 1957 with a French light 'plane invasion (4 SAAB 91B Safirs, Nord 854, Paul Aubert Super Cigale), the Turbi G-APFA before it grew a canopy, a *flyable* G.A. Cygnet G-AFVR and the parasol Hirtenberg HS.9A G-AGAK (which no longer exists). The next Garden Party had bad weather and became 'Wet Waltham' but it was great to see the D.H.86A from Southampton.

My first two Garden Party visits were to Radlett in 1946 and 1947; Radlett was actually a special extra day to the first post-war SBAC Shows. The Show moved to Farnborough in the next year and in the fifties saw many exciting new types from British Industry including the V-bombers, the magnificent Princess flying boat, Britannia, altitude-record Olympus Canberra, speed-record-breaking Fairey Delta, Gnat, Hunter and numerous others. In 1996 at Farnborough I was so pleased to record '50 years since my first

SBAC show' and met Alan Wright (of Civil Aircraft Register fame) with the same thought.

Farnborough also attracted many support and visiting aircraft. I well remember my old Hillman Minx breaking down (half-shaft fracture!) on the way at Newbury and hiring a car to make it to Farnborough '59. I returned later in the week behind Reg Bloomfield on Dave Saul's motor bike to pick up the car and see the visiting aircraft at Blackbushe. We watched from the runway end, seeing a USAF Globemaster 2, French Navy Bretagne and Portuguese Navy Lockheed Harpoon. The latter was certainly a rarity but little did I realise that I would fly in a Confederate Air Force Harpoon at Harlingen just 29 years later!

The Bristol Orpheus was well under way in the fifties and flight-proving and development continued at Filton on a single seat Gnat, Fiat G.91 and a little known F.86 Sabre conversion. One day, I saw all three jets, nicely lined up in front of a 'cherry picker' hydraulic lift, obviously ready for a photo session. I sneaked across the airfield with nobody around. As I was leaving, I looked back and saw three men watching and obviously wondering who was the cheeky intruder.

My great passion to photograph every different aircraft variant gradually waned as the field widened and I became interested in *flying* in these machines. Having become involved in the flying display scene, I was meeting many of the aviators on the other side of the fence, opening up flying opportunities.

But that is another story.

CHAPTER 20

CHRISTCHURCH CHRONICLES

by

TED GOULD

(as told to

PETER G. CAMPBELL)

MESSENGER 4A G-ALAJ

This aircraft belonged to the Royal Artillery Flying Club; early in 1956 they brought it back from their base in Germany as there was no real requirement for it over there, so it was then based at Christchurch, and various club members had the opportunity of flying it. I flew it quite a lot and thoroughly enjoyed it; it was a very nice aeroplane.

In March Tommy Marshall had got the offer of a Gemini, G-AKFU; I can't remember whether it was just on loan or not, but anyway it was based up at Boston, in Lincolnshire. So on the 14th of March John Pothecary and I, and another chap called Colin, who worked in the hangars, set out in the Messenger to collect the Gemini and bring it back to Christchurch; 'Poth' was flying the aircraft.

On the way there, as so often can happen, an embarrassing situation arose personally in that I wanted to 'spend a penny,' and gradually this wanting became urgent, and then necessary. We were just over half-way there by this time. I mentioned my discomfort, which was greeted with scorn, I may add, by the others, but I knew that I was going to have to find some way out of this predicament. I did find a cup (or maybe it was a Thermos top) which we had used previously for some coffee and relieved my embarrassment into this cup, which was looked on in disgust by the other members of the party.

The next thing to consider was how I was going to dispose of the contents of the cup; it was a little bumpy and the aeroplane was floating around a bit, so I thought of what seemed at the time a

162

marvellous yet obvious solution: to release the contents out of the window. I pulled back the sliding section of the canopy on the starboard side and offered the cup to the slipstream. Unfortunately it must have been at the wrong angle, because instead of emptying itself *outside* the aircraft it emptied *inside*; the contents did a sort of complete turn round the back of the inside of the aircraft and finished up on 'Poth's' head, neck and hair. This caused a scream of disgust, anguish and so forth (not surprisingly, I suppose), and in the excitement he more or less put the aeroplane on its back; this was rather disconcerting for me too as I had released my belt to help the operation, and I now found myself thumping around all over the cockpit. At the same time 'Poth' was crying out in disgust, cursing and swearing, and furiously trying to wipe this stuff off. I told him not to be a bloody baby and make such a fuss over a small incident like this, for which I was rewarded with just a deep glowering look (although we are still good friends to this day, I should add!).

Anyway, we completed the journey to Boston without further incident. I was to return solo in the Messenger, with 'Poth' and Colin in the Gemini, but on the way back the weather, which had been very good up till then, began to deteriorate (this seems to be the usual story when relating flying memories!) until there was a lot of mist and low cloud and light rain. Up to this time 'Poth' and I were going more or less together in loose formation, but by the time we got down to the Newbury area it was getting very difficult to keep in visual contact. The Gemini had radio but the Messenger didn't, so there was still no way that we could communicate with one another except by hand signals. Finally it got so bad that things were absolutely impossible; I had lost 'Poth' completely by this time (it later turned out that he had radioed ahead to Hurn and they had advised him of better weather further south by Ringwood, so he had climbed up out of the worst of it and had kept going). I tried various different heights, but to no avail, and then I spotted Greenham Common, which had recently been taken over by our friends from America.

Without further ado (I couldn't call them up, of course), I just came in, without even doing a circuit, and landed safely. I noticed as I came in to land on the main runway that there was a C-47 by the end of it waiting to take off, props ticking over. As I landed, I carried on taxying, and eventually turned off the main runway onto the hard standing, not far from Flying Control.

I stayed there for several minutes, still in the aircraft, wondering what to do next. Then, suddenly, all hell broke loose: Tannoys which I should think you could hear on the South Coast shouted "Unidentified aircraft, landed on Runway So-and-So." It seemed as if a state of emergency had been declared. The next moment several Jeeps roared up, full of police with machine guns, and whatever else they carry.

I opened the side of the canopy, looked out, and there was a very thick-necked gentleman with a raucous voice, who shouted: "Get out of that aircraft, you. Put your hands up." This incensed me, especially coming so soon after all the unpleasantness of the outward flight, and then the awkwardness of the emergency landing in bad weather. I stood up in the cockpit and said loudly in my best upper-class British voice: "Would you kindly not address me in that manner. I'm not in *your* bloody Air Force." At that his manner changed and relaxed somewhat – he even called me "Sir."

So they took me over to the CO, Colonel Smythe I think it was, who was a very friendly bloke, and he explained the necessity for the security arrangements; this was as near as they got to apologising to me. I can understand now why all the people who used to come to this country from the States – film stars and other celebrities – used to say how wonderful *our* policemen were.

I was given the opportunity to meet several of the pilots there, and then a message came through from the pilot of the C-47, who had taken off to do a VFR flight to Manston, that he had had to abort and come straight back because of the bad weather; this of course lent credence to my perfectly true story that the weather was too bad for me to continue, and that's why I'd had to land there. They were very nice to me, and gave me a drink in the Mess, and then they escorted me to a hotel in Newbury where I was going to have to spend the night. I think the two rather charming ladies in the Hotel (the Chequers, I believe it was) looked rather askance when a crowd of American policemen escorted me in there, especially as I had no luggage.

The next morning they saw me off, and I had an uneventful flight back to Christchurch.

Following that incident, several officers came down to see me at my home in Bournemouth, and they were very interested in starting a social and flying club at Greenham Common, which I believe they did.

So perhaps some good came out of that landing after all.

AUSTER 5D G-AGLK

Rebuilding 'GLK, one of my early efforts, was quite an interesting experience, and the aircraft itself was a bit special in that it was the first civilian Mark 5 Auster after the war, being used by the

Ministry of Civil Aviation. I bought the bones of 'GLK from an engineer called Roy Webb, a friend of mine from Botley, Southampton. After a forced landing in a freshwater lake in South Wales it had been taken out of the water, drained off and stored for a while, and then Roy Webb had bought it.

There was no engine with it when I acquired it, but having been a Ministry aircraft the fuselage had been originally sandblasted by Austers and then protected with aluminium paint, so even after the ditching and storage I could find no corrosion at all when I stripped the aircraft right down.

I'm pretty positive that I didn't use the wings from that aircraft; I had another pair of wings, but I can't really recall where they came from.

I then made an arrangement with Austers through Wally Walpole, the manager of the repair section (and a very good friend of mine) whereby Austers agreed to rebuild the fuselage for me. As the aircraft was a Mark 5 and had originally had a Lycoming engine, they would do a modification to what later became known as J/1N standard and install a Gipsy Major. They had never done this before in a Mark 5, but agreed to do the work at a very nominal figure. I supplied the engine, a brand new one that was quite easy to obtain from surplus stocks.

Austers rebuilt and recovered the fuselage, using new wooden components, and fitted a number of modifications which would later become standard practice on J/1N Alpha conversions; these included a new moulded windscreen and rounded-off Autocrat-type rear windows, four seats, a larger fin and rudder, and also a long-range tank. I rebuilt the wings and also finished the other modifications that they supplied most of the parts for, but it was all done for a very reasonable cost.

The aircraft was finally finished in August 1957, was airtested on the 13th with John Pothecary, and was found to fly very well. On the 16th we flew it to Tarrant Rushton, where it was painted, and on the 23rd we flew it back down to Christchurch.

(While mentioning John 'Poth', can I just say that my friendship with him has always been a very good one and goes back a long time; we learned to fly at the same time at Thruxton. Later Tommy Marshall and I lent him the Moth 'AWO to help him build up the 100 hours necessary for his Instructor's Licence, and he also flew the Drone on various occasions. He was Chief Instructor at Christchurch before joining Silver City and flying Bristol Freighters, and then, later, BAC.111s with British United until he retired. Of course after that he was then at Shoreham for some years before moving down west quite recently, so he's really quite near us now. My wife and I are looking forward to seeing both him and Jenny a lot more in future.)

I flew 'GLK extensively, and in April 1958 I took my wife Barbara and our two children to Paris. We didn't leave Christ-church until fairly late in the day; we had decided that we'd stay the night in Brighton, and actually I was quite glad when we reached Shoreham as the flight had been getting very bumpy, and I was told after I had landed in what I thought was a very short distance that the wind was 40 knots!

The next day we had a very nice and enjoyable flight over the channel (non-radio, of course) to Le Touquet, and then map-read our way down to Paris; it was quite amazing how suddenly the Eiffel Tower appeared out of the mist on our port side. We then easily found our way to Toussus-le-Noble, just south of the city.

We had a very enjoyable few days in Paris, except for my feet! With all my passengers being female, I was allowed very little in the way of baggage, and had only the one pair of shoes with me. The Paris streets were very hot to the feet, and even now my children remind me of the time when they and their mother went off round the Louvre, whilst I sat in abject misery with tortured feet by the Winged Victory statue at the entrance!

On the way back conditions got a bit hairy due to poor visibility; fortunately my wife spotted the canal and railway line that led directly to Le Touquet, and we just tootled along at a very low height and turned and lobbed into the aerodrome. We had to stay there overnight because the fog was so bad; even the Silver City Bristol Freighters were grounded. The next day the weather had improved a bit and we made it home safely.

In the June of that year I took my wife Barbara and a friend, Flight-Lt. Roger Mann, down to the South of France in 'GLK; Roger was by this time a very experienced Service pilot and we shared the flying. We went over the Dordogne area, and right down to Carcassonne and the gliding centre at the Black Mountain; wherever we landed we were given a marvellous welcome.

The return trip was relatively uneventful, although we were fogged in once or twice. We visited a lot of airfields and saw some of the old aircraft that were still there ever since the German occupation during the last war. But by the time we reached Poitiers the weather had deteriorated so much that, although we took off on the next leg, we had to return to the airfield. At this stage Barbara was getting somewhat concerned, and elected to complete the journey by train and boat! We duly met up with her a couple of days later when we eventually reached Lympne.

I eventually sold 'GLK only because the Royal Artillery Aero

Club had recently lost their Auster, when a young lieutenant was killed in a crash on the hills behind Shoreham on the way home in very bad weather. They were without an aircraft, and badly needed another because of all the bookings, so I sold 'GLK through Major-General Bill Hughes (the Chairman of the RAAC), who became a very good friend of mine. They had many happy years of flying in it before it was sold to a new owner at Shoreham. *['GLK is still airworthy and is now based at Biggin Hill – Ed.]*

I later rebuilt several more Austers, including 'GYD & 'JYB, although we are now talking about the early sixties *[the exploits of 'GYD in 1953 in the hands of Major Christopher Draper are recorded in Chapter 11 – Ed.]*.

'JYB was actually a hybrid; I had two fuselages, a J/1 Autocrat with rear damage and a Mark 4 with front damage. I took both of these up to Austers on the roof of my car (I had a big Ford Zephyr in those days), and Wally Walpole's department did a splendid job of cutting them, joining them together and then reinforcing them, with full official approval, of course, and then I had one very good fuselage. Austers were quite intrigued by all of this and wanted to put a photograph of it in their house magazine, but when I went to collect the rebuilt fuselage there wasn't any camera available, so the opportunity was lost.

I had a spare pair of wings (I can't remember exactly where they came from) which I completely overhauled; all the bolts and fittings were renewed and the spars were examined, and the ARB surveyor approved all of that. Of course this type of aircraft was given a full C. of A. and had to be signed out by the ARB surveyor as well as a licensed engineer.

Strangely enough I can remember that aircraft very well. I had an engine on which I'd done a top overhaul, and had had the magnetos and carburettors checked, and so forth, and all this was signed out, of course. I took it down to Christchurch and assembled it in the Auster; it went up together very well and I remember that the ARB were coming in the next day or so, and I did an air test on it, and that aircraft, I can remember, flew just like a bird. There was no adjustment necessary on the rigging of the aircraft, nor was any needed on the engine: even the tick-over was perfect. I remember just taking it up on the air test, as I needed to do for the C. of A., and it performed beautifully. All the figures came out remarkably well; it was a delight to fly, and seemed very light.

I remember I sold it to Tommy Marshall, who was short of an aircraft at the time, but after that it was resold to the Shaftesbury Flying Club at Compton Abbas, near Shaftesbury. *['JYB is still airworthy, and is based in Lincolnshire – Ed.]*

CHAPTER 21

AEROVANALIA

Edited by

PETER G. CAMPBELL

(With personal contributions from 'Ladi' Marmol & Rex Nicholls, and press cuttings supplied by Charles Tomkins, 'Ladi' Marmol and Peter Amos.)

[The Miles Aerovan, like the dinosaurs, was a great success in its own time but alas is now no longer with us. Only a few bits and pieces remain, stored with the Miles Aircraft Collection.

The twin-engined Aerovan was perhaps the first real all-purpose aircraft. It could lift a payload of a ton, and was used for carrying such diverse cargoes as motorcars, ponies, pigs, furniture, parties of school children and Father Christmas! In the harsh winter of 1947 G-AILF was fitted experimentally with skis; amazingly, colour film footage of this exercise still exists.

The standard Aerovan had two Cirrus Major engines, but one, G-AKHF, was converted by Miles to take two Lycomings of increased horsepower, which in turn necessitated the fitting of enlarged fins and rudders. This aircraft was based at Shoreham in the early fifties but in 1954 was exported to Italy as I-VALK and was reportedly still in existence there in the late sixties.

During the fifties most surviving Aerovans visited Shoreham at one time or another for attention by F.G. Miles Ltd, the last recorded such visit being by PH-EAB (ex-G-AHXH) in 1959. Possibly the most well known Aerovan in later years was G-AJOF, which was converted by Miles to take a Hurel-Dubois-designed high aspect ratio wing in 1957 and was then reregistered G-AHDM.

In 1958 OO-ERY (ex-G-AJOG) was repurchased by Devonair Ltd, who had owned it previously before selling it in Belgium in 1952. The intention was to renovate it and then use it on charter work in the West Country, but because of problems relating to the legal ownership of the aircraft it was never restored to the British

Register and languished at the back of a hangar at RAF Chivenor in Devon for several years. On a personal visit in 1961 I was asked if I would like to purchase this Aerovan; probably every visiting enthusiast was asked that same question, but in those days we did not have that sort of money (so what's new?) and we were certainly not as conscious as we would be today of the importance of preserving our aviation heritage. Eventually OO-ERY was ignominiously burnt on a Guy Fawkes bonfire on the 5th of November 1963.

The accounts that follow will give an indication of the amazing versatility and ruggedness of the Aerovan – Ed.]

NEW DRILL FOR THE AEROVAN

[Reprinted from the "Miles Magazine", Vol.4, No.3, 1947, by courtesy of Peter Amos of the Miles Aircraft Collection and with further details supplied by Charles Tomkins.]

Out on one of the large Northamptonshire farms, the ravages of melting snow and torrential rain had set a serious problem to the early sowing of summer crops. Acres of ploughed land lay deep in mud and only a long spell of warm, dry weather could have saved a serious delay in the summer harvest. To wait for such a spell of weather was precarious to all who lived by the land.

And so it happened that the enterprising Mr J.W. Tomkins of Apethorpe, near Peterborough, took the matter into his own hands and became the first farmer in England to sow wheat from the air. It was on the 1st April this year *[in 1947, after the memorable winter of snow and ice – Ed.]* when Mr Tomkins started his experiment. Loading his Tiger Moth with 60 lb of wheat, he flew at a height of 50 ft and at an air speed of 64 m.p.h. The distribution of grain proved satisfactory and in view of the fact that it had been raining for 20 consecutive days, Mr Tomkins decided to enlist the help of anyone who would be willing to cooperate and who had a larger and more suitable type of aircraft.

A telegram to Miles Aircraft received their full-hearted co-operation. The following day an Aerovan *[G-AILF, which was the one that had been fitted with skis during the winter – Ed.]* was ready to do the job. Overnight the staff had gone to work on the aircraft and had fitted a hopper on the floor of the freight compartment. A slide, which could be opened to a pre-determined position for starting or stopping the flow of grain, was fitted to the bottom of the hopper, and a hole was made in the Aerovan floor immediately below it.

Although the scheme was only decided upon on Wednesday, April 2nd, the Aerovan was ready on Thursday morning. Unfortunately fog covered Woodley Aerodrome and take-off was delayed until the middle of Good Friday morning.

The pilot of the Aerovan was our Sales Pilot, Squadron Leader Jimmy Nelson, and with him went Michael Booth who acted as Technical Adviser.

On arrival at Mr Tomkins' farm at Apethorpe, a strong wind was blowing and conditions did not appear suitable for the immediate work of sowing wheat. However, despite the wind, Farmer Tomkins had his plans ready for action and with his advisers and the pilot, they discussed the principle of operation and set to work on the first plot of 50 acres. The drawback of the first attempt was undoubtedly the strong gusts of wind which constantly blew the aircraft off an even track.

Progress was held up for two days while awaiting suitable weather. During this interval, the hopper on the Aerovan was enlarged. It was now possible to run a complete length of the field without filling the hopper, the filling being done during the turns. With this improvement the sowing runs became much more accurate.

On Monday, sowing of the plot was completed. About 4 bushels of wheat to the acre were sown at first, followed by about 3 bushels to the acre towards the end. Flying at a speed of about 75 m.p.h. at a height of 50 ft the Aerovan sowed over 10 acres of a 400 acre field in three trips in a period of two hours.

[The 'Farmers' Weekly' quoted a time of 4½ hours for some 40 acres, i.e. about 10 acres per hour, double the sowing rate quoted in the 'Miles Magazine'; it went on to say that "spectators saw the corn come down with the 'swoosh' and patter of a hailstorm." The 'Farmer and Stockbreeder' reported that "it took half a minute to fly the 400 yard length of the field, and when the run was finished . . . the plane circled in readiness for the next run. The complete circuit took about 2½ minutes to finish. Though the grain passed through an opening that was barely six inches wide, the wind scattered it over an 8 yard wide cast." – Ed.]

After the grain was sown, a tractor pulled a set of eleven harrows over the ground. This was a troublesome job on the muddy ground but was an important item in the successful completion of the task . . .

When experiments had been completed at Mr Tomkins' farm, the Aerovan started work again at another farm, after much consideration had been given to the general organisation of such work. The equipment on the aircraft was considerably modified and

170

the hopper was altered so that it could hold about 2,000 lb of seed, all of which could be loaded into it while the aircraft was on the ground. This enabled two crew to be dispensed with *[German ex-prisoners of war – Ed.]* and saved not only their additional weight but the upsetting in balance of the machine when the sacks were being emptied into the hopper. The hopper itself was moved from the original position to a position forward of the main wheels. This had the effect of keeping the aircraft evenly balanced at all times, disregarding the amount of seed it contained.

The marking technique for the second operation was considerably altered. Two individuals, one stationed at each end of the field, held white flags. The aircraft would fly directly into the wind and the hopper slide opened immediately the aircraft was above the initial marker. Depending upon the amount of wind drift so the marker moved around until he was in a position at which the aircraft would drop the seed within a foot or so of the required position. The slide was closed when the aircraft passed over the other marker. In this way wastage of seed was reduced to nil.

With these alterations the Aerovan was able to sow a 10-12 yd spread of seed from a height of 50 ft at a ground speed of 70 m.p.h. and the distribution of the seed was better than that completed by hand broadcasting.

From these trials, most of the problems were overcome. It remains to be seen just how far reaching an effect these experiments will have on the future of seed-sowing in this country, but from the satisfactory results obtained it would seem obvious that the aeroplane has a place amongst the farmers' mechanised instruments.

*   *   *

QUICK-CHANGE FEATURE OF NEW FLYING SIGNS

[Reprinted from the 'Advertiser's Weekly' of June 16th 1953 by courtesy of L.C. 'Ladi' Marmol.]

In the past neon signs have been fitted underneath the wings of aeroplanes, but this has not always proved entirely satisfactory. A new method has been developed by an ex-Czechoslovakian glider pilot, L. Marmol. The practical application of the method has been worked out by Claude-General Neon Lights Ltd.

A framework of one inch diameter tubular steel measuring 27 feet by 3.5 feet is fitted to each side of the aircraft, each framework carrying two signs, one superimposed on top of the other and consiting of 36 inch Claudgen neon-filled (red) letters.

Among the legends which have been supplied are "Colds? Try Bac-O-Vac" on one side of the 'plane and "Bac-O-Vac for Coughs" on the other. *[I have also seen a photo showing an advertisement for Persil! – Ed.]*

The method of fixing these glass letters to the framework has been designed to enable a quick change to be made to a different legend from a library of letters. A flasher operates each sign in turn enabling both legends to appear at two-second intervals.

The power gear consists of a petrol-driven generator, and to eliminate any risk of fire the generator is enclosed in steel. Safety cut-outs have been included which automatically switch off the transformers in the event of a high tension short circuit anywhere on the sign.

The company, Air Ads Ltd, is based on Southend Airport, and owns four 'planes, styled "Aerovans", each capable of carrying nine passengers or freight. Some flights have been made over the London area, but much more successful were flights over seaside towns where, providing an unimpeded stretch of low ground, the beach and promenade presented a virtually captive audience of holiday-makers – with both leisure and inclination to contemplate any out-of-the-ordinary event. Blackpool, Southend and Ilfracombe are a few of the resorts visited.

The neon letters stood up well to the past very hard winter and despite the hazards of flight and landing there have been no breakages.

* * *

SOME OF MY EXPERIENCES IN GERMANY

by L.C. 'Ladi' Marmol

Apart from the neon advertising version of the Aerovan I used it for many other purposes. After the war the RAF were accustomed to using the German submarine fortifications at Heligoland for target practice until as late as 1955. When they finally stopped, my aircraft was the first civil one to land on the dunes there (on the 12th July 1955) with Prince Luis Ferdinand von Preussen aboard, in order to initiate a passenger service for German hayfever sufferers, as the island had a 'zero' pollen count.

On the 5th July 1956 my Aerovan G-AJWD unfortunately lost the port propeller in flight on the Belgium-Germany border with three passengers and a spare engine on board. The propeller cut the cable of the second engine, missing my wife, and I managed to land in a 20 acre oat field. It was the first flight after a new C. of A. and it was obvious that the port propeller had not been tightened sufficiently. Some two months later, the wood structure of the aircraft was repaired on the spot by Mr Ottley, the designer of the Ottley Gliding Towing Hook, and a new propeller was fitted. I can recall that I flew over the spot whilst delivering a Tiger Moth to Germany, whereupon Mr. Ottley gave me a big wave; I managed to capture that moment in a photo.

Later, while I was returning to the UK in the Aerovan and flying over France near Lille I lost the starboard propeller at 1,500 ft. At full throttle I managed to maintain height, but after some half an hour the oil pressure was dropping and the aircraft was gradually descending. Near Dunkirk I was forced down and, with a big gap in the floor of the Aerovan, I landed in a wet potato field; the front cockpit collapsed, the main spar came down on top of me and I was unable to move or release my Miles harness.

Fortunately, there was a farmhand close by who cut the belt harness and pulled me out from under the main spar. On this occasion the starboard propeller had been *over*tightened.

*　　*　　*

AN UNCOMFORTABLE SURVEY FLIGHT

by Rex Nicholls

One day in 1954 I was on a training flight from Croydon in a Tiger Moth with a pupil, and as was customary I put down at Shoreham. As I arrived I saw Meridian Air Maps' Aerovan G-AJKP; its engines were running and a close inspection revealed Jean Bird at the controls. Seeing me, she beckoned me over and asked if we would like to join her on a test flight. We had the time – "about an hour," said Jean. The Aerovan's cabin contained three spare seats, two of which my pupil and I occupied. The floor was covered with a considerable number of batteries. These powered a camera mounted in a gimbal ring which in turn was mounted over a large circular hole cut in the floor of the hinged rear door which formed the tail of the fuselage pod. Next to Jean's seat up front in the 'bay window' was another which the camera operator occupied when he was not using the equipment.

Jean took off and we climbed steadily on a north-easterly heading. Jean said something about it being too hazy for photography, but levelling off at around 5,000 ft we flew on until we crossed the Thames. To the north the weather was gin-clear, whereupon Jean decided that a photographic sortie was 'on' after all. She vacated the pilot's seat and invited me to take over and climb the Aerovan to 10,000 ft while pressing on towards the Norwich area. I spent about an hour flying the Aerovan, a novelty for me in that there was nothing of the aeroplane ahead to judge the climbing attitude. Jean then took over again and began a slow flight exercise, first on a westerly heading, then east. Back and forth we flew and my pupil and I sat in our seats. To wander about upset the aircraft's trim considerably, as I had noted during the long climb.

By this time I was desperate for a loo but there was no way relief could be obtained. No empty bottles or tin cans anywhere! However there was a gap of about two inches between the gimbal ring and the edge of the hole cut in the floor. Although to move towards it would upset the trim I was getting really desperate by now. I asked the camera operator about the possible use of this gap.

"No," he said, "we've tried that but it blows back in!"

It was quite chilly at 10,000 ft, and we had left our flying suits in the Tiger, which didn't help.

At long last we landed back at Shoreham – we'd been airborne a few minutes short of five hours! Full relief was achieved only after ten minutes in the loo – the system had nearly seized up! A lesson had been well learned about pre-flight checks.

This was the last occasion I flew with Jean. A little over three years later, on December 17th 1957, she was flying the same Aerovan when it suffered an engine failure soon after take-off from Manchester and crashed: Jean and three others died.

[It is thought that the prime cause was a faulty fuel pump, but to this day some of the details of the incident have not been explained entirely satisfactorily: we may never know for sure – Ed.]

CHAPTER 22

THOSE WERE THE DAYS

by

ERIC. M. BELL

At the beginning of the 1950s, I was a member of the 1402 squadron Croydon Air Training Corps (ATC). I had always been fascinated by flying machines for as long as I can remember, so when our CO asked for volunteers to help out at the ATC Gliding School, Hamsey Green, near Croydon, I jumped at the chance. Here at last, I thought, was an opportunity to get airborne.

I was there every available hour, ready to do anything that would get me into the air. The school owned four machines, all single-seaters, a Dagling SG.38 and three Kirby Cadets. My brief, along with the other enthusiastic cadets, was to make myself useful. I was young and had a lot to learn so I was willing to work hard, driving the retrieving car (my first driving experience), operating the winch, repairing gliders, painting hangars, making tea etc., and for all the donkey work I was rewarded with instruction for straight and level gliding. I might add that all gliding instruction was carried out first on the primary Dagling and then on a Cadet – all solo gliders. So your first gliding experience was completely alone: there were no dual gliders in those days.

Strange as it may seem, our instructors were all civilians, and very keen individuals. Although I did not know it at that time, one of these instructors was going to provide me with opportunities in the flying world that I could only dream of then, due to lack of finances. His name was Mike Conry and he became one of my closest friends; he was then a small-time actor who was obsessed with getting airborne. I, like most cadets, soon became bored with doing straight and level, which was all that was allowed at that time.

Mike then came up with the idea of starting our own gliding club, which he began to organise. He obtained from a farmer the use of a field at the top of Tipsy Hill in Surrey, overlooking a valley 500 feet below. We also obtained an old Dagling glider with metal

175

wings, a retrieving car, and an old converted Sunbeam car for a winch. The farmer let us have an old barn which needed repair, and we turned this into a hangar and bunkhouse. Most members were asked to pay 2/6d (12½p) per week into the kitty, and Mike registered the name 'Croydon Gliding Club'. We soon had a large membership and were gliding the whole year round, doing circuits and staying aloft a lot longer than we could have done in the ATC.

It was during this time that Mike suggested that flying times would be even greater if we could stop all the running around which gliding involved, and every one agreed. He then had an opportunity to buy a crashed, off-the-register, 1930 Kronfeld Drone with a Douglas motorcycle engine, G-AEDB. Mike managed to talk a builder into letting us keep it in an upstairs room in his Streatham business premises, and asked the lads to drop something into the kitty for spares etc. Everyone was very excited at the thought of real flying, but this turned to disappointment when they saw the flying machine and engine, which appeared to them only fit for the scrapyard. Mike, it seemed, was the only one who could envisage this piece of scrap ever flying, but his enthusiasm rubbed off on them and about sixty hopeful lads started work. In small parties at weekends and evenings the 'optimists' turned up to work, overhauling the airframe and engine, but gradually numbers dwindled and after about two years when the job was finished there were only four stalwarts left.

The problem now was where to fly it. Mike managed to get the private airfield owner of Hamsey Green to agree to keep it there in his hangar with his Blackburn Bluebird aircraft. The next problem was getting the Drone out of the builder's premises. The unfortunate builder had to agree to demolish the upstairs outside wall so that we could lower it onto his lorry, but this we did and we reassembled the 'plane at Hamsey Green. Then one very still and sunny Sunday afternoon Mike suggested it was time to give the Drone a few ground runs and perhaps a test flight. He donned a flying helmet and goggles and belted up. I pulled the rope round the starter pulley a few times and success – the engine burst into life for the first time, sounding like a giant bee; the noise brought out a few people from the houses nearby.

Mike waved 'thumbs-up' and then taxied out. It was like the 'Blériot days' all over again. Mike had never before piloted a powered aircraft, and after two or three runs up and down the field he gave another 'thumbs-up' and with a big smile he was away. We could not believe our eyes as he cleared the boundary hedge. He made four circuits of the field and landed triumphantly.

After approximately forty hours local circuit flying we had an offer from 'THE AEROPLANE' magazine to enter the Drone in the forthcoming Vintage Fly-In at White Waltham. To transport the 'plane by road was very expensive, so Mike decided to fit an extra fuel tank and fly first to Denham, which he would use as a temporary base, before he attempted the last leg of twenty-five miles to White Waltham. He had no navigational experience and had to find his way using known landmarks, and even with the extra fuel there was no room for error. In his low-flying aircraft, being able to read the names of railway stations through his binoculars would prove invaluable.

It was a fine summer's day when Mike set off. A friend and I motored to Denham airfield while the other friend saw him off from Hamsey Green and 'phoned us to say that Mike was on his way. We waited and waited, listening and scanning the sky. At last, through our binoculars, we spotted a 'plane in the distance and heard the familiar bee-like engine. Mike had made it, and, as it turned out, with just a pint of fuel to spare. We were all as excited as if it had been man's first flight.

A few days later, the White Waltham Fly-In took place, but the weather was gusting at times to forty knots. Mike was not sure whether it was suitable to make the short flight but as the wind speed decreased he decided to have a go. I was at White Waltham airfield waiting for him, but he did not arrive. I learned later that he had crash-landed into a ploughed field at Gerrards Cross and was badly injured. He was taken to hospital suffering from a broken pelvis and other injuries. The Drone was a write-off once more, but thankfully Mike made a full recovery and was soon flying again!

Mike then established his Company C.A.B. at Croydon Airport and formed the Central Flying Group, where keen lads of eighteen years and over could join with a chance of obtaining flying lessons at £1.16s (£1.80) to £2.8s (£2.40) per hour, according to the time devoted by a member to the group's activities. Mike had acquired parts of crashed Tiger Moths and decided to build one sound machine out of these with the help of the twenty members, who worked under trained supervision in the corner of a rented hangar. The airframe and engine were periodically checked by the ARB, and by the end of one year's hard part-time work, and with only four members still attending, a Certificate of Airworthiness was obtained. We were delighted but still needed a fully qualified pilot to test-fly and complete the necessary form before the Tiger could be considered operational. Every Saturday and Sunday we would drag the machine out onto the tarmac hopefully, asking various pilots if they would take the first flight; they would agree to do it but always at a future date. Then one afternoon a tall bespectacled gentleman approached, introduced himself as Trevor Prytherch, and asked why the aircraft was not in the air. We told him the story and showed him the paperwork, and after a thorough visual inspection he agreed to take it up. While I booked it out, Trevor, who was a schoolmaster, donned his flying helmet, goggles and jacket and, with the blank flight certificate, climbed aboard. I swung the prop, and after five nail-biting minutes our Tiger was airborne. It was a successful thirty-minute maiden flight and when Trevor returned, the completed flight certificate showed that only a few minor adjustments were necessary. What an achievement for all of us!

Trevor had obtained his 'A' licence before the 1939 war through the Civil Air Guard, and he also held the third autogyro licence to be issued in the UK. He said he would be pleased to join our group as an instructor, and taught many of us to fly. He clocked up so many flying hours on the Tiger that he was able to obtain his Assistant Flying Instructor's Licence. Trevor was never happier than when he was in the air, and became a great friend to all who knew him.

There were many memorable incidents connected with the Tiger Moth while Trevor was with us: one, as I remember, occurred on a Saturday afternoon. As usual we would operate from the perimeter track of Croydon Airport, and to save fuel the engine would be kept running and Trevor would remain in the cockpit all the afternoon. If someone was just on a joyride, the ground crew would remove the forward stick by withdrawing the pin, and leave it on the ground. On one occasion, after Trevor had been for a short break by the hedgerow to respond to the call of nature, he jumped into the front seat; the next pupil, who had just installed himself in the rear seat, had only done two take-offs and straight and level flights. After his usual command "scalded cats", which meant "throttle forward and take off", the beginner started to ascend, when to his horror Trevor realised that his control stick had been left on the grass below and he had no means of controlling the plane. He dare not let his pupil know, so he carried on, giving his usual cheery commands, as if nothing was amiss. Landing was going to be 'tricky' (Trevor's word for 'disastrous'). By now the ground crew, realising the situation, wondered whether to contact the emergency services but decided that the sight of them might panic the pupil, so we just watched and prayed. After three hair-raising attempts, the 'plane landed safely, and no one was more surprised than the novice to be told that he had done it completely on his own. That pupil finally soloed in only four hours, thanks to Trevor's composure in a major crisis.

We kept the Tiger Moth for approximately three years and many more members obtained their licences on it. As far as I know it was finally shipped to Australia.

Mentioning Australia reminds me of another story concerning Mike Conry. One day in the autumn of 1955 Mike and I were sitting in the Croydon canteen over a cup of tea when someone came up and told him that there was a lady who wanted to come and see him along with her son of eighteen. Apparently the son wanted to fly out to Australia with his mother; the father was already out there, and the family had sold their house and were purchasing a Proctor so that they could go out and join him. Several people had told them that Mike Conry was the best person to teach him how to fly the Proctor, and that is why they wanted to see him.

While we were waiting for them to arrive, Mike casually remarked to me: "I wonder how many hours he's got in. I can't see much chance of him getting to Australia."

That same morning the lady and her son arrived, introduced themselves, and explained why they wanted to make the trip, which she was financing in full from the sale of their house. Mike had a good look at the son's log book, and it transpired that he had only recently got his Private Pilot's Licence on a Tiger Moth, and that although he had been in a Proctor he had never actually flown one. (Incidentally, the Proctor was a far heavier machine to handle than a Tiger, and therefore not one to be flown lightly!) Also, he had done very little navigation except on his cross-country exercises. So Mike had to say to them that quite honestly they hadn't got a hope of doing the trip.

Mum was quite upset at this remark, and stated that she was willing to pay top money for her son to have lessons, every day if necessary. But Mike was a very definite sort of person: he said emphatically that if they both didn't want to kill themselves the lad would have to have a lot more general experience of flying before he should ever think of taking on such a trip.

Nevertheless Mum was undaunted and she kept on pestering Mike many times over the next week or two to take on her son, saying she didn't mind how much it cost. Eventually on one Saturday morning she got her way; he relented and agreed to give him a go and see what he was like. He said to me: "You can come along as well, Eric, and sit in the back with Mum!"

Of course she was overjoyed at this offer (the prospect of the flight, not me sitting next to her!), and Mike said: "Well, I'm not promising anything, but let's give him a go."

So he sat him in the left hand seat and off we went. Mike was obviously a bit tensed up – he was a very good instructor, but he could be a bit aggressive when instructing, as he was a very confident sort of person; he was certainly very wary about this chap. Incidentally this was in Mike's Proctor, G-AKDZ I think it was. So we taxied out. Even on the take-off we had a bit of a problem; the Proctor had a tendency to swing to the left, and it was quite a heavy aircraft to handle. Mike got quite annoyed; I can remember feeling the aircraft swinging, whereupon Mike gave the lad a jab in the ribs and said: "Correct it!" We managed to get off the ground all right, but you can see that it was a bit of a handful.

Anyhow he told him to follow a course to take us down over Gatwick, which in those days was nothing like the size it is now. It was a bit misty, and Mike asked him if he could fly on instruments, which he wasn't very used to. Also Mike had to operate the radio, which was another skill the lad had not yet got the hang of. So Mike told him to concentrate on the flying, and he'd deal with the radio.

When we got down to Gatwick, Mike then said: "I'll take over now," and put the aircraft into several turns to disorient the novice pilot, after which he said: "Now you pick up the bearing and get us back to Croydon."

It wasn't long before we found ourselves over Aldershot and then Basingstoke; Mike was following all of this and was letting the lad have his way, but he wasn't going to let him go too far off course. So he gave him another poke in the ribs – a very hard one this time, which was quite normal – and told him the bearing to get us back to Croydon. The landing wasn't all that hot either; he bounced a few times and Mike got a bit upset. We got out, and Mum said to him: "What's he like, then?"

Mike had no doubts: "Well, he's nowhere near ready to go to Australia; that's out of the question."

However he did give him quite a number of lessons after that, and eventually the great day dawned one Sunday morning in November – they were ready to go. Extra fuel tanks had been fitted in place of the two rear seats, and there was also a dinghy aboard.

When I arrived on the tarmac that morning, there were crowds of people gathered: cameras, press, radio and so on. While I was standing there, someone I knew from work came across and spoke to me and said: "Why are you here, Eric, watching this chap?"

I said: "Well, I've been following his progress, and wondering whether he'll make Australia."

So he said: "Well, in fact he happens to be my cousin! His Dad's gone on to Australia by boat, and we think they're absolutely ridiculous to try and make this trip."

I might mention that most of the people at the aerodrome – the mechanics and everybody else who worked there who'd been

'Ladi' Marmol shows the neon tubes fitted to the Aerovan for advertising purposes during a trip to Germany in 1955 (via L.C. Marmol)

'Ladi' Marmol overflies his Aerovan G-AJWD, under repair after its landing near the Belgium/Germany border in 1954 (L.C. Marmol)

Messenger G-AILL after the forced landing on the disused wartime airstrip at Donat-Ems, near Chur (via E. Bell)

The Rheinwaldhorn (11,165 ft), photographed from G-AILL at 9,500 ft (via E. Bell)

Would-be pilot
Eric Bell in a
Dagling primary
glider at Croydon
(via E. Bell)

A Kirby Cadet
glider at Hamsey
Green (via E. Bell)

A real survivor –
the Proctor 3 G-ALJF
(E. Bell)

Ken Hamilton in an Olympia sailplane awaits a launch at Lasham in 1958 (via K. Hamilton)

BOAC Britannia G-AOVF takes off from Heathrow c. 1958 (via A. Jackson)

Ron Paine shows off the clean lines of the Miles Hawk Speed Six G-ADGP
(via R.R. Paine)

A throughbred line-up at Baginton (Coventry) in the early fifties: Ron
Paine's Speed Six, Jimmy Rush's Falcon Six, Geoffrey Marler's Falcon
Six, Ernie Crabtree's Gemini 3A, with a Proctor and another Gemini
in the background (via R.R. Paine)

Irene Shackleton poses for her husband in front of Sycamore G-AMWG before their 1954 flight (E. Shackleton)

Fox Moth G-ACEJ of Giro Aviation on Southport Sands (via E. Shackleton)

Aero 45 OK-FHP at Baginton in 1958; some work, others play! (E. Shackleton)

following the whole story for several weeks – were starting to place bets on the lad. Mike reckoned that he'd never make it past Calais, his first planned stop, although many of the others thought he'd get a bit further on than that. But Mike insisted that he wouldn't even be able to land the thing at Calais.

Anyway, they took off in a blaze of glory, cameras going and reporters scribbling, and then we went into the canteen to wait.

Eventually a lady from the control tower came down and told Mike: "You've won your bet."

Mike said: "Never!"

She replied: "Yes, they were landing at Calais in a cross-wind when it all went a bit wrong. They weren't injured, but a wheel came off, an undercarriage leg collapsed, a wing was torn off, and the whole thing piled up."

Mother and son continued on to Australia by a scheduled flight, and the aircraft was brought back a few days later to Croydon for repair; I remember seeing it up on trestles. Many people at that time reckoned that it was not repairable, but it was all put right eventually, and I think it was shipped out to Australia in the spring of 1956, the year of the Olympic Games there.

Another Proctor came into my life not long after that episode. Although my occupation was an aircraft design engineer with Vickers Armstrong (now British Aerospace), a lot of my free time was spent helping to overhaul and inspect light aircraft parts, draughting etc. for small firms at Croydon Airport. Usually I was paid by flying time on various light aircraft, often Proctors. Having been connected with Mike's company in purchasing ex-RAF Proctors, I became very knowledgeable on their modifications, and how to assess their general condition. I thought therefore that it would be a good idea to sort one out for myself and undertake a C. of A.

In a copy of 'THE AEROPLANE' magazine dated April 26th 1957, an advert appeared: "Private owner wishes to dispose of three Proctors at £125 each, ex-RAF." I applied for details and back came a reply from an ex-Group Captain, who advised me to go for the one at Croft-On-Tees, a private airfield just outside Darlington.

Trevor and I flew up to view this aircraft on May 12th 1957. We were shown it by the manager who looked after the field and hangar. With wings folded, covered in dust, and the RAF roundels still on, the aircraft had not been moved since 1948. The engine plug blanks bore labels stating "Engine inhibited, dated 1948: RAF." The engine had not been run since that time. Trevor and I swept all the dust off, and dragged the Proctor outside. The manager's aircraft was the only other machine there. Otherwise there were just farm tractors and other bits of machinery in the hangar.

The field had one hard runway, used during the war, and now this airfield was only used on race days for the Catterick races nearby. The manager supplied us with fuel, oil, a set of plugs etc., and a starter truck. We pumped up the tyres, chocked the wheels, sat in the cockpit, primed and pushed the starter. With four revolutions of the prop the engine burst into life, burning off the inhibitor – there was smoke everywhere. The engine ran as sweet as a nut, with no mag-drop at all. We gave it an hour's running time, then as the weather was grand we taxied out onto the runway and then up and down it once or twice. Soon we had it a foot off the ground – what a thrill! I had already spent some time with a torch giving it a thorough inspection; its modification state was excellent – only three compulsory mods to do. This looked like the one for me.

On May 18th 1957, I phoned the Group Captain in Canterbury and told him I was not a company dealer, just a keen aircraft enthusiast with a very small bank balance. We both came to an agreed selling price of £65. He informed me that the three Proctors were registered in his name when he left the RAF and he could not afford to continue paying hangarage rent. I sent him my cheque for £65 for the sale of a Proctor 3, RAF serial number Z7252, airframe hours 1199, engine hours 224 since new in 1948.

I could not believe I was now the proud owner of my very own aircraft. The next problem was where I was going to carry out the C. of A. and convert it into a civil aircraft. It had three seats – two in the front and a seat for the radio operator in the rear. I wanted to convert it to four seats and dual control. The fabric of this aircraft was camouflaged so it would require respraying. The airfield's manager said we could use the hangar and for a small charge have the use of benches, trestles, jacks and power etc.

Summer was approaching, so I decided to carry out the work up there, with the help of a licensed engineer. I found an old-timer in Vickers' inspection department named Bill, who still held engineering licences for Proctors. He agreed to spend his three weeks holiday in Darlington helping me to carry out the overhaul. On May 31st 1957, Trevor, Bill and I went up to Darlington from Croydon to survey the work and agreed to a start date. Although the aircraft was in fine shape there was a lot to be done.

On June 27th, Bill and I contacted the local ARB who visited us and carried out a full examination. They handed us the work list which necessitated a complete strip-down; there was nothing left unseen. De Havilland's engine inspector did likewise for the engine and selected a cylinder to be stripped to search for signs of corrosion.

The work began and the whole aircraft was completely dismantled, with many parts renewed. Numerous car trips were made from my home in Croydon to Darlington with materials. The ARB examined everything that was dismantled and also what was left intact, and then told us to rebuild the airframe and the engine. I arranged for the dual control assembly to be manufactured and the blind-flying panel to be calibrated. The paperwork was raised for these items. All new tyres were fitted and new engine hoses assembled. I also managed to acquire a brand-new plastic cockpit dome. Having helped with converting Proctors at Croydon, I had good contacts for spares.

I then applied to the Ministry for a civil registration, which was G-ALJF, No.R1516/2 dated 10th September 1957. We had engine runs, flight tests etc., but unfortunately the whole work had taken more time and money than we had contemplated.

The complete C. of A. had taken 595 hours (between three of us). The cost of materials was £321, and labour, accommodation and travel expenses worked out at £200 (2 persons only), making a total of £521. The aircraft had initially cost me £65 and was advertised for sale in 1959 for £700.

G-ALJF eventually flew into Croydon on 22nd January 1959, where a full C. of A. was obtained.

Many problems were encountered that are too involved to mention, but I found the whole experience very interesting; I had learned a lot, and it was most enjoyable.

G-ALJF was used in the making of a TV film in 1988, starring Stephanie Powers as Beryl Markham, who in 1936 was the first person to fly across the Atlantic from east to west. It is one of only two Proctors still airworthy today in the UK, although I believe that several more are being rebuilt; it flew into Brooklands on September 3rd 1994 and I had the pleasure of flying a circuit in it, piloted by Frederick Moore (Cobaircraft Company Ltd of Biggin Hill), who keeps it in excellent condition. It is a real old timer, and still going strong.

Sadly Mike Conry died aged 49 in July 1972 and Trevor Prytherch died aged 78 in January 1995.

CHAPTER 23

HORSE MANURE, COAL SCUTTLES AND EGG BOXES

by

KEN HAMILTON

[NOTES ON THE AUTHOR: Ken Hamilton was born in 1926; on being called up as a teenager during WW2, he requested to join the RAF, whereupon he was drafted into the Army. He served in India until 1947, when he returned to the UK and resolved to have flying lessons a year or so later. In fact he then became enamoured with gliding and has done much more of that than powered flying, having notched up about 3,400 flights. He is now retired and lives in Pembrokeshire, but still flies when he has the opportunity.]

You may well ask: "What on earth has the title of this piece got to do with aviation?" If you will indulge me for a moment, I will elucidate.

My love for aviation commenced in 1930 as a four-year-old living in Liverpool. On hearing the occasional biplane flying overhead I would dash to the back yard to watch it with awe and envy. One day, the most noisy of aircraft (or so I thought) was about to come through the roof; I went outside to see no less than a huge airship (either the R100 or R101, I couldn't tell at the time) at very low altitude. What a sight!

My dear old Gran, with whom we lived, would further kindle my interest by telling me stories of a lady friend of a youthful 84 years who loved aerobatics in 'Stringbags'; this gutsy lady eventually met her end after a fall from a pavement kerb! So I was convinced that flying was safe, and the seeds were sown at an early age for what would be a life-long love affair. Some of you may also be of my 'golden age' and will remember the excitement of the air aces – Lindberg, Amy Johnson, Amelia Earhart etc. – heady days!

Then at the age of seven we moved to Catford in London. Here there was a lot more flying activity. I clearly recall one dashing aviator skywriting 'PERSIL' in smoke. "Is he on fire and leaving his name for posterity?" I asked my mother.

"Stupid boy," she retorted.

My father, a ship's engineer, came home on leave about that time. I had got wind that much flying could be seen at a place called Hendon Aerodrome, and after much nagging and pleading my father surrendered and took me to Hendon. It was a glorious summer's day (as they all are in our childhood memories). So there was I waiting with bated breath for the air show to start.

My father said: "Stand up, look, it's the King (George V) and entourage driving in splendour in front of us."

"Boring," said I; "what about the flying?"

My most vivid recollection of that day was seeing biplanes flying wingtip to wingtip linked with lengths of rope – clever!

Now to come back to the reason for the title. Round about 1937 there was an airshow advertised at Biggin Hill. Of course I wanted to go. Alas, my mother was not well at the time and couldn't take me, so I said I would go on my own. All was reluctantly agreed except the finances: somehow I had to fund this trip. On a penny a week pocket money, which was always quickly spent, there was indeed a problem. I suppose this was the start of my young entrepreneurial business ideas; three courses of action suggested themselves at the time.

Firstly, what about shovelling up horse manure and flogging it round the neighbours for their gardens? This proved a reasonable success.

Secondly, how about filling up coal scuttles for old ladies on my way home from school? This achieved only limited success.

Thirdly, there was a fish shop in Catford which sold Polish eggs (they must have been pretty stale by the time we got them!); but they came in wooden crates and I could buy these for a penny each. I sold the first one, as was, for twopence, and so it started. From these humble beginnings I moved on to chopping them up and selling bundles as kindling wood at threepence each.

So, slowly but surely, the necessary entrance fee was raised (two shillings, I think it was), and I was now in a great state of excitement about my solo adventure to Biggin Hill. But how was I going to get there? Yes, you're right, by 'Shanks' Pony', and naturally on the day the sun was shining!

For the first time a brand-new Lysander was on static display: a funny-looking beast, I thought. Shortly after that came the time in my life when I first discovered the quirks of life's 'good news' and 'bad news'. During the day I had met another lad, with his Mum, whom I then palled up with (the boy I mean!); anyhow, we shared our sandwiches, and I expressed my young life's desire to go for a joyride, but at 5/- a time this was way beyond my financial resources.

My new pal's Mum then said to him: "Darling, would you like a flight? Because if you would I'll pay for both of you."

"Yes, rather," said he.

Can you begin to imagine my joy? I was ecstatic.

That was the 'good news'. Joyrides commenced after the display, but you know what's coming next, don't you? The 'bad news' – the little 'toerag' *chickened out.* And so I lost that opportunity. I don't think I have ever in my long life felt so let down – a truly crushing blow. Hopefully you are now wiping away a tear of sympathy for my shattered dream!

In 1938 when there was the threat of war I was sent away from London back to Gran's at Liverpool. When the panic subsided I returned south and we moved to Eastcote in Middlesex, where we were when the war really did start. Now, like most other boys, what could be better to fire the imagination than a Spitfire or Hurricane in which to stooge around the skies as an air ace? As soon as possible I volunteered for aircrew, but failed the medical due to a pierced eardrum. There were three of us who volunteered at the same time. The other two were accepted but never flew Spitfires; they were in Bomber Command and neither survived. I played soldiers in India, and the nearest I got to flying was watching the DC-3s in and out of Dum Dum, Calcutta.

Funny old life, isn't it? I had to be content with driving Tank Transporters but at least I survived and was able to return home in 1947 with my ambition to learn to fly still intact.

At Elstree airfield they used to do 'trial lessons' for 15/-, a lot of money in those days. Somehow I scraped it together and booked my lesson in an Auster. Now we're talking! I actually got to touch that thing that sticks out of the floor for a few minutes. Fantastic! The bug had bitten me ferociously.

A small diversion here: during this flight the instructor told me that it was from this very 'plane, G-AGXT, that the sawn-off parts of a guy called Setty (he of car-dealing notoriety) had been dumped into the Thames. Should I have been impressed?!

Now another problem loomed: to take flying lessons would cost me £4-10s an hour – beyond my reach. So I planned what I thought at the time a clever 'scam'. I'd book further 'trial lessons,' being careful to get a different instructor for each one. With the help of different sunglasses, hats, scarves etc., I felt I could cheaply learn a bit more, but I was rumbled when one day there was a last-minute change of instructor.

"*You,*" he said, "can b***** off unless you take a full course."

So that's what I had to do, b***** off.

Not to be deterred, I went to Denham, hoping to pull the same stunt. But word had got around, so: no money, no fly. Things were desperately serious – what to do next?

Well, it would be a few years before I could take to the skies again; every spare minute was taken up by establishing a business (*bona fide* of course!). Then in 1957 I read a newspaper article about the Duke of Edinburgh flying a glider at Lasham. I had vaguely considered gliding purely on cost-effective grounds, so if it was good enough for His Nibs it was good enough for me.

Off to Lasham I went, and had a long wait for an air experience flight. The instructor was Brian Masters and we flew in a Slingsby T.21 training glider. We reached the dizzy height of 400 ft with him 'pole-bending' on the launch. Then there was a big bang and the nose came up.

"What the hell was that?" I asked.

It was a cable break, but we came down to a smooth landing, and then a relaunch. The top of this one was between 900 and 1,000 ft: silence – am I in heaven? This is better than you know what . . . Yes, yes, this is for me. Floating on air and with an open cockpit the visibility all round was fantastic. When we got down it was straight into the office to book a week's course for the autumn of 1957.

The instructors for the course were Derek Piggott, Brian Masters and Ann Welch. The flying was terrific, though too cool for any thermals, so most flights were only of four or five minutes duration. There was plenty of opportunity for muscle development on the ground, though, pushing and shoving the T.21s around. The accommodation was in bunks housed in old wartime Nissen Huts, and the washhouse was equipped only with cold water and the ubiquitous aluminium bowls.

I thought: "Hell, am I back in the army again?" But by the time the course was finished I have to admit I was obsessed.

Now came my first solo, on the 4th November, in a T.21, name of *'Daisy'* (we also had a *'Fanny'* and a *'Rudolph'* – guess the colour of its nose). So there I was, sitting at the launch point, fully briefed, and the co-pilot's seat occupied by a bag of ballast.

"All clear above and behind, take up slack," then all out and off I went into the blue. At the top of the launch, the release, and I looked across to Derek. "Oh! my God – this is just a bag of ballast!" I was truly on my own; "stay calm and do as you've been taught." Bliss, total bliss – I had three more solos that day.

187

In the next three years I spent as much time as possible in the air in gliders, and took further powered-flying lessons at Denham Lasham, Blackbushe and, yes, even Elstree, gaining experience in Austers, Taylorcrafts, Chipmunks, Tiger Moths, Colts etc.

In those distant days, if my memory serves me right, by holding a Silver 'C' Gliding Certificate you could get your Private Pilot's Licence on reduced flying hours, subject to all other requirements being met. And that is how I got my PPL. However, I have to confess that my true love is gliding, and the romance is still with me. From the moment you leave the ground there is a wonderful feeling of freedom; just like a bird you get lifted to new heights and the feeling is magical (oh! do shut up, that sounds very 'Mills and Boon').

To be fair, there are many frustrations in gliding, like going for your Silver 'C', needing 5 hours duration in thermals, and managing 4 hrs 58 mins, with the inevitable bitter disappointment. But then better luck on another day with 6 hrs 10 mins. Sadly I missed my Gold 'C' height on a couple of occasions by small margins – *c'est la vie!*

Over the years I have been fortunate to have flown both powered aircraft and gliders in Germany, Italy, Austria, France and America, and wonderful experiences they were too. Every flight is different in some way and we all have many tales to tell, so please allow me one last indulgence (or perhaps a few more than that).

On a particularly good day at Lasham there would be at least 14 gliders soaring and stacked over the airfield (Heathrow holding had nothing on us). As the sea-breeze front weakened we had to come in, but the problem on this occasion was that the runway was busy at the time with a Dan Air Comet 4B (Dan Air had their main-tenance facility at Lasham), plus miscellaneous small planes and gliders. Being near the top of the stack meant that safe landing areas were diminishing on both runway and field by the time I was coming in; I don't mind admitting that the adrenalin was flowing freely!

Another 'hairy' event took place at Blackbushe in an Auster. On climb-out I was confronted with a trainee parachutist over the main runway at low altitude. I often wondered if he reported a 'near miss'; I bet he was more traumatized than me by the incident though. Incidentally, that particular Auster had more fumes in the cockpit than the M25 and I refused to fly in it again.

In the early sixties I had the chance to go to the Aosta Valley in Italy. The flying here was different from anything I'd previously experienced. Amongst those majestic mountains you really did feel as free as a bird, soaring from valley to valley. Also it was easier here to attain greater height, making the scenery below even more breathtaking. I was flying a Blanik (which was new to me), and on one flight above the snow line at about 9,000 ft I noticed a climber standing on a rocky outcrop above me. So back along the mountain face I came at eyeball level and waved – no response. So I turned and came back again and this time waggled the wings – still no response. When I related this to the Italian CFI he fell about laughing and told me that it was a statue of some poor soul who had fallen from that spot. So the next day I ignored him (the statue, I mean, not the CFI – one doesn't ignore CFIs, does one?).

Later, in the Black Forest in Germany, I had this little German instructor, complete with leather Gestapo-style coat and hat (I'm sure that Herr Flick from *'Allo 'Allo* must have been modelled on this guy); he had limited English and my German was even more limited. Well, off we went for my check flight, thermalled up to about 1,000 metres and levelled off. I have to tell you at this point that back then, no aerobatics or cloud flying were allowed in Germany without ATC clearance. After we had levelled out, he said (or rather I *heard* him say): "Now ve 'av a loop."

So I carried out all the pre-checks, and had stuffed the nose down on this K.13 to about pull-back speed when I heard this chap in the back screaming: "Nein, nein, nein!"

So I slowed down and levelled out, whereupon he said: "Vot vas you doink?"

I replied in my best German: "You sprecht 'now we have a loop'."

He answered as he clicked his heels (or was it his teeth chattering?): "Nein, nein, I said 'now ve 'av a *look*'."

But who wants to *look* when you can *loop*? I heard he avoided British pilots from then on.

There are so many happy memories in reminiscing about those post-war days, and as I said earlier the love of flying doesn't diminish. Even now, with a slightly 'dicky ticker' I still manage the odd flight, though not solo. My wife also spoils me with the odd surprise. For my 60th it was a helicopter ride, and last year for my 70th she got me strapped into a Microlight for an hour's flying over our beautiful Pembrokeshire – and, yes, the sun shone!

Now its time to shut up and raise a glass to the magnificent sport that so many of us enjoy or have enjoyed.

CHAPTER 24

FLYING THE WHISPERING GIANT

by

CAPT. ARCHIE JACKSON

[NOTES ON THE AUTHOR: Archie Jackson was born in Chile in 1922; he joined the RAF in 1941, learning to fly on Tiger Moths at Watchfield in England and Airspeed Oxfords in Alberta, Canada. With a total of 124 hours he was awarded his wings and was commissioned that same year. In 1942 he was seconded to BOAC to fly the Empire flying boats on the route from Poole, Dorset via Foynes (Eire) to Lisbon, Bathurst (Gambia), Freetown (Sierra Leone) and Lagos (Nigeria). These famous flying boats had been stripped of all soundproofing, carpets etc. to save weight. The passengers were in wartime service but wore civilian clothes as Portugal was a neutral country. There was no cabin service and boxes of cold food were provided: nor was there a bar. Several flying boats were lost in accidents and were replaced by Short Sunderlands.

After demobilisation he studied for the civil pilot's 'B' Licence and then joined the Chilean national airline, then equipped with DC-3s and Lodestars. Early in 1947 he was recruited by Air Vice Marshal Don Bennett of 'Pathfinder' fame for British South American Airways, which operated Lancastrians and Yorks. The airline gradually extended its routes so that both the east and west coasts of the southern continent were served, along with Bermuda, Nassau, Jamaica and Cuba. Delivery to BSAA of the Tudor, which featured a pressurised cabin, raised hopes that the Company would compete more effectively against foreign airlines operating Constellations and DC-6s, but the unexplained disappearances of two Tudors in the Western Atlantic doomed the future of BSAA and it was absorbed by BOAC, Archie being assigned to the Argonaut fleet.

He finally retired at the end of 1976, having logged 22,000 hours and spent twelve happy years flying the superb Vickers VC-10. He then entered Oxford University where he obtained an Honours Degree in Modern History in 1980, subsequently working as a tutor and college librarian. He has written numerous articles for aviation magazines, and his published books include an autobiography, 'Both Feet in the Air,' 'Pathfinder Bennett – Airman Extraordinary' and 'Imperial Airways and the First British Airlines.']

The year 1954 was a disastrous date for the British Overseas Airways Corporation. In April yet another crash of a Comet 1 had put an end to jetliner operations for several years to come. In November the crash landing of a Britannia in the Severn estuary served as a warning of delays to the introduction of the big turboprop transport to the national airline. Sir Miles Thomas, BOAC's Chairman, had spent months looking for second-hand Lockheed Constellations to fill the gap in capacity caused by the withdrawal of the Comet. It was a prudent move on his part to order ten Douglas DC-7s as an insurance against late delivery of the Britannias.

BOAC had ordered 15 of the smaller version of Bristol's turboprop airliner for its southern and eastern routes. The larger version, the Britannia 312, 18 of which were to follow, was intended to operate to North and South America and the Caribbean. Both types were powered by the Bristol Company's own Proteus engine.

The introduction of the Britannia on the North Atlantic route, hopefully years ahead of Boeing's 707 and de Havilland's Comet 4, was to herald the withdrawal of the piston-engined aircraft. BOAC had been operating the Boeing Stratocruiser. Even so, the prevailing strong westerly winds over the ocean meant that for a few years to come a refuelling stop at Shannon (or Prestwick, Keflavik, Goose Bay or Gander) would continue to be necessary.

In the early post-war years those of us who were flying to Africa, the Middle East, the Indian sub-continent and Asia, were rather envious of our colleagues on the western route. We called them the 'Atlantic barons' because they were paid extra money for doing battle with the rigours of the winter weather. In addition they had the opportunity to bring home food and goods which were still in very short supply in a Britain that remained subject to strict rationing. We did not face the same dangers from icing but we were familiar with the line squalls and thunderstorms prevalent in the monsoon season, the dust storms which rose up suddenly to reduce forward visibility to a few yards. Storm warning radar was not available to us.

191

I had flown with British South American Airways to Latin America and the Caribbean and subsequently to BOAC's eastern routes. I was keen to add to my experience by flying to North America. Since 1949 I had been flying the Argonaut, which was a pressurised version of the DC-4, powered by Rolls Royce Merlin engines. This reliable, if noisy, aircraft was certainly an improvement upon the Avro Lancastrians, Yorks and Tudors that we had operated in BSAA. I put my name down for a posting to the Britannia 312 and waited . . . and waited. The main reason for the late introduction of this aircraft was an icing problem which afflicted the unproven Proteus engine, causing loss of power or even a complete shutdown. It was 1958 before I began the conversion course. This involved a three-hour written examination paper, many hours spent in a simulator and finally the pleasurable experience of handling the Britannia myself.

In the Argonaut a take-off at maximum weight from an airport some thousands of feet above sea level in the heat of the day could be a hairy experience, and positively terrifying if an engine failed. The take-off performance of the Britannia, even allowing for the mild English climate, and airports not much above sea level, was a revelation. Within the cockpit and passenger cabin the noise level was very low, the vibration negligible. Spectators near to the airport were astonished at the quiet 'whoosh' that accompanied the Britannia's departure from the runway, and the rapid rate of climb.

My first flight across the North Atlantic was as a supernumerary pilot. As this journey was to prove the aircraft no passengers were carried. We took off from Heathrow on a late summer evening and refuelled at Prestwick. From there the flight to Boston was expected to take 11 hours. The decision as regards the fuel to be carried was based upon that flight time plus the fuel to be consumed if a diversion was to be made to the further of two airports listed as alternates on our flight plan. Most captains then added a further small percentage of fuel to cover an unexpected deterioration of weather or stronger adverse winds.

The normal crew complement consisted of two pilots, a flight engineer and navigator. Radio communication in clear speech on VHF or HF was the responsibility of the pilots. Over the oceans the navigator depended primarily on the Loran system. Master and Slave stations on land transmitted pulses which the navigator interpreted from a cathode ray tube. Then he referred to his chart which was overprinted with Loran chain lines. The Britannia also carried a periscopic sextant for astro-navigation.

Useful assistance was obtained from Ocean Station Vessels, usually called weather ships, mainly operated by the Americans.

The position of these vessels was marked on the navigation charts. Their crews were responsible for reporting sea and weather conditions including the upper winds and temperatures at various flight levels. They had a good record for assistance to shipping and in 1947 rescued all on board a Boeing flying boat which was running out of fuel and had alighted on the ocean.

Equipped with radar they were able to identify airliners passing within their range and could pass to an enquiring navigator his aircraft's bearing and distance from the ship. These vessels were withdrawn when the long-range pure jets came to be fitted with the present-day inertial navigation system, a spin-off from the space programme. This provided such accurate fixes that flight crews no longer bothered to ask for help from the weather ships. It was my first opportunity to test the usefulness of the storm warning radar. By revealing the thunderstorm core rather like the X-ray of a hollow tooth it allowed the pilot time to alter course and avoid a very rough ride.

I was also able to recognise the entry of ice crystals into the engine intakes and the successive modifications which prevented the engines from shutting down. Deflectors had been fitted into the engine air ducts to keep ice crystals from accumulating. In addition glow plugs, made of platinum alloy, were added to relight the fuel-air mixture as soon as any interruption occurred. These projected into the flame tubes, the crew being warned by the momentary flicker of the needles of the engine instruments. For those in the passenger cabin the visual consequence was more dramatic, particularly at night. A long column of flame would suddenly emerge from the engine!

Depending upon the track being flown, the Canadian coast was crossed over Labrador or more usually Gander, Newfoundland. Thereafter the navigator could have a rest and the pilots tuned in one radio range station after another on the assigned airway, reporting overhead each one as the flight progressed. Over the entire route it was possible to pick up weather forecasts and actual reports covering all the major airports.

On this proving flight, after landing at Boston we continued to New York. The weather had been excellent over the whole route but the storm warning radar with its range of about 100 miles had proved useful in its alternative function. One could tilt the scanner down to reveal coastlines, rivers, islands and built-up areas. The following day an unexpected change to our programme occurred when we were ordered to fly to Gander and collect passengers delayed there through the engine failure of an American Airlines Constellation. Subsequently we flew to Bermuda, Nassau and

Montego Bay (Jamaica) and terminated our outward journey at Caracas (Venezuela). Our route home took in Trinidad and Barbados before a night stop in Bermuda. The direct flight to Heathrow from the island took 9 hours 24 minutes, a new record at that time.

As the Britannia progressively took over the services to North American cities, I made frequent journeys to Chicago and Detroit. These were reached after a stop at Montreal. Owing to the strong prevailing westerly wind it was not always possible to make a direct flight to this city. Before I left home I would receive a telephone call from BOAC Operations advising me of the weather en route and the shortest time track. With this information I had to decide where to refuel along the way and whether to choose Gander or Goose Bay. Particularly in winter the weather conditions on the eastern seaboard were as much a consideration as the strength of the winds.

In those days, the hours which an airline could require the flight crew to work were far longer than they are today. Moreover all our departure times were scheduled around nine o'clock or later in the evening. To compensate for the long duty period two bunks were provided, one above the other, just aft of the flight deck. Even so it was not easy for a captain to relax comfortably when each weather bulletin reported deteriorating conditions at his destination and possible alternates. The greatest worry concerned reports of freezing rain. An aircraft descending through cloud into freezing rain could become so encumbered with rapidly forming deposits of ice that the extra weight and effect on the flying controls could force it down.

The air conditioning system kept the passenger cabin at an acceptable temperature but the same could not be said for the flight deck. When the air temperature outside the aircraft was exceptionally low we would sit wearing overcoats over our uniform jackets to combat the cold.

During winter operations in North America the runways sometimes became covered by snow, slush or frozen ice, despite the best efforts of the airport authorities. When the ice was present the runways were gritted to allow effective braking. But the only person who could give a reliable report on the effectiveness of this measure was the last pilot to have landed. No one was particularly keen to be the first to try. When a thaw took place ice and snow melted to produce slush. After the failure of an airliner to take off from Munich, when lives were lost in the resulting crash *[this was the Ambassador G-ALZU carrying the Manchester United football team, on the 6th February 1958 – Ed.]* every pilot was made aware of the loss of forward acceleration caused by even an inch of slush.

Before that accident very few operating manuals even mentioned slush.

In the early days of BOAC operations into Detroit and Chicago there were only a couple of flights from London each week, but Montreal was visited more often. With the introduction of the Britannia a service to the Caribbean was opened. In freezing conditions it was necessary to have the aircraft sprayed with de-icing fluid immediately before departure. In winter, piles of snow were banked beside the taxiways and great care had to be taken to ensure that the outboard propellers did not make contact with them. On our return from the brilliant sunshine of the Caribbean limited use of reverse thrust was essential as the propellers created a sudden snowstorm that quickly obscured forward vision.

The continuous flow of aircraft in and out of New York and Chicago made it important to listen very intently to the controller's rapidly spoken instructions. At that time medium frequency radio beacons rather close to each other served as holding points before an approach to New York's Kennedy Airport was authorised. This was normally towards the only runway provided with an instrument landing system. However it did not follow that one would be cleared to land on it. Such was the volume of protest aginst noise from the local community that on descending below cloud one was often ordered to veer off and make a visual approach to another runway.

Chicago O'Hare airport was even then one of the busiest in the world. To cope with the traffic the controllers required pilots on their final approach to fly much faster than the normal speed and to keep uncomfortably close behind the airliner immediately ahead. If one was tempted to reduce speed the controller issued a stern rebuke accompanied by a threat to send one back to the holding pattern. The final words "clear to land" were not heard until the preceding aircraft was turning off the runway. By that time one might be as low as 200 ft.

Such pressure was not applied at Detroit's Wayne airport but not many European airlines put in there and we were sometimes confused by their non-standard jargon. "You are clear to the orchard." This was the original name of the airport in bygone days. "Call over the tall trees." Very confusing. In Britain a pilot abandoning his attempt to land declares that he is overshooting. The Americans use the term 'go around.' On one occasion I reported that I would overshoot when, due to a simple bulb failure, I did not obtain the necessary green lights on the instrument panel signifying that the undercarriage was locked down. I was therefore extremely surprised to find an ambulance, fire engine and foam tender racing along beside the runway as I touched down on my second approach.

The Britannia subsequently reduced the flight time across the North Atlantic as compared with piston-engined propeller aircraft but this advantage was swiftly eroded by the entry into service of Boeing 707s, Douglas DC-8s and BOAC's own Comet 4. First class passengers inevitably chose to travel on the pure jets and our Britannias were relegated to all-economy and charter flights. Indeed an extra row of seats was fitted alongside the two crew bunks and the passengers seated there were treated to the sight of their flight crew taking it in turn to disappear for an hour or two behind the curtains.

It has always been the custom for captains to make periodic visits to the passenger cabin. This personal contact had been backed up by hand-written bulletins on the progress of the flight. With the number of passengers increasing as each new long-range airliner appeared this practice fell into disuse and the introduction of a public address system permitted messages to be broadcast both from the flight deck and the galley. Some captains made minimal use of their new toy. Others were much more verbose and I recall a message sent up front with a ten dollar bill. The pilots were informed that there would be a further sum if they remained silent until the conclusion of the flight.

I made my last flight on a Britannia flying the band of the Royal Scots Guards to Buenos Aires in November 1963. BOAC had begun to accept deliveries of the Vickers VC-10 and thereafter the last of their propeller-driven airliners were withdrawn from service, and readily found buyers among the independent charter companies.

BOAC had been disappointed with the economics of the Britannia. A huge weight of electrical equipment involved a lot of servicing, and maintenance costs in all departments were high. But ultimately the engines had performed well. Time between overhauls was progressively extended, and their new owners undoubtedly benefited from the considerable expense which BOAC, as the initial purchaser, had incurred.

CHAPTER 25

THE OTHER SIDE OF THE FENCE

by

BERNARD MARTIN

[NOTES ON THE AUTHOR: Bernard Martin was born in Uxbridge, Middlesex on 1st May 1941 into a household where his elder teenage brother was already a member of the National Association of Spotters Clubs, and learning to crawl between countless copies of the 'Aeroplane Spotter' and 'Aircraft of the Fighting Powers' left an indelible mark.

The proximity of Northolt, Heathrow and Denham airfields during the formative years also contributed to a hardening of aviation interests. Working with the Ministry of Supply from 1959 and via the Ministries of Aviation, Technology and Defence to early retirement from RAF Strike Command HQ in 1991 allowed the seed to germinate.

Bernard is probably more widely known for his editorial and compilation duties with AIR-BRITAIN (the International Association of Aviation Historians) having been particularly involved with researches into the UK Register. Coincidentally, in 1969 he took over the BCAN editorial mantle from Denis Fox, extracts from whose writings are included elsewhere in this book. He eventually handed over the reins in 1981 and has since been continuously involved with the annual and popular AIR-BRITAIN FLY-IN which he had introduced in 1978.]

During the fifties I was still at Grammar School in Middlesex, but living under the approach path to the main runway at Northolt, being twenty minutes or so by bus from Heathrow and some fifty minutes by bus and legs to Denham enabled me to keep an eye on aviation activities with some ease. Given that I was a teenager throughout the times covered by this book, the title of this particular passage reflects the plight of an aviation enthusiast compared to the illustrious writers with whom, editor permitting, I share this valuable space.

Having said that, compared to the opportunities today, occasioned by the understandable need for safety and protection of property from light-fingered personages using the aviation enthusiast mantle as a cover, there were many occasions in the fifties that I found myself happily indulging my hobby on the right (from an enthusiast's viewpoint) side of the fence. The friendly grass airfield at Denham in Buckinghamshire was a case in point. Maybe it was the air of innocence that a teenager evoked in those days, but upon presenting myself to the CFI 'Wilbur' Wright (I vaguely recall that his real name was Denis, but the tag adhered heavily to anyone with that surname in those days!) I invariably gained permission to enter the parking area adjacent to the Flying Club to note the aircraft and take photographs.

A look at some of my 1957 log books shows that on the 23rd June I was greeted with the usual sight of the Flying Club's three Miles Hawk Trainers G-AFBS, G-AIDF and G-AJZH. G-AIDF was always notable for being a dark red overall and wearing distinctive undercarriage spats. It is perhaps a tribute to the care with which the local Club endowed their mounts that G-AFBS has survived to this day and is on view with the Imperial War Museum at Duxford.

The Club also had the Taylorcraft Plus D G-AHAI on strength and more of the type were to be seen on walking the half mile or so around to the hangars on the north side of the airfield where Nightscale Aircraft Services had their G-AHUG and G-AIIU. I always recall that enthusiasts were permitted to step into the hangars if Mrs Bickerton (the airfield owner) was not on site at the time. I did have a slight advantage over some contemporaries if there was any problem of access, as her husband, Dr Myles Bickerton, happened to be the optician used by our family and, if there was any dispute, Myles would often confirm that he had given permission for a quick viewing!

On another slightly earlier occasion, the 28th July 1956 to be precise, I recall definitely being the other (right) side of the fence at Denham! In those early days of television any Outside Broadcast was quite an event, and a regular series saw an intrepid group of cameramen and their motley support crew setting forth for a rare OB. The opening sequence (in various shades of grey) always showed one of the OB wagon drivers pressing the starter button with those immortal words "We're starting now!" Although much of the broadcast was genuinely live, some elements were the subject of telerecording earlier in the day.

Having noticed several large vehicles and miles of cabling in and around the airfield earlier in the day, I guessed that something was afoot and found myself among a crowd of onlookers in the hangar area that evening.

Nowadays we would call the event a Fly-In and a remarkable collection had been assembled for the benefit of the BBC viewing masses. I recall that Douglas Bader had been elected to make the opening sequence and he duly departed in the Spartan Arrow G-ABWP so as to arrive back at the appointed moment as if he had just casually flown in – to be greeted by more than the usual number of Club members! It was quite an evening of activity and my log shows that I recorded more than fifty aircraft that evening including 12 Autocrats, 7 Tiger Moths, 5 Hawk Trainers, 3 Aiglet Trainers, 3 Provosts (from 2 FTS for the occasion), 3 Geminis, 2 Proctors and single examples of a Moth Major, Chipmunk (the unconverted G-AORE/WB757), Cessna 172 (the resident VP-KNO), B.A. Swallow, Hirtenberg HS.9A, Moth Minor, Luton Minor (the infamous G-AFIR), Whitney Straight, Monarch, Plus D and Auster J/4.

One enduring memory of the evening entertainment for me was to be shouted at by Raymond Baxter. He had been enlisted to interview various worthies amongst the aircraft and, unlike the mobile radio-mikes of today, his large lollipop was attached to many yards of thick cable linking him to the OB vans. While I was squatting down in true photographic fashion to obtain a better angle on the real stars of the evening, I was blissfully unaware of a fast-moving snake rapidly approaching me as he tracked along the line in front of the hangars – hence the shout. Another example of what could be experienced on the other side of the fence!

Visits to Heathrow (or in fact as we knew it then, London Airport or LAP – to rhyme with map) were made virtually each weekend and on weekdays during the school holidays. Since these were my pre-car days, I walked many miles from the North side (Bath Road) around to Hatton Cross and the Great South West road to literally view from the other side of the fence into the Hunting Clan and Pan American hangars. Although today's enthusiasts would give their eye-teeth for such a sight, on the 25th April 1957 my log shows an 'also present' list on this South-side parking line-up of a C-46, a KLM DC-3, three Avro Yorks, three US-registered DC-4s, two USAF C-121 Constellations, a TWA L-749A Supercon-stellation, a USAF C-54, a Viking and an Icelandic Viscount. Such was the quality of movements in those days that these were sometimes regarded as not quite worth the hike from the Central roof-gardens!

For the Christmas and New Year period of 1956/57, an opportunity arose to stay with a cousin who then managed a seafront clifftop hotel in Newquay, Cornwall. Knowing of my aeronautical bent, the said cousin had a quiet word with the Station Commander at RAF St. Mawgan, which was a few miles along the coast. Thus it was on the 2nd January 1957 that I found myself disembarking from a bus at the decidedly un-New-Year-like hour of 0830 at the main gate of the RAF station. Duly presenting myself, unescorted, to the office of the Station Commander, I was asked to wait while a couple of servicemen were given a dressing-down for some misdismeanours. Thereafter, I was happily taken to the main hangar where the Shackleton MR.2s of 228 Squadron were housed and being readied for the day's circuit training. An accompanied flight-deck visit and crawl from one end to the other was undertaken, the latter being rather 'interesting' when negotiating the open bomb-bay and raising the thought of what it must be like when flying at a few thousand feet instead of merely above the hangar floor!

Three of the four 228 Sqadron aircraft later came to life with a beautiful roar of the Griffon engines and, joined by two MR.1s of 220 Sqadron, performed circuits for much of the morning, admired by myself standing a few hundred yards from the active runway. I closely examined four of the based Whirlwind HAR.2 helicopters in their RAF Rescue yellow scheme, and also discovered two Anson 12s and one Anson 19. Also visiting was a Canberra PR.7 of 50 Sqadron, which was based at that time at an airfield not very far from my present home! Apart from typical technician banter about my being from the 'Daily Express' because of my notebook jottings, I was left to my own devices for several hours for a most enjoyable morning. This extract is noteworthy if only to highlight how attitudes of the RAF have been forcibly changed by unhappy circumstances in the past 40 years.

Later that year, on the 30th August 1957, a first pilgrimage was made to Bovingdon in Hertfordshire, again by public transport; this also presented a need for stamina, requiring two buses from my then home town of Uxbridge to Chesham and then tying up with an hourly (and for those pre-privatisation days a rare) ride on a Rover bus en route to Hemel Hempstead, which passed right by the end of the main runway at Bovingdon. Here I installed myself with a recently-acquired simple camera and indulged in watching circuits by the based Meteor F.8s WK672 (pale blue overall), WK927 (camouflaged) and NF.14 WS848. Other visitors included RAF Coastal Command Dakota KP208, a Varsity, a Balliol T.2, Italian AF Fairchild C-119 and a Morton Air Services Dove G-ANAN, although I never did discover what the latter was doing there! There were also numerous C-47s of the based HQ 3rd AF USAF and two visiting C-54s. Also scattered around were 6 Ansons, 3 Chipmunks and some 5 more PR Meteors. Although on this occasion I was very firmly on the public side of the fence, an irritated serviceman arrived in a Land Rover (on the inside of the fence) to complain that my presence by the runway fence was distracting his Meteor pilots while landing. My expression of surprise and disbelief that they would surely have had far more on their minds than a stray personage on the ground while performing their landing approach did not seem to satisfy the individual – nonetheless I stood my public ground!

1957 was also notable for being the year that I made my first-ever visit to Croydon! Again, I had to resort to public transport for the long journey from West to South London. Happily in those days, Uxbridge was blessed with many bus routes, including those of the Green Line whose flat-fronted coach-type vehicles (the early RF types for the transport enthusiast) undertook longer journeys through the Capital. We were fortunate in having three such routes, emanating from High Wycombe, Amersham and Chesham which terminated in Godstone, Caterham and somewhere else to the south-east of London which mists of time have driven from my mind. However, the relevance is that one of these travelled all the way through central Croydon where one changed for a conventional double-decker (RT type) to Croydon Airport.

I shall never forget that first-ever visit on the 14th July 1957, not so much for the aircraft as having to shelter from the rain against a hedge waiting for the Airport Enclosure to open at 1400! When it did open, however, the rain turned to little more than a drizzle and the first aircraft to be logged arriving were no less than three Zlin 226 Akrobats and two supporting Aero 45s in Czechoslovak markings; these were en route for the National Aerobatic Championships at Baginton. I soon also noticed a high-wing single-engined type lurking by the Air Couriers hangar and this turned out to be my first overseas-registered Piper Tripacer D-EHAN. Naturally, Tiger Moths and Austers were a common sight, but these were accompanied by Chipmunks (then increasing in numbers from recent RAF demobbing) and many Morton Air Services Dove and Heron movements, as well as the latter with Vickers and Shell. Examples of the Hornet Moth, Leopard Moth, Proctor, Gemini and Hawk Trainer kept me satisfied until starting the long journey back home. An instant resolve was made to contact Rollasons and Air Couriers for permission to visit their hangars at a later date.

In fact, my return visit was not that much later, on the 3rd August 1957 and, having got the bug, again on the 23rd August! Highlights of these conducted tours were many, but mention must be made of the countless ex-Rollason civil Tiger Moth conversions which included HB-UBF, OO-SOC and OO-SOK for overseas export as well as some 20 or more fuselages stacked upright along the side of the conversion hangar awaiting their turn. The memory of these visits also includes the *smell* of the workshops, be it dope or paint spray or simply wood being cut to size. In later visits, we were also privileged to be able to scale the walkways at the rear of the Rollason hangar, where one could glimpse over into the adjacent MTCA Accident Investigation hangar in which gruesome remains were re-assembled roughly into their former aircraft shapes.

Another first visit for the year was to Blackbushe on the 19th August, then still very active with scheduled and charter services with famous operating names including Eagle (with Vikings), Airwork (with Vikings, Hermes and a Consul), Dan-Air (with Dakota and Heron) and Britavia (with Hermes). The visit was another accomplished by tortuous public transport, culminating in a Southdown service from Camberley, which returned some three hours later from Basingstoke, so the walk back to the A30 from visiting the US Navy hangar had to be carefully timed to avoid another three-hour wait (although would it really be a shame to be stranded at an active airfield?). My first sight that day upon disembarking from the bus was an Indian Airlines DC-4 VT-CZT – not a bad start – followed by a Karl Herfurtner Viking D-ADEL (with Eagle) and a Westair C-46 N4894V. Dragonfly G-AEWZ was also noted lurking behind the Britavia hangar and the USN complex revealed R4D-8 17108 and a Beech SNB-5. My log also notes that 6 Hunters and 5 Javelins also flew over during the day: with hindsight the latter were probably from Odiham.

During 1958 an expedition was made to Southend Airport – it was quite a journey in those days without automotive transport and even when public transport was more accessible than it sometimes seems today! The reason for the major effort was to see the countless Percival Prentices recently demobbed by the RAF and held by Aviation Traders for potential civil conversion.

Having written in advance, we were greeted by the Tower staff and driven over to the area in the centre of the airfield where the majority of the Prentices were stored. There we were left to our own devices to log, view, photograph at will and then wave to the Tower when we wanted to be collected. I remember that it was a hot July day and I almost decided to give up logging and recording aircraft after over 90 Prentices had been examined.

In addition the proximity of the main runway allowed excellent views of departing LTU DC-4 D-AMIR and their Vikings D-BABY and D-BALI as well as the countless Air Safaris, Overseas Aviation,

Universal and Channel Airways Vikings, not to mention the Air Charter Bristol Freighters on the Channel Air Bridge ferry flights. I also recall examining the various wrecks around the airfield including Avro Tudor fuselages, Harvard wrecks, even more Prentices and the unique ATEL Accountant G-ATEL parked with the other 95 Prentices. This was truly an amazing occasion (all the more so as soon afterwards I lost my Prentice logs with all the ex-RAF fuselage Code Letters etc.) and one that will never be repeated, and even more enjoyable for being – with pleasurably granted permission – on the other side of the fence.

A holiday in South Devon in August enabled me to make my first visit to Honiton, alias Exeter Airport, and by courtesy of a taxi from Torquay (affordable even by a teenager in those days, with a little parental contribution) the seemingly Thirties-style terminal was entered and a Jersey Airlines Heron, Gemini from Guernsey and Taylorcraft Plus D from Fairoaks were espied on the apron. However, it was the aircraft from the joint 3/4 CAACU that really captured my attention. The hangar and area to the left of the apron contained three FB.5 Vampires (VZ302/17, VZ304/24 and WA450/20) all wearing fluorescent orange bands around the fuselage, wingtips and at the base of the rudder. Seeing some Balliols elsewhere on the field prompted a sortie to the Control Tower, where permission was happily granted for me to pass through the barrier and inspect the hangar (later West Country Aircraft Services) containing no less than 14 Balliol T.2s. Ten of these wore yellow fuselage bands while the others had the fluorescent red prevalent in those days. Also hangared and eagerly inspected were the two Mosquito TT.35s (RS718/49 and TA719/56) with the target-towing scheme of black and yellow stripes beneath the wings; they were also equipped with ML winches for towing banner-and-sleeve targets for their anti-aircraft sorties over Dartmoor. Other towing activity noted during the day was Dakota G-AMVB which made a low run with a magnetometer trailing behind.

As a footnote to this visit, where the hospitality of officialdom to visiting enthusiasts was pleasantly accepted, little did I know that a few years later I would be handling the MOA contract with Exeter & Plymouth Airports Ltd for managing the target-towing facilities. When I visited under these auspices as the Ministry representative, I received even more hospitality! Later on, I made a visit to witness trials of a new banner-collection method involving Scimitar aircraft. This involved erecting a couple of poles some distance apart rather like the sides of a goalnet, over which was draped a long cable attached to a banner or sleeve target lying on the grass.

The Scimitar then approached at low level with deck-landing hook extended and caught the cable, then proceeding to the training area with the target trailing a safe distance behind – thus avoiding the need to have a winch fitted to the aircraft. The reference to a 'safe distance' was no idle remark as some gunners were adept at missing the target and hitting the cable!

Looking back to the fifties, the underlying impression at most airfields was that the enthusiast was regarded as a welcome intrusion and, if politely approached, most operators would allow hangars to be entered and notes and photographs taken. Forty years later, I would like to once again express my deep gratitude and thanks for their allowing me, on many occasions, to venture on *the other side of the fence.*

CHAPTER 26

WINGS OVER NORFOLK

by

DENIS KIRKHAM

Until 1957 light aviation in Norfolk consisted of a small number of privately-owned aeroplanes operating from fields rather than any recognised airfield. Apart from one machine, a G.A. Cygnet, they were all conventional in that they were of tail-wheel configuration and few if any were fitted with radio or other navigation aids. Three were Austers, one (somewhat dilapidated!) a Proctor, and one a Gemini. Not surprisingly, two were operated by their farmer owners, one involved a doctor and the dilapidated Proctor was owned by a group of Americans based at Sculthorpe: it permanently resided in the corner of a field at Docking, protected from the sheep by mobile pens and from the elements by a haystack on the prevailing wind side.

The pre-war Norfolk and Norwich Aero Club had had the good sense to purchase some ex-RAF Tiger Moths, which were kept in store, but for one reason or another had made no progress towards becoming operational with them. Their pre-war base at Mousehold Airfield had been bombed during the war and later built upon by the local Council; although plenty of disused airfields surrounded Norwich they all had concrete runways, presenting the obvious difficulties for tail-skidded Tigers with no brakes! So inertia somehow developed. Swanton Morley, arguably the best grass airfield in the country, was still in use by the RAF and perhaps a 'wait and see' policy was understandable. Eventually the Aero Club was able to negotiate the use of that airfield, sharing it with the gliders of the Air Training Corps – but not before they had been persuaded to sell their Tigers to Elwyn McAully, a 30-year-old ex-Merchant Navy Officer and Air Traffic Controller who had arrived in Norfolk to become Senior Air Traffic Control Officer with the Americans at Sculthorpe.

McAully's arrival in Norfolk changed everything. Here was a personable, capable, enthusiastic, recently-qualified (at Fair Oaks) and could-be ruthless private pilot, determined to establish a flying group and to get airborne very quickly. He called a meeting at Fakenham, attended by 32 people, all meeting for the first time. Having outlined his plans, he invited cheques for £25 each to get an aeroplane bought: eighteen cheques were handed over, and the Fakenkam Flying Group was formed with a Committee of six members on the 14th June 1957. On the 17th the Committee agreed to approach the Air Ministry for the use of Little Snoring airfield (an ex-Mosquito base). The next week, all members attended to consider a Miles Whitney Straight (at £400!), but on the 29th a quorum agreed to buy Tiger Moth G-ANCS from Crewdson Aviation at Gatwick (happy days!) for £325. On the 1st July McAully flew the aeroplane to Norfolk. Not a bad rate of progress, you might think?

Fred Ringer, a friendly farmer (one of the Auster private owners), had kindly agreed that the Group could operate out of Summerfield Farm's field at Docking, and that is where the aeroplane was temporarily based pending approval from the Air Ministry re Little Snoring. That was where I also became acquainted with the Proctor!

Mac (McAully) had already invited an American KB.50 pilot to become the Group's CFI, and instructional flights commenced on arrival of the aircraft. Lt. Cecil Rhoads had considerable experience instructing on T.6 Texans (Harvards to us) in the States, prior to moving on to the KB.50s which were the tanker version of the B.29 Superfortress. He was a superb instructor and the Group's membership expanded rapidly following the extensive Press publicity which followed. By the end of the year the use of Little Snoring had been agreed with the Air Ministry and an additional Tiger, G-ANFO, had been purchased. By the end of the decade the aircraft operating from Little Snoring included (or had included) Proctor G-AHBS, Hawk Trainers (Magisters) G-AKPF and G-AJHD, Autocrat G-AHHM, Tipsy Belfair G-AFJR, Tiger Moth G-AOIP, Gemini G-AOXW and BAC Drone G-AEKV.

The Group's original Tiger, G-ANCS, had become a Constructive Total Loss shortly after the move to Snoring, arising from a landing accident when the pilot-in-charge failed to observe that a large pile of sugar beet had been stacked at the approach end of the runway! I can still recall my horror when turning onto the airfield in my 1932 MG J2 to see the fuselage and tail assembly of G-ANCS sticking up vertically from the centre of the sugar beet pile. It was our first major accident (although the pilot was unscathed) but, regrettably, considerably worse accidents were to follow. G-ANCS was eventually rebuilt, many years later, and returned to Norfolk, being based at Felthorpe, where on the 16th March 1985 her owner Mark Norman kindly allowed me to fly her once again.

The Felthorpe Flying Group was in existence before the formation of the Fakenham Group but its structure was somewhat different in that its aircraft was the privately-owned J/1N Auster G-AJEB operated by Jack Last, but also involving George and Eric Jarvis. At that time (i.e. during the fifties) it was possible to claim a government rebate on fuel purchased and used in an aircraft owned and operated by a Group; the Group ultimately had to be not less than five people sharing the use (pilotage?) of the aeroplane so that no one person logged more than 20% of its total flight time. Returns had to be made and the rebate varied depending upon the type of engine involved. I remember that it was 14/10d (74p approximately) per hour for the Gipsy Major. Jack was an ex-RAF Beaufort pilot, now a miller; George had a nursery (for plants, not people), and Eric farmed at Beck Farm near Felthorpe which provided the flying field. Eric subsequently got his Licence with the Fakenham Group and George (then aged 65) also joined the Group, ultimately buying Tiger G-ANFM from Mac and basing it at Felthorpe. The rebate scheme was apparently seen as a method of encouraging private flying, and justified because it was considered that in a national emergency those pilots would be available, and able, to fly the majority of the aircraft types then in use in the RAF: shades, perhaps, of the Civil Air Guard and ATA operations?

The returns were rarely vetted and the scheme was of course wide open to abuse. With Tigers and Magisters available at about £400 with 1,800-hour-lifed Gipsy Majors you will see that, if every flight was 'stretched' a bit (1½ hours for every one hour actually flown) the rebate would more than justify the 'using up' of the engine hours. Neither Felthorpe or Fakenham were any more dishonest or naive than similar Groups throughout the country, and certainly all of the pilots involved would have jumped at the chance to help out in a real emergency.

The Fakenham Group rapidly replaced Tiger G-ANCS with the pale blue G-ANFO which I see from my log book that I first flew on the 8th November 1957 under instruction from Flt. Lt. Z.W. "Danny" Kaye, who had become the Group's CFI in place of Lt. Cecil Rhoads. "Danny", a Polish fighter pilot, was at that time instructing on Hunters at the CFE at RAF West Raynham. He was a superb pilot, and liked and respected by all, so his death in a mid-air collision over Cambridge in 1960 caused considerable distress. More of that later.

I referred earlier to the 'obvious difficulties' arising as a result of operating a tail-skidded aeroplane from concrete runways: they were twofold. Firstly, the tail skid would rapidly be ground away and would be of little if any help in steering the aircraft on the ground at the end of the landing roll or whilst taxying. This difficulty was easily overcome by replacing the standard spoon-shaped skid with a flat rectangular plate about six inches in length, drilled to accept a chunk of iron itself six inches long by two inches in section. The two retaining bolts were, of course, recessed deep within the iron 'shoe'. These 'shoes' were produced by one of the members, kept at the airfield, and each pilot was responsible for changing them when it became obviously necessary.

The second difficulty was overcome by making all landings 'wheelers': this involved touching down on the main wheels only and progressively moving the stick forward as the speed decayed until the tail skid finally dropped onto the runway at, I suppose, about ten to fifteen knots – certainly well below the 39 knot stall onto the runway following a 'three-pointer'! Fortunately, all runways were then serviceable, giving a choice of six directions to select as the nearest into wind. Nevertheless, if a swing did start to develop at the end of the landing roll Danny's instructions were to "cut the switches." The overall technique, once learned, was simple and entirely effective. All taxying involved someone holding each or one wingtip, depending upon the wind strength.

By early 1958 Tiger G-AOIP joined the Group, followed by Proctor G-AHBS: air races were being held on the occasional Sunday over a triangular local course: aerobatic instruction was available: and weekly meetings, talks and lectures took place, first at the Bell Inn in Fakenham, and then in the Clubhouse which we had erected at Little Snoring. This was a wartime 'prefab' home which we had purchased, dismantled, for £120. Enthusiasm was such that every task produced an excellent response from the majority of members – and the membership was expanding rapidly. These were indeed halcyon days! Shell and B.P. supplied windsocks, navigational protractors, air-law cards etc. free of charge, a local brewery (Morgans, now long-gone) supplied a diesel-powered generator and floor covering for the Clubhouse, and FOC and the Air Ministry (Lands Department) charged an anual rent "for the right to fly from the runways and the use of one T-type hangar" fixed at £75 annually. Resulting from our close ties with the USAF at Sculthorpe (McAully and another seven USAF members) we were regularly invited to their Officers' Club Saturday night functions: massive T-bone steaks, dances and Jayne Mans-field (once only!). This close associaton stood me personally in very good stead when I force-landed in near-darkness at the Base on the 28th September. This is how it happened.

Flt. Lt. "Danny" Kaye had been posted from RAF West Raynham to RAF Debden in mid-1958 but had undertaken to continue to act as our CFI, and regularly arrived at Little Snoring on a Saturday or Sunday for a full day's flying. He would fit in as many students as possible, and on that particular day fitted in a 'late arrival' which led in turn to it being a close call to get him back by air to Debden and return by air to Snoring in daylight. I needed more cross-country experience and so was a natural choice – apart from my volunteering – to ferry him in the Tiger. Cars with their headlights on were to be positioned along the active runway at Snoring for my return, in the event that dusk or darkness beat me to it. So off we went; the flight to Debden was uneventful, but I noticed with some unease that several houses had got lights on by the time we landed. "Danny" rapidly got out of the front cockpit, secured the straps, patted my shoulder and I took off, the engine having been left running, of course. I did not "climb to 2,000 ft, setting course over the airfield from the reciprocal side" but turned onto course immediately after take-off, throttling back to cruise power (1,800 revs) at 2,000 ft. Normal compass behaviour followed!

After about fifteen minutes on course (roughly!), with house lights now proliferating, I decided to apply full power – less half an inch – on the throttle to get back before complete darkness. I abandoned any pretext of map-reading but simply steered the compass course. By the time I must have been only ten miles or so from Snoring I had decided to act on advice that Jack Last had given me some time before: "just steer for the coast east of Wells-next-Sea, turn left until you see the long entrance to Wells Harbour, turn left onto 180° and you will be over Snoring within ten minutes." That is what I did but (a) I could no longer read the compass, (b) I could not see the tank-top fuel gauge indicating any contents, and (c) I suddenly remembered that increased power equates with increased fuel consumption!

My relief on seeing the cluster of lights indicating Fakenham turned to one of horror, after orbiting it, to see that someone had moved the church and the market square – either that or it was not Fakenham at all. Almost immediately after my third orbit I saw a set of runway lights a short way over to the west and headed for them with no hesitation at all. Arriving overhead the airfield which I realised was Sculthorpe, with its KB-50s parked along one runway, a green Verey light was fired onto the grass area in front of the Tower followed by another fired into the air and then another onto the grass. I made the tightest circuit and best landing I have ever made onto that grass. McAully was on duty in the Tower; he had been at Snoring before my departure, realised it was me in some difficulty and acted true to form in every resect. A Major Green, Duty Officer, greeted me with: "Yeah, say, do you guys in this country usually fly first-world-war aircraft at night with no lights and no radio?" He then told me exactly what he thought of me – and bought me a Coke! It took the presence of a local magistrate, Col. Labouchere, several hours and the promise by McAully to get the Tiger off the airfield at first light before I was "released from (albeit friendly) custody." The Cold War was of course very active at that time. Did I "learn about flying from that"? I certainly did.

It also illustrates the part that excessive enthusiasm, inexperience and increasing pressure and concern can play in undermining confidence; from the ground I was seen to fly fast, heading north, less than a mile from the western boundary of Little Snoring airfield and on my return I was seen to be orbiting Walsingham (Fakenham, as I thought), less than two miles to the north-west of Snoring!

From the earliest days of our Group our flying had been influenced and enhanced by the experience of our service-trained instructors. Graham "Taffy" Rich (ex-Spitfires and with an AFC), a diminutive Welshman, helped out and Boleslaw "Bob" Stramik (Polish and ex-desert Spitfires) flew regularly as an Assistant Instructor. As a result, formation flying was taught and practised as soon as enough Tigers were available. George Jarvis' G-ANFM with the Group's own G-ANFO and G-AOIP flew regularly together, taking off in formation from the runways at Snoring and practising tied-together 'vic' formation flights. This led to the Group being invited to appear overhead Oulton Broad on the final day of the Regatta Week in 1958: a formation fly-past followed by a 'Prince of Wales Feathers' break and individual aerobatics to complete. My log book records two hours passenger time as I was flying with Colin Labouchere (Henry's older brother) who was a very good aerobatic pilot (and I certainly was not!). However, my part in the proceedings was to play a trumpet (trumpet facing downwind of course!) from the rear cockpit during the final fly-by. I cannot remember whether this idea was mine or Jimmy Hoseason's, but he was the Regatta Secretary and had organised our participation sometime after joining the Group. He also handled the commentary and to this day I do not know what he said to describe this bit of folly! It is indicative of the terrific spirit of fun in the flying during that period with no shortage of volunteers to publicise and help the development of the Group. Jimmy went on to form the Waveney Flying Group at Seething, now widely known as an established and thriving organisation.

By early 1959 Mac had bought a Magister (Hawk Trainer in civilian guise), G-AJHD, and I see that I checked out in it on the 1st of March. Dire warnings were given regarding the port wing dropping on stalling and "on no account attempt to lift it before unstalling" – it did and I didn't. I don't remember any problems with the aeroplane at all; a marked trim change when selecting flap and a need to get it just right when landing crosswind due to the single-strutted oleo undercarriage not liking sideways influences. A large and effective rear windscreen and superb lever-operated brakes – all in all a delightful aeroplane to fly. She was rapidly joined by G-AKPF (in my log book for the 5th April 1959) which had been purchased by John Fell (currently Hon. Sec. of the North Norfolk Strut of the PFA) who made her available to Group members. She was then a very attractive pale blue, and now one of only three Magisters still flying in the UK (and the only one in the pre-war all-yellow paint scheme).

The following weekend (12th April), I flew Auster Autocrat G-AHHM after a check ride with Jimmy Hoseason, who had bought the aeroplane shortly beforehand and subsequently undertook a quite ambitious flight in it to North Africa and return. Long before the days of GPS and with a crystal-type radio as the only navaid apart from the compass, it was quite an undertaking. I never liked the compass mounting in Austers, which required a mirror mounted above the compass in order to read it. Apart from that it was a comfortable, reasonably quiet (Cirrus Minor-engined) aeroplane to fly and I enjoyed it. One of our most memorable flights in 'HHM again involved Oulton Broad Regatta; someone had suggested that attaching a downward-facing loudspeaker horn to each of the lift struts, with suitable batteries secured in place of the rear seat and with a hand-held microphone, would enable airborne broadcasting and announcing to be carried out all along the Norfolk and Suffolk coastline – to publicise the Regatta of course. No sooner suggested than done: the equipment should weigh no more than a passenger, but what about the drag? Hmm, we were forty years younger then, of course, and as I recall it the first flight after attachment of the loudspeakers was made without the batteries on board to see whether the extra drag alone created a marked deterioration in performance, particularly on climb-out. Strangely, it didn't, despite the fact that first position flap was not selected and that Felthorpe was grass and had a shorter runway than Snoring.

The air test of the effectiveness of the equipment in terms of broadcasting proved that it was necessary to throttle right back before making any announcement, as engine noise otherwise drowned the sound. It also demonstrated that the increased drag steepened the glide considerably! This meant that our subsequent coastwise passage would have indicated a roller-coaster trace looked at horizontally: 1,500 ft to 500 ft to 1,500 ft etc. – but it worked and the day was perfect.

At one point we landed at Seething; flying cross-legged is never advisable and we definitely needed to land! The ex-B.24 runways at Seething were visible and in fair enough condition, so we landed, only to be met by a local farming man who was in fact delighted to see an aeroplane at Seething again. After establishing that we were not (any longer) in trouble he chatted away, and from that humble beginning the Waveney Flying Group came into being with Jimmy Hoseason at the helm.

Although this particular series of flights did not give rise to any mention in the local press, probably because they were not forewarned, the flying activities at and from Little Snoring were regularly and enthusiastically reported by Freddie Fletcher, the local Eastern Daily Press reporter, who came to be a regular visitor at the Clubhouse. Another Freddie, not famous at that time, was a local reporter with the Kings Lynn News & Advertiser and had joined the Group as a Full Flying Member, having previously flown Vampires in the RAF. I remember him as a pleasant but fairly reserved sort of a chap and he didn't stay with the Group for long. Indeed, amongst the papers I still have from those early days when I was Hon. Sec. of the Fakenham Group is a letter requesting the refund of his £25 share as he was "a bit short" at the time. Refund was duly made; a few years later he could have bought the Group – his surname was Forsyth, and few people today have not heard of him as a novelist.

The publicity given locally to private flying was far more positive in nature than seems to be the case today. I have newspaper cuttings and associated photographs which reflect this approach. It doubtless encouraged the dormant pre-war Norfolk and Norwich Aero Club to call a meeting, reported under the headline "Aero Club's New Aim Will Be Private Group Flying", at which the Club Chairman, Mr A.A. Rice, announced that the Club proposed to change its policy and to promote private group flying. That did not in fact happen but the Club ultimately secured the use of RAF Swanton Morley and gradually built up its membership to reestablish its pre-war reputation.

In so far as I was concerned, the fact that the Cromer Town Crier had been enabled to do his stuff ("Alfie will Fly to Cry") from the front seat of one of our Tigers gave rise to a further batch of enquiries for details of Group membership. The Press report and photograph did the trick, as I doubt that he could have worn his

212

funny hat or have been heard whilst airborne; he did however wave his bell.

In the November of 1958 we had organised a Rally at Little Snoring, which had been attended by a number of well-known personalities and interesting aircraft. Prior to his move to Sculthorpe, Mac had been Air Traffic Controller at Dunsfold, where of course he had become friendly with Neville Duke. At the time the French-built Emeraude was beginning to appear on the scene and he, I believe, had agreed to demonstrate it in the UK. The Rally had been fairly hastily been decided upon, despite the potential for bad weather in November, in order to get the Emeraude to Snoring with, of course, Neville Duke in it. The Press report read: "The Rally's thrills and variety dispelled their disappointment at the non-appearance of well-known test pilot Neville Duke who, it was thought, might be testing the paces of his midget aircraft the Emerald. He could not fly in because of a broken propeller. He is a personal friend of Mr E. McAully, Chairman of the Fakenham Flying Group." ("midget" and "Emerald" are 'journalese'!)

Despite the non-appearance of the Emeraude, and more particularly its pilot, the Rally was a great success; it brought Norman Jones and a contingent from the Tiger Club to Snoring for the first of many times. Sue Burgess at that time was a widely-acclaimed parachutist, later to become the wife of Sqdn. Ldr. Peter Phillips, test and demonstration pilot; Joan Short also attended, owner of the first Turbulent to be seen in Norfolk.

The locals – including the public and the members – had never experienced anything like it. All were allowed to mingle freely with the aircraft: it certainly couldn't happen today, and perhaps shouldn't have happened then. Nevertheless it was the first of many subsequent rallies, aerobatic competitions, air races and displays enjoyed at Snoring. It was so successful that in the the following September, after a fairly desperate call for help from Harold Best-Devereux on behalf of the PFA, the annual PFA Rally was held at the field. I recall our concern at watching Harold line up to land, and then touching down in the stubble of the recently-harvested field between the runways, breathing a sigh of relief when he was safely down, and then being amazed when he emerged from the two-seat aircraft (was it the PFA's Turbi?) together with his wife and very new-born baby. Happy days!

Earlier in the year we had suffered our first great loss and this was perhaps a warning, or reminder, that sad days would equally form part of our lives in flying as they do in all other areas. Lt. Cecil Rhoads was killed in a USAF KB.30 Jet Tanker aircraft which crashed at Diedenberg-les-Ambleve in Belgium, some ten miles from the German border. He was a real friend and a very popular instructor during the critical early months of the Group. His flying knowledge and ability was such that we had considered him indestructible. I never make a climbing or gliding turn without still hearing his voice and the slightest of sideways pressure on the stick away from or into the turn. I owe him a lot and I was deeply saddened at his loss.

During 1959 twenty lady members of the British Women Pilots' Association held a special Rally at Little Snoring, which included a competition for the then new "Faith Bennett Trophy". The trophy, a cup, was awarded to the pilot gaining most points in a general flying ability and navigation contest. It was won by Janet Ferguson, then a flying instructor at Elstree. This was the major event of the weekend, which was a great success, including as it did other events such as flour bombing, formation flying, a dinner dance at the Officers' Club at USAF Sculthorpe, a parachute jump by Ken O'Rourke (a Valiant pilot and Group member) and a final "flypast of Norfolk towns to show Norfolk people that amateur aviation is very much alive in the county." (Press report.)

Undoubtedly the most unusual aeroplane which I had the pleasure of flying was the BAC Drone G-AEKV in November 1959, which Mac had recently bought (reputedly for £100 from someone at Shoreham). Its arrival at Little Snoring was announced by the noise of its engine long before the little aeroplane arrived overhead. I never got higher than 700 ft, but I can't remember whether that figure was dictated by personal preference or the decision to stop the temperature gauge moving into the red. The engine was water-cooled and overheated very easily. The speed range, climb, cruise and stall, was very narrow with relatively few knots difference, and with a 'pusher' engine and seating so close to the ground visibility was superb and landings were 'a piece of cake'.

I remember being asked by Mac to avoid overflying Fakenham or Walsingham because of the noise the Drone made. Ultimately one of the Group members who lived in Walsingham conveyed the message to us that several people in the village were threatening to use their shotguns as "the damn thing not only makes too much noise but it stays in the same place too long making it." Mac then decided to sell it to avoid potential trouble for the Group as a whole, but not before it provided quite a spectacle, flown by Jimmy Hoseason wearing a bowler hat, at the Norfolk Gliding Club's first major Rally at Tibenham airfield in April 1960. Every available aircraft from Little Snoring plus the Tiger Club's G-APDZ (the 'Bishop') flown by Mac in the lead participated in the rally display. We flew over in a large formation, all except the Drone, which was too slow but really stole the arrival honours with its shape, its noise, its speed (or lack of it), and Jim's bowler hat clearly visible in the cockpit!

The founder members of the Norfolk Gliding Club had contacted me in early 1958 regarding the possibility of sharing Little Snoring now that the Fakenham Flying Group had become established in its usage of the airfield. Ernie "Joe" Cunningham, one of the Gliding Club's provisional committee, was an old friend, our having been at the same school and ATC squadron together, and so far he and his fellow gliding enthusiasts had been frustrated in their attempts to find and rent a suitable field from which to get started.

Following an informal meeting it became clear that there were practical difficulties which would create problems for both sets of fliers, making the idea a non-starter; however we were able to put forward some hints as to how best to approach the Air Ministry (Lands Dept.), and to relate our approach in endeavouring to gain support from a PR point of view with the local public and certain officials. We also, naturally, offered any practical support we could otherwise give.

In 1958 the Gliding Club was established and at the beginning of 1959 the Air Ministry offered them the use of the runways, a hangar and part of the Control Tower at Tibenham, an ex-USAF B.24 base. By 1960 they owned and were operating two aircraft, a Slingsby T.21B two-seater and a Tutor single-seater, together with two syndicate-owned Olympias. Six members had qualified to fly solo, all having been trained entirely within the Club. Launching was usually by tow-car, occasionally by aero-tow. Superb progress, in the flatlands of Norfolk! Small wonder that all the Fakenham-based aeropanes and pilots supported their first Open Day 100%. A memorable day for me in more than one respect as I participated in a formation of three Tigers with the leader inverted as one of the display features. I had previously arrived overhead Tibenham singly, breaking away from the large 'gaggle' formation with leaking fuel (as I thought) streaming past the port side of the rear cockpit. I finally returned to Snoring in superb evening conditions knowing that the day had been a huge success all round.

My participation on the display formation was not as P.1; Bob Stramik (ex-Spitfires) was doing the piloting, I was filming. Barry Tempest, another founder member of the Fakenham Flying Group, was flying the other Group-owned Tiger and Mac was in front flying the Tiger Club's G-APDZ which had an inverted flight fuel system fitted. Take-off was conventional, converting to "leader inverted" following appropriate hand signals (no radios) just prior to the flypast. I still have it on film: it worked like a charm.

My leaking fuel scare was caused by my front cockpit passenger being sick; being a considerate sort of a chap, despite his distress, he did not want to make a mess in the aircraft so lowered the port hatch and deposited his breakfast over the side. It 'wetted' the rear windscreen and the left shoulder of my flying suit, but, wearing helmet, goggles and oxygen mask (to keep my face warm) I didn't realise what it was until we were on the ground and stopped. He was very sorry; I was very pleased – no fuel leak after all!

The Gliding Club were delighted with the day: 1,000 cars and 3,000 people attended. We all 'had a ball' and the weather had been perfect.

Another interesting aeroplane which arrived at Little Snoring in 1959 was the Tipsy Belfair G-AFJR. This had been bought by Tony Southerland and his brother Tim, both farmers and keen members of the Group. Tony, now sadly deceased, was a great character and on the Group Committee as "Social Member"; any 'old flyers' who may have visited Snoring and met Tony will know how well he lived up to that title. He farmed at Burnham Thorpe and one of his huge barns (a listed building) provided accommodation for some of the best 'barn-dance'-type parties ever held in Norfolk. They were particularly popular with visitors, including Tiger Club members with whom we had close friendships, "Lolly" and Lewis "Benjy" Benjamin, Norman Jones, "G.B." Golding-Barrett and dear old C.P. "Bish" Nepean-Bishop having become familiar faces at Snoring.

However, I digress: back to the Belfair! It was a side-by-side two-seat low-wing Belgian-designed monoplane powered by a Walter Mikron engine; the cabin was, to say the least, cosy! The centrally-mounted stick providing dual control seemed a strange arrangement at first but presented no problem in operation. The starboard seat was slightly to the rear of the other, and in order to have access to the single throttle, which was mounted on the port side of the interior, it was necessary to place one's left arm around the back of the occupant of what should be the P.1 (port-side) seat if flying the aircraft from the P.2 (passenger) seat. Quite comfortable and quite cosy. Small wonder that some pilots elected to fly 'in charge' from the 'wrong' seat when taking young lady passengers aloft!

Tony made the aircraft available by arrangement to other members, and I had many happy flights in that aeroplane. He and I would go on pigeon-scaring operations over the farm, but my most enjoyable flight with him was a visit to USAF Wethersfield to discuss participation in their proposed air display. Inevitably we

216

were plied with several Cokes during our stay, necessitating an emergency landing on the then disused airfield at Shipdham on the way home. Nothing was wrong with the aeroplane – the emergency related to the occupants' bladders. Shipdham is now a thriving Aero Club (Arrow Air Centre) and maintenance organisation, but at that time it was deserted.

I understand that G-AFJR still exists, and is being rebuilt to static display consition in Brussels. Shortly after Tony acquired the aircraft the Felthorpe Group bought a similar one, the open-cockpit Tipsy Trainer G-AFWT (always referred to by the members as "'arfwit"!), and they operated it successfully for several years.

One aeroplane which visited Snoring fairly regularly was the Gemini G-AOXW owned by Aubrey Buxton; he allowed Mac to fly it and this enabled four of us to fly down to Blackbushe (via Denham) in order to visit the 1959 Farnborough Air Show. I remember it as a quiet, roomy and pleasant aeroplane to fly although I did not solo in it. Its owner was a very experienced private pilot and and I recall him recounting one of his adventures which I believe was later to have a bearing on the tragic loss of Bill Higgins and passenger in the Auster G-AHHM on the last day of 1959. The story went like this . . .

Shortly after the Suez crisis, Aubrey was returning in a private aircraft and, over the Mediterranean and low on fuel, contact with Air Traffic had been lost, the result of either radio malfunction or a vengeful Egyptian controller. Uncertain of his position, he had flown low over a small ship and had dropped a weighted message onto its deck seeking its assistance. I cannot remember whether he planned to ditch alongside or to ask the crew to indicate by some means the direction to the nearest land; suffice to say that he did obtain their assistance and lived to tell the tale. It made quite an impression at the time on those of us who heard it, Bill Higgins included.

Bill had flown in Halifaxes from North Creake during the war and had met and married a local girl. He was a Scot from Dumfries and, as well as being the Group's Hon. Treasurer he was a very active (and probably the most popular) member; he had a great sense of humour and a ready smile for everyone. On one occasion, sharing a flight together in one of the Tigers (where intercom was at that time via Gosport tubes) we were spiralling down to get a closer look at a Regatta on the River Yare when he suddenly anounced, at about 500 ft: "I have control."

Earlier, when we were at 2,000 ft overflying the Yare he had asked: "Do you want to go down for a closer look?", knowing of my interest in sailing.

When I had responded: "Good idea," he had presumed that I would be in control during the descent – and the rest can be guessed! We laughed about it later of course, with him taking the blame, although my inadequate reply to his query had created the misunderstanding as to who *was* in control.

At about 9 a.m. on the morning of New Year's Eve 1959 Bill took off from Little Snoring together with a friend, Brian Grimmer, bound for Dumfries via Newcastle for the traditional celebrations with his parents. The weather was fine but hazy and there is little doubt that he would have planned to follow the coast northbound after crossing the Wash to Skegness as his landfall. However, shortly after one hour later, the skipper of a coaster some 11½ miles north of Wells-next-Sea saw the Auster "coming up astern at just above mast-head height on a southerly course." It then "veered off, banked, returned at a lower height, level with my bridge, when one of the occupants threw a white object, which I took to be a message of some kind, but it fell short and into the sea. This manoeuvre was repeated six times, the last missile being a bottle. All of them fell into the sea. As the last missile fell the 'plane nosedived into the sea. Just prior to the 'plane crashing we heard the occupants shouting but were unable to distinguish the words."

Both men were pitched out of the aircraft, which sank immediately. Bill's body was recovered, but Brian Grimmer's was lost. At the inquest, Mac attempted to explain the 'double the drift on the reciprocal' aspect, and the possibility of failure to do so with a south-westerly wind and hazy conditions leading to some alarm when the Norfolk coast would fail to appear on time, but all was conjecture, of course. I have little doubt that the Mediterranean story Bill had heard earlier played a part, but whatever happened it was a tragic end to nearly three years of flying and a good fellowship – and the downside was set to continue into 1960.

On May the 12th 1960 Mac was killed in G-APDZ whilst practising aerobatics over the airfield. Two months later, on the 7th of July, "Danny" was killed over Cambridgeshire in a mid-air collision between the Varsity he was flying and a Vampire, and five months after that Jack Last was killed at Seething when his Tripacer was blown over, striking him in the process, whilst being moved on the ground during a freak storm. I was familiar with the old Latin adage which translates into "Adversity Strengthens" and it proved to be true as we moved into the sixties. The Fakenham Flying Group was renamed the McAully Flying Group following an Extraordinary Meeting which I called at the end of May, and by common consent in recognition of the tremendous leadership which Mac had given.

In 1961 53 aircraft attended the then biggest Rally staged in Norfolk. The Norfolk Youth Flying Club, sponsored by the Education Committee, came into being as an offshoot of the Group, and the Waveney Flying Group became established under the leadership of Jim Hoseason on the Fakenham pattern. New horizons opened up in the shape of participation in Battle of Britain Day displays at RAF Coltishall and elsewhere, new types of aircraft began to become available 'on demonstration', tricycle under-carriages began to proliferate and things began to change in so many ways.

I have many happy memories of flying since the fifties, but none surpass the fun, freedom and comradeship of that era, and I count myself fortunate, albeit in a small way, to have been part of it.

CHAPTER 27

THE THROTTLE BENDERS' UNION

by

RON PAINE

(as told to

PETER G. CAMPBELL)

[The Throttle Benders' Union was mentioned briefly in Chapter 6 in connection with air racing; but what was it exactly, and did it achieve its objective? For the first time, the story of its formation and purpose is told by one of the small band of members, Ron Paine. Ron was one of the foremost figures in aviation in the fifties; apart from owning and racing the Miles Hawk Speed Six, he ran the successful company Wolverhampton Aviation Ltd, which had had an agency for Miles aircraft since just after the war. After the collapse of Miles in 1948 they had bought up Gemini and Messenger airframes, establishing a small production line for the types at Wolverhampton. This company then begat Derby Aviation Ltd, who operated Marathons and DC-3s, and later Ron was one of the founders of British Midland Airways.

In more recent years Ron Paine has been instrumental in the rebuilding of the famous red D.H.88 Comet G-ACSS (the winner of the 1934 England to Australia Air Race), which flew again for a short time a few years ago before a reluctant decision was made to ground it for the sake of preserving it safely in one piece – it was not the easiest of machines to get the mastery over; now it is on static display at Old Warden. Subsequently Ron organised the building, from scratch this time, of another Comet in the USA, an exact replica of G-ACSS; this one is flying very successfully and appears at all the major airshows.

He still has several plans up his sleeve (or, more accurately, in a safe place!), but only time will tell whether they materialise. Surely, if anyone can make things happen, Ron can! – Ed.]

To get air racing back 'on the map' after the war, the Royal Aero Club had to promote the sport; I was very much involved with the RAeC and also with the Association of British Aero Clubs, and we began to approach the owners of a number of airfields to try and kindle their interest in being a host airfield for racing. The first airport to respond positively was Southend, and in fact the 1947 Southend Air Race was promoted by the City Fathers. I took part in that race in a Magister G-AHNU and won it!

Within the next month or so we had requests from Newcastle, Yeadon (Leeds/Bradford) and four or five other major airports, all wanting to put on air races. We selected a short list of the airfields we thought most suitable to host the event in future years, and then named the event the National Air Race. The intention was that, to compete in the prestigious King's Cup race, which was going to be run that year at Coventry, a pilot entering the National Air Race would have to get a good enough placing, and enough points, for him to qualify.

Whilst this was all going on, we were endeavouring to get the manufacturers of aeroplanes, and the fuel companies, to once again put into being what had been the standard practice before the war. These companies had traditionally sponsored air-racing events by providing fuel, oil and other consumables free of charge for the competitors' aeroplanes. If you won the race, and were using a certain type of sparking plug or tyre and so forth, then you got a bonus payment for that, and the company would also use your aeroplane for advertising their wares; this applied to petrol and oil too, of course.

Unfortunately, at this time, the fuel companies did not feel that they could support us, and we felt that they were being very mean on the subject. So we tried from all angles, but we couldn't move them. However, whilst we were at a Newcastle event in 1949, the six of us who had been meeting regularly at the races met the Shell representative, Joe Taylor, whom we all knew, and we asked him once again if the company would be prepared to reconsider its position. The six of us worked hard with him all over the weekend, but to no avail; we had also tried again with Esso and also with Wakefield's, the oil company, but without any success.

Just as we were leaving Newcastle to go back to our various aerodromes, Nat Somers said: "You know, we'll have to get a union going!"

It was all fun; the whole thing was fun, of course. And so everybody was laughing and joking, and the next thing that happened was this: Col. Preston was informed that Nat Somers was going to entertain us all at Ciro's Club in London to officially form the 'Throttle Benders' Union'. We invited the cartoonist 'Wren', 'Mossie' Preston and so forth, and it was a fantastic evening; that is where it was born.

For the record, the six of us involved were Nat Somers, Tony Cole, Geoffrey Alington, Fred Dunkerley, Jimmy Rush and myself (we co-opted Walter Bowles later).

The 'Throttle Benders' Union' was a very closed shop. We six had sowed the seeds at Newcastle, but we were still working to get sponsorship; and then, out of the blue, Eric Hall, who was the service manager of the Auster Aircraft factory at Rearsby, mentioned that he knew that the managing director of an oil company by the name of Ragosine was very anxious to help, and was prepared to give the members of the Union a refill of oil and provide the oil for racing. So we met him and we accepted his offer. For the first race of the next season, 1950, Ragosine oil was made available to us, and of course we took advantage of this, drained our tanks and put Ragosine oil in.

The response to Ragosine was so good because all of us who were running aerodromes were buying Ragosine oil; we had taken Shell out and put Ragosine in! This applied to Fred Dunkerley at Manchester, Nat Somers at Elstree, and so on. Anyway, we all made it our business to push Ragosine oil.

It was really successful; you can imagine the 'buzz' that was running around the industry at that time, but you've got to remember that we were a very small organisation, and it was getting quite embarrassing for the Esso and the Shell representatives to come along and put up their hospitality tents and so forth! But this is precisely what the Union had been formed for: we had achieved our aim of getting sponsorship.

Now Ragosine were so thrilled with all of this that they then said that they would pay for all the fuel being used as well, which was at the time being supplied by Shell. So we finished up with both fuel and oil paid for by the Ragosine Oil Company: and not just the six of us – all the other pilots were by this time benefitting from this generosity.

All this was done in a very sporting nature. The next thing that happened was that, although Ragosine was paying for the oil and petrol, we decided to change the brand of petrol we used from Shell to Esso! All the other racing pilots tended to use Shell (which was now being paid for by Ragosine), and they too defected to Esso. This was the straw that broke the camel's back; the petrol companies could not stand this. We had a race at Coventry, the 1950 King's Cup I think it was, where we changed over. The next season both Shell and Esso came forward and said that they would support the air-racing. Of course we were asked to use their products. So we went to Ragosine and thanked them very much. Their managing director was delighted – not only had he got some more customers but he had done a wonderful public relations job for us. Mind you, he had already made it very clear some time before that his company would stand down immediately we achieved our object, so no feelings were hurt. Ragosine were a British firm who, like a number of other companies both before and after, did a deal with a manufacturer whereby they could sell oil under their own name.

So those were the aims and objects of the 'Throttle Benders' Union', to get all of this sponsorship going, and of course, once we'd achieved that, the whole thing more or less died, although we did meet each year at Ciro's for a while. It was a lot of fun, but at the same time it had helped to put the whole of the air-racing scene on a much firmer footing for the future.

One or two other things may be of interest. We had a special motif painted on each of our aircraft to indicate that we were members of the 'Throttle Benders Union', and this can be seen in photographs taken in the early fifties. Also Jimmy Rush made a special contribution (he was based at Newcastle, and that's how we got the Newcastle races going, because he involved the Newcastle Corporation). Jimmy was in the glass business, and he arranged to have seven special sets of glass goblets made up; he then got an artist up there to hand-paint them all with the aircraft and names of the members of the Union. We all had a set and they're really a unique (well, almost unique!) momento of those days.

*   *   *

[Ron Paine has also contributed the following experiences which, although nothing to do with the TBU, are well worth mentioning here – Ed.]

MY CONNECTIONS WITH MILES AIRCRAFT

By the time I had set up the civil divisions at Burnaston (Derby) and Wolverhampton Airport after the war, Miles Aircraft were producing the Gemini and the Messenger, and we became the Miles agents for the Midlands. This introduced me to these two types, but at the time we had both of the flying schools operating Magisters, along with a Whitney Straight and a Monarch. When Miles ceased to operate in 1948, I bought the Speed Six and a number of other Hawks from the Receiver, and it became clear that we could also do something useful with the remainder of the production line of the

Geminis. I also went to Northern Ireland and brought back the Messengers, which had been produced there in limited numbers. It turned out that there was a severe shortage of Messenger wings, and so I got permission from the ARB to modify Gemini wings by filling them in where the nacelles would have gone for the Gemini engines, and then fitting them to Messengers; we converted about six in this way, including our demonstrator G-AILL. It added a bit to the weight, but it was acceptable.

I was also responsible for converting all the ex-RAF Messengers for civilian use. We bought them from the Air Ministry, collected them from Lichfield and converted them at Wolverhampton.

At about that time Miles had put two Gipsy Major 1C engines into a Gemini in place of the normal Cirrus Minors; after the flying tests were completed the aeroplane was then sold to Nat Somers as the Gemini 1C, and he won the King's Cup in it at Elmdon in 1949.

John Houlder, of the Houlder Brothers shipping line, was a great friend of mine, and he said that he would like one too, so I bought a fuselage and all the necessary parts from the receivers at Miles. Then Nat Somers lent me his aeroplane, and with that and the drawings that I was able to get from the receiver, we then produced the first Gemini 3A from the Wolverhampton stable. That was a success, and so then we went on to buy up the production line and turn out a number of Gemini 3As; they too proved very successful.

Early one morning I received a call from Douglas Bader (who was the Managing Director of Shell Aviation Ltd), and he said he was on his way to see me. In his typical fashion he said: "I want three Geminis, but I want them yesterday."

The outcome was that we first built G-AMGF for him to his standard; when he proved to be happy with that, he then ordered one for Trinidad and one for Venezuela.

That was the start of a very nice relationship with Douglas. We then got him to race Jean Batten's Gull in the *Daily Express'* Air Race from Shoreham in 1951. At the time, Douglas was writing for the *News of the World'*, and he got them to enter it. His joke was that it would have been quite something if he could have won the race for the *News of the World.'*

Douglas has often been reported as being a difficult fellow to get on with. While I agree with a lot of what has been said, he was not like that with his 'own kind', if you follow me, those people who knew about aeroplanes. If a potentially embarrassing situation blew up I would just walk away from it.

I flew with him an awful lot; it is true that he stood for no nonsense, but he was a good chum. You had to know your subject with Douglas, and you had to be up with him, and trying to beat him at everything all the time. There was always this competitive element that crept into everything he did, which presumably stemmed from the time when he had had to single-handedly learn to use his two tin legs effectively enough so that he appeared to be walking fairly normally; that must really have been a daunting challenge. Douglas didn't mind if he lost out on some competitive activity, the important thing to him was that it had to be competitive, more or less whatever it involved. You would be flying with him, and you'd say: "We've done an hour or so's flying, and you've made a bit of a pig's leg of that, haven't you?", and you woke him up that way. He was a very good chap.

Later, it was necessary for some modifications to be made to his Gemini. We had put the Gipsy Major engines in the same nacelles that had contained the original Cirrus Minors; they were a tight fit as you can imagine, and the arrangement wasn't very accessible for servicing. So in 1955 the aircraft was taken down to F.G. Miles Ltd, who had reformed and were operating from Shoreham at the time. There they fitted Aries nacelles (the Aries was a further development of the Gemini with two Cirrus Major engines), and at the same time put in bigger brakes. They also fitted an ADF loop on top of the fuselage and an 'eyebrow' strake on the fuselage each side of the front of the cockpit. This was quite an interesting little exercise; if you looked at an original Gemini, there were slats on the front of the wings just inboard of the nacelles to deaden the early stall warning. We found that to take those off and put on the 'eyebrow' did exactly the same job, but it was simpler and lighter and at the same time more aerodynamic.

*　　*　　*

OUR AIR SURVEY CONTRACTS

After the war, I received a request from the Canadian Company Aero Surveys, who wanted to buy some aeroplanes that they could do some photography and survey work with over most of Canada. So I then approached the Ministry and we bought a 'parcel' of about twenty Mosquito B.35s, which had a blower on one side. Aero Surveys wanted them to fly at 40,000 ft, and my job was to get them from the Ministry, overhaul them, put HF and radio into them, and certify them to 40,000 ft; that of course meant that we had to test-fly them up to that height. Finally we had to fly them to Ottawa, which of course meant fitting long-range tanks to them all. As far as I know, the aeroplanes were still there until a few years ago.

Following on from there, they knew that I was operating Ansons, and they wanted to know whether I could rig up an Anson to take a magnetometer, because if so, they would offer us a contract to fly over the North Sea surveying potential oil field sites. They sent the magnetometer over, and I bought a Mark 1 Anson, which would take a payload of a ton, and put all the electronics into it, including 1,000 watt generators left and right, and an arrangement by which I could drop the magnetometer on a coil to trail behind the aircraft when in flight.

Staff from Aero Surveys then came over to this country; we gave them an office and we worked together for four years. During this time I purchased two more Ansons and we covered Turkey and parts of Africa, including Sierra Leone, surveying for minerals, as well as most of the UK oilfields. I fitted Decca Navigators into the aircraft, and we then surveyed the whole of the North Sea; so the oil fields that you are seeing today were all surveyed with an Anson. We would go backwards and forwards, up and down, using the Decca Navigator, and the information was all recorded by the equipment on board the aeroplane, so we needed to have a crew of three on board. I kept G-AMDA and it's now on display at Duxford; I had bought that one brand spanking new.

Later, when I was operating Dakotas, I fixed up one of those with long-range tanks and so forth, and went on survey work with that.

I was also co-founder of British Midland Airways, and was responsible for opening up Castle Donington eventually. We started with Dragon Rapides, and then Dakotas, and I also bought three Marathons, and then some redundant Argonauts from BOAC.

Another interest of mine was the flying club at Elstree. John Houlder had taken the lease for Elstree aerodrome, but I took over and started the Elstree Flying Club. Our club aircraft at Derby and Wolverhampton were all painted in a pale green, just like our first demonstration Messenger G-AILL, so this is why the Austers and Magisters based at Elstree sported the same colour scheme. As time went on, we dispensed with the Austers and Magisters (we must have been almost the last operator of Magisters, although I think that Denham still had a few). I then formed the London School of Flying, who had about ten ex-RAF Chipmunks.

And that's how the fifties ended!

CHAPTER 28

EXTRACTS OF FOX

Edited by

PETER G. CAMPBELL

[NOTES ON THE AUTHOR: One of the most prolific writers on the aviation scene in the fifties & sixties was Denis Fox; the material that follows is reproduced here by kind permission of Air-Britain (Historians) Ltd, in whose journal 'British Civil Aviation News' it first appeared, and with acknowledgements to Denis Fox.

Air-Britain, which will celebrate its 50th anniversary in 1998, is an international organisation of aviation historians and enthusiasts; many members are also pilots.

Denis was a tireless worker for Air-Britain for many years, and during the fifties & sixties he was to be seen at most flying events both large and small with his notebook and cigarette, neither of which he appeared ever to be without. He was always after the really interesting snippets of news for the magazine, and, as he wrote in a letter to me once: "If I can't find any scandal I'll have to invent some!"

This chapter comprises a selection of extracts from his contributions to BCAN between 1954 & 1960. These well illuminate three of his main attributes: firstly, his shrewdness in keeping his finger on the pulse of aviation events, secondly, his cynical sense of humour which so often came through in his writing, and thirdly, his wonderful way with words – Ed.]

28th AUGUST, 1954: VINTAGE BANK HOLIDAY

Taking advantage of the freak of nature that provided two consecutive days of flyable weather, the Vintage Aeroplane Club staged its most successful rally to date, on August 1st and 2nd. Such was the weather on the Sunday that no fewer than 53 visiting aircraft elbowed their way into Denham's modest confines – with the result that the local cricket pitch was impressed into use as an aircraft park. The groundsman's comments are not yet available!

First over the fence was the Bagley-Tiger combine G-AMCM, hotly pursued by the much hoped for, but little expected Puss Moth G-ABDF, flown by Air-Britain member John Jakeman. Its arrival marked the successful culmination of three months' hard labour at Elstree where it has been rebuilt by its owners, its C. of A. being renewed on the previous day.

The events of the two days followed the accepted pattern of vintage informality, though not all of a strictly vintage nature. Some immaculate formation flying by the vintage biplanes contrasted sharply with the Porteous-Aiglet act in G-AMYI, as did the skill of Ron Gillman's balloon bursting in Cadet G-ACHP compare with the lack of skill displayed by the legion of enthusiasts who hurled themselves into the air with similar intent. In the middle of Monday's proceedings was witnessed the forcible abduction of a young lady by the driver of Arrow G-AJAM. His criminal intentions became obvious when the more intimate items of the lady's clothing began to descend at regular intervals from the circling Arrow. With a clanging of bells, Tipsy G-AFWT arrived at the scene of the crime, bearing two helmetted 'Bobbies,' and after a prolonged chase the Arrow was brought to earth and its driver arrested. The now scantily-clad passenger was last seen proceeding into a place where further pursuit was morally impossible.

Height judging, individual demonstrations, supply dropping and a 'radio-controlled' G-ACHP (with a very human control concealed in the rear seat), completed the supporting bill. The supply dropping was virtually identical to bombing – with the addition of parachutes – thus rendering the attendant ballistics incalculable. Air-Britain, in the shape of the Bagley Tiger, having collected a free lunch for arriving undetected, went on to win the latter item hands down, with the Hon. Gen. Sec. in the front seat to keep the nose down . . .

*   *   *

[A.J. Jackson relinquished the Editorship of BCAN in May 1957 to give him time to complete his famous work 'BRITISH CIVIL AIRCRAFT 1919-1959', and Denis, who up till then had been Honorary General Secretary, then took over the editorial 'hot seat'. His first editorial described how he felt about this . . . – Ed.]

MAY 25th, 1957: THIS IS THE JOURNAL THAT JACK BUILT

The very thought of being required to step into the editorial shoes of A.J.J. is sufficient to produce trepidation in bulk, for they are the shoes of a giant personality. They will take much to fill.

Our own trepidation is blended with the pleasure of being asked, and the sorrow of realising that all good things must end. To Air-Britain, Jack has been a very good thing indeed, and will continue to be so in other capacities. Upon BCAN has been built the very structure of our Association, for it was this publication alone which kept Air-Britain solvent in the early days. Had it failed, Air-Britain would have failed, and it is fair to say that we have to thank this good friend for the fact that we are still kicking.

The Jackson era has seen the production of the last two hundred and two issues of this paper, and your new Editor intended to produce statistics to evidence the vast amount of work this has entailed. The intention was abandoned in despair after counting 2,325 entries in the 'new allocations' columns alone. It all adds up to the fact that the worthy Jack is very entitled to rest upon a forest of laurels. However, we well know that he is poorly versed in the art of resting, and none of us will be at all surprised if we hear that something else is cooking in the industrial area of Olivia Drive.

In keeping with its past, we firmly believe that the future of BCAN is bright – despite its new Editor. Those worthy assistants, John Bagley and Rod Havers, continue to produce the goods, interesting aeroplanes are currently two-a-penny in the register, and our jungle telegraph is in good order.

To conclude this, our first Editorial, it is our solemn duty to record BCAN's unqualified disapproval of a truly horrific piece of vandalism which heads the current list of new allocations.

We refer, of course, to the abortion of G-AHDM, which letters properly belong to the now defunct H.P. Halton 1 "Falmouth" of BOAC. This ended its life in an even more dramatically modified form than the new holder of its registration, for it was the leading lady in the film 'No Highway' – and caused Mr Honey as much consternation as is currently being experienced by ourselves. The new holder is, of course, our old friend G-AJOF [formerly a Miles Aerovan 4 – Ed.], c/n 6403, and is now sporting a pair of Hurel-Dubois wings. Hence the fraudulent conversion.

* * *

SEPTEMBER 28th, 1957: BULL AND BUSHE

In common with numerous enthusiasts, it is our annual pleasure to allot the first week in September to the Farnborough/Blackbushe circuit. The pleasure is enhanced by the opportunity it affords of meeting our members and readers in more natural surroundings than those obtaining at an Annual General Meeting.

In recent years, weather conditions have tended to push the

event into the Winter Sports category, and the pencil and notebook, formerly the standard identification marks of an enthusiast, have yielded to a uniform mantle of plastic raincoat and goose-pimples for all ranks.

By way of compensation to those who managed to thread their way through the jungle of flying bricks, electronic ironmongery and lethal pyrotechnics, was the sight of a new light aeroplane, the Auster Atlantic – and a very snappy one, too! We wish it well, and it is welcome to grace the pages of our registers.

*   *   *

OCTOBER 26th, 1957: SENTIMENTAL JOURNEY

Evident at Croydon on 29th September was the fact that the new BOAC colour scheme is contagious and that the Airways Aero Club has caught it. Their Chipmunks and Aiglets are breaking out in white tops and blue vertical tail surfaces, as is the Morton Consul G-AIOS, which is used by the Club . . .

The real object of the visit was to fulfil a desire to ride in Tiger G-ACDC, a desire which has been nursed ever since it arrived there in 1953 along with a million of its clapped-out fellows. With BCAN's former Editor driving from the back seat – and the current one acting as his crash buffer in front – G-ACDC sprang into the air, in close company with three other Tiger Club machines on a formation flight to Sandown. With Nepean Bishop acting as an airborne sheepdog, the formation duly arrived there in good order, and local sports were indulged in. Among the sports was an abortive attempt by a USAF C-47 to land there from Northolt, while all hands made ready to pick up the pieces. After a single attempt it returned hot-foot to the mainland, followed after a respectful pause by the now five-strong Tiger gaggle.

It is little realised that G-ACDC is not quite the same aeroplane as it was at Baginton, for it suffered major damage in a take-off crash at Croydon on 6th September. The accident was witnessed by the Editor, whose language was horrible to hear. A new propeller, three new wings, a new tail unit and half the undercarriage were replaced by Rollasons with prodigious speed in time for it to reappear at the Garden Party on the 15th *[at Wisley – Ed.]*.

*   *   *

DECEMBER 28th, 1957: RING OUT THE OLD

The imminent withdrawal from use of 1957, and the very recent disposal of Christmas, makes this an apt moment to look back at the year which has gone . . .

Brushing aside the post-Xmas shambles of blunt corkscrews, time-expired cigars and clapped-out wishbones, we look back at a year more interesting than most – a year which has produced a fascinating variety of newly-registered aeroplanes. From Boeing 707, through Vanguard, Britannia and Comet 4, way down the scale to Atlantic, Alpha and Turbi, it has been a vintage year. It has seen the Viscount, Heron and Dove continuing to enjoy themselves, with Twin Pioneer, President and E.P.9 joining the fun. We have seen the Tiger Moth refuse to lie down, and we are agog to see the Prentice get up. We have seen everything.

Naturally, all this has kept us extremely busy, and furious application to the Register has successfully and mercifully insulated us from the facts of life. Such matters so vital to the national well-being as skiffle groups, non-iron shirts and runaway heiresses leave us serenely unmoved so long as our heads are firmly buried in the pages of the Register. Thus engrossed, it would require our typewriter to be struck by lightning to produce any visible emotion at all. Yes, in these days of mass-hysteria, a hobby – even one as curious as ours – is a distinct asset. Long live our hobby! Long live the Register! Long live our Assistant Editors!

* * *

JANUARY 11th, 1958: RING IN THE NEW

That the close of 1957 also closed a chapter in the BOAC story is evident . . . After almost fourteen years of service, the York has finally been retired from BOAC's fleet. We are surprised that the event was allowed to pass without even the smallest spark of emotion.

However there is one spark . . . – a very bright spark named G-AJDR – which has no more right to that title than the baby's pram. It was G-AJDR once, but since 1950 it has been progressively fitted with the wings of G-AKMU, the fuselage of G-AJRU, the wings of G-AJRT (once fitted to G-AJRU), and the maker's plate with the c/n 1750 belonging to G-AJRS. It might well be happier at Boscombe Down – home of the Bustard Flying Club. *[This aircraft is still flying, but now as G-AJRS, with the Shuttleworth Collection – Ed.]*

* * *

MAY 10th, 1958: OXFORD MARKET

At Kidlington on 26th and 27th April was staged a new event – the "Sales Weekend" of W.S. Shackleton Ltd. Whether the object was to sell aeroplanes or to provide a gala for the enthusiasts was not clear, but the latter's requirements were met in full, and a good time was duly had . . .

In the sale park, not for sale, but as an example of its type, was the Bishop Tiger – the aerobatic *'Bishmoth'* G-APDZ. This remarkable aeroplane was put through its paces with all the youthful abandon of its namesake, and among its secret weapons was revealed an electrically ignited smoke generator.

The thunder of Bishop's demonstrations was partly stolen by the simultaneous arrival from Eastleigh of the famous D.H. 86 G-ACZP. In a smart new coat of paint, and driven by the redoubtable V.H. Bellamy, it was the sensation of the day.

*   *   *

JUNE 14th, 1958: RINGING THE CHANGES

[Amongst the changes of ownership, it remains to be seen to what use the Dragon Rapide] G-APJW will be put – when it is converted – by Tarmac Ltd. Destined for missionary operations in darkest Africa, it may now instead patrol the jungle between Watford and Luton in support of Tarmac's commitments to the first stage of the new London to Birmingham motorway. The contractor responsible for the remainder of the road has also threatened to introduce aeroplanes to the bulldozers, but the marriage has yet to be effected.

*   *   *

JUNE 28th, 1958: ISLE OF TIGERS

Whit Monday, May 26th, saw the occasion of the Tiger Club's annual rally and race meeting at Lea aerodrome, Sandown, I.O.W. On the eve of the event the Club scrambled from its bases at Croydon and Fair Oaks, and flew south to 'weigh in.' From the comfort of the coupé G-AOXS we were provided *en passant* with food for thought at the sight of Tiger G-APFN awash in Langstone Harbour – with which it became intimate on April 29th.

After an entirely honourable night spent at a girls' hostel, the crews re-emerged to find the airfield exhibiting nearly all the characteristics of a paddy field. Mopping up operations were put in hand, and the show was on . . .

An unhappy accident overtook Lt. Cdr. Jack Overbury's demonstration of the Turbulent G-APBZ, which struck the ground before recovering from a stall turn, and was destroyed. A Whirlwind XJ729 was present for a demonstration, and its capabilities were most convincingly proved by the rapidity with which it conveyed the injured pilot to hospital at Ryde.

The show went on, and among other items was a demonstration by Ian Forbes of the extraordinary slow-flying properties and short-field capabilities of the HDM.105 G-AHDM. Its performance is so impressive that one can almost forgive it its registration marks.

* * *

JULY 12th, 1958: THE ROYAL AERONAUTICAL SOCIETY'S GARDEN PARTY

The most sensational feature of this year's Garden Party was the quantity of water which fell upon it. . . . Undaunted, the show went on. . . . Among other evergreens was the annual duel between the Hurricane G-AMAU and the Spitfire 5B AB910 (G-AISU), and the immortal Swordfish G-AJVH to prove that high-density seating is nothing new. On this occasion it was pursued, overhauled and boarded at the eleventh hour by a gentleman astride a penny-farthing bicycle . . .

The few visiting aircraft which managed to defeat the weather included Hastings TG606; this brought a party from Henlow, which produced the Dakota at the 1957 party. One is entitled to ponder on their choice of vehicle for the 1959 party . . .

* * *

AUGUST 9th, 1958: THE BLIGHT FIGHTERS

Were it not for their high cost of replacement, agricultural Tiger Moths would undoubtedly reign supreme in the latest cancellations, for an outbreak of potato blight has provoked unprecedented activity in the crop-spraying market. Inevitably, the blight is enlisting support from the local obstructions, and the English rural scene is fast acquiring a strata of bent aeroplanes. Among many casualties is the Chipmunk G-APMN . . . which is due to perform at Farnborough next month, whereat the SBAC will be sprayed on from a low height.

* * *

SEPTEMBER 13th, 1958: ELSTREE TWOSOME

With breakfast patrols an extinct pastime and tea patrols decidedly on the wane, Elstree's revivalist meeting of August 10th made a welcome event . . .

No records are claimed to have been broken by the party, but we would challenge anyone to produce a collection of more than nine Hawk Trainers at any single event today!

Among static items, the most fascinating was the wreckage of a Proctor 'registered' N3725N – and many furrowed brows were seen in its vicinity. This proved to be G-AIZA, disposed of by the Rank Organisation *[after being used as a film prop – Ed.]*.

The other half of the twosome was effected on August 23rd, when a private meeting was held to welcome a number of French visitors. Unfortunately weather conditions over the English Channel were poor – as the Editors were able to personally confirm – and the only visitor from France was the Emeraude F-BIRA. The most significant aeroplane present was the very long-awaited Druine Turbi G-AOTK, seen in public for the first time since its maiden flight at Hatfield on August 9th.

* * *

OCTOBER 11th, 1958: BIGGIN OR BENBECULA?

Our readers will have noticed that 16.5% of the undermentioned aircraft *[in the Changes of Ownership column – Ed.]* are based at Croydon, in company with about eighty others. Enough has already been said about the MTCA's obsession to assassinate the place, and it is significant that not a single new civil airfield has been initiated by the Ministry since its formation. The briefest glance at a pre-War map of airfields in the London area leads one to suspect that successive Ministers compete for a secret challenge trophy, awarded to the Minister whose tenure of office sees the greatest number of closures. The trophy will presumably be won outright by the Minister who closes London Airport.

Very rightly hallowed in Royal Air Force circles, Biggin Hill as an alternative is patently absurd *[though we all know now what happened within just a year of this comment being made – Ed.]*, and the suggestion that Hendon be used was killed at birth – presumably because it was a reasonably intelligent suggestion. The Minister is being pressed to "think again" about Croydon – which is something he very obviously hasn't bothered to think about at all. As there are less than three months to go, perhaps he would care to start thinking?

* * *

DECEMBER 13th, 1958: ELEPHANT TO LET

Turning to the ridiculous, we had hoped that by now we would be applauding the belated application of some common sense to the Croydon fiasco. But no; we have only the very dubious satisfaction of confirming yet again that common sense – like water on a duck – is a proscribed commodity among 'planners'. Everybody wants to use Croydon and nobody wants to use Gatwick – so it is entirely natural that the former should be closed and the latter opened.

Even the afore-mentioned duck would be hard-put to match such progressive genius.

The 'planners' who failed to cultivate peanuts in Tanganyika have calmly cultivated £7.5 million of concrete at Gatwick – but by a small oversight they forgot to enquire whether it was wanted. The current 38 scheduled movements per week (largely the same aeroplane going and coming) speaks for itself. Henceforth we can be very sure that people will be compelled to use it, irrespective of their wishes; the planner's face requires to be saved, and it will be saved – no matter how many tax-paying faces are trampled in the process.

*   *   *

MAY 23rd, 1959: ON BEING SOME BIRDS

May 9th saw the start of the biggest-ever gliding event, when the 1959 National Gliding Championships commenced at Lasham – attended by the unbridled enthusiasm, the funny hats, and comic-opera vehicles which so characterise the movement . . .

A surprise was provided by the Agricola G-APFZ standing in the middle of nowhere, and inscribed "Aerial Agriculture Ltd. Unit No.1" . . . As we departed, it was being approached by a group of small boys – so we can only hope that G-APFZ still exists.

Reverting to the gliding; even as we write, the records are being broken. Mrs Anne Burns has flown her Skylark 3B to Northumberland, and Cdr. H.C.N. Goodhart has gone one better and jumped the border into Scotland with a similar machine. To the normally accepted hazards which attend such events have been added two new ones; at the USAF base at Greenham Common, the juvenile enthusiasm of its inhabitants is such that guns are pointed at gliders which land within its confines, and the hapless drivers are given (almost) the full Chicago treatment. Nearer at hand, the neighbourhood of Lasham was in the grip of foot and mouth disease and gliders accidentally landing within certain areas were likely to remain *in situ* until de-bugged – or whatever one does to cure a diseased glider.

*   *   *

JULY 25th, 1959: THE JOINT IS JUMPING

Quite the most extraordinary collection of allocations has erupted into the bottom of this page, and a number of equally exotic vehicles are in fairly imminent prospect. This encouraging state of affairs calls for some comment . . .

The regular appearance (on paper) of Gyrocopters gives us

235

furiously to wonder whether a recurrence of the Pou mania is about to break out. Those who were present circa 1936 will recall that the United Kingdom was practically knee-deep in bent Pous; doubtless our current Police State will suppress any outbreak of bent Bensens. The latest specimen lurks in Fifeshire, and may well be a straightforward conversion of a set of motorised bagpipes.

[After discussing other 'rare birds' such as a civil-registered Hunter (G-APUX), and the first UK-registered Tripacers, a Super Cub, Comanche, Cessna 310 & Mooney 20, Denis concluded as follows: – Ed.]

All this convinces us more than ever that there is a market for a sophisticated light aeroplane – a market big enough to absorb the early production models which are a pre-requisite to export. Many of our famous manufacturers owe their fame to the fact that they once built aeroplanes. Some of them would do well to abandon their profitless tinkering with supersonic bricks, and revert to the more mundane but money-making process of building saleable aeroplanes.

*   *   *

AUGUST 8th, 1959: ON A SAUCER, OUT OF COWES

The creators of the Saro SR-N1 Hovercraft have been hard-put to decide what they have created – whether it be a flying machine, a ship, or a 'thing'. Its recent adoption of the Class B marks G-12-4 remove it from the latter categories, and B.C.A.N. is now solemnly required to admit its existence.

*   *   *

OCTOBER 24th, 1959: CROYDON CLOSURE

[This piece was not actually originated by Denis Fox, although it was edited by him for inclusion in this particular issue of BCAN: the supplier of the information was K. Galpin. However the subject matter seems so appropriate and in this context so very emotive, that in my view it just begged to be included – Ed.]

A very substantial chapter in the history of British aviation was closed on the evening of September 30th as the last few aircraft left Croydon for ever. The last airline service was operated by Morton's Heron G-AOXL, at about 6.30 p.m., followed shortly by Dove G-ANAN making an empty positioning flight to Gatwick. From Vendair's hangar, Auster G-APJX, Proctor G-ALJF, Gemini G-AJWE and Anson G-AHIB trickled out and took off into the gathering gloom towards Biggin Hill, while Chipmunk G-APTS from the Airways Club hangar only just made the deadline; it had been painted in Surrey Club colours which were still damp when it took off on what I am sure was its first flight. Proctor G-AGWB took off, came back, and finally took off again, and the Piaggio P.166 G-APVE prepared to make the last flight out of Croydon. Suddenly, Gemini G-AJWE returned at speed, landed, and prepared to dispute the 'honour' with the P.166. After some jockeying for position, this was conceded, and G-APVE was followed into the air by G-AJWE at 7.45 p.m. Thus, fittingly, a British aircraft was the last to leave the sacred soil.

A last snoop round all the hangars revealed that Rollasons are the only people to stay put; construction work will continue at Croydon, but final erection will be at Biggin or more probably at Redhill where the Tiger Club have ensconced themselves . . .

Biggin's 'civil area' is now leased to Surrey Aviation Ltd in the persons of J.R. Maitland, of Maitland Air Charter, and E. Drewery, of G-APSZ. Plans are afoot to make Biggin Hill a centre of private aviation in the south of England, and we look forward to their early fruition.

[Despite the 1959 closure, Mike Stroud tells me that a number of aircraft have landed at Croydon since then, and that three small Air Shows took place during the eighties; a grass strip of about 700 yards is still available (at a pinch) in the public open space that used to be the Airport. More recent shows have been not allowed, one reason quoted being because a very rare, if not unique, clump of grass was out there somewhere which could be irrevocably damaged by landing aircraft! Apparently this rare specimen has now been moved to Kew Gardens. So there may well still be some ongoing dispute over who did, or will be able to, finally make the last flight into or out of Croydon – Ed.]

*   *   *

NOVEMBER 14th, 1959: DINORNIS MAXIMUS
– THE GIANT MOA

As is now common knowledge, the civil aviation interests of the MTCA, and most of the Ministry of Supply's activities are to be absorbed by the newly-hatched MOA – the Ministry of Aviation – which will produce a spate of nominal changes of ownership for this page in due course! For those who have never made its acquaintance, the MOA is/was a large, extinct, flat-breasted bird, ostrich-like, and incapable of flying. A native of New Zealand, the MOA was exterminated by the Maoris before the Europeans arrived, but mummified heads have been found. Events may yet prove that the Maoris were right . . .

*   *   *

APRIL 9th, 1960: ON MERGING AND SUBMERGING

The list of changes is rather less profound than it appears at first sight, and much of the padding is due to Airwork paving the way for the merger of its airline interests with those of Hunting-Clan. The possibility of Chipmunks operating their Safari services to Nairobi and Salisbury is thus diminished . . .

For the agony column comes news of the impending closure of Blackbushe, a veiled threat to close Stansted, and a similar threat to Speke. Upon the last-named the local authority desires to erect housing units ('houses' in olde English), while at Blackbushe, the worthies of Yateley (pop. 2,036) talk of acquiring that king-size hangar of the US Navy for a village hall – negotiations to acquire the Pacific Ocean for a Parish swimming pool having presumably broken down . . .

*   *   *

APRIL 23rd, 1960: 10,000 UP!

Overlooking the minor sins of omission, duplication and manipulation perpetrated by the keepers of the archives, G-ARAA is the 10,001st registration allotted since the International Convention of 1928 decided that Great Britain was to be the sole user of the nationality letter 'G'. To celebrate this event, the Editors prepared the following table showing the approximate dates when each new registration sequence was initiated. Apart from being a (not infallible!) guide to the date when any particular aircraft was registered, the table shows how the number of aircraft coming onto the Register has fluctuated with trade cycles, wars, surplus sales of Prentices and other disasters.

For completeness, the first two sequences used are also included, although this rather spoils the title of this note, G-ARAA being the 11,347th registration in the complete sequence!

G-EAAA	May 1919	G-AHAA	Jan 1946
G-EBAA	Jan 1922	G-AIAA	Aug 1946
G-AAAA	Jul 1928	G-AJAA	Jan 1947
G-ABAA	May 1930	G-AKAA	Jun 1947
G-ACAA	Aug 1932	G-ALAA	May 1948
G-ADAA	Nov 1934	G-AMAA	Apr 1950
G-AEAA	Jan 1936	G-ANAA	Jun 1953
G-AFAA	Jul 1937	G-AOAA	Feb 1955
G-AGAA	Oct 1939	G-APAA	Mar 1957

238

*   *   *

MAY 14th, 1960: THE LUNATIC FRINGE

Against that splendid backcloth of the Sussex Downs in Springtime, Tangmere's former satellite at Westhampnett (alias the Goodwood Motor Circuit) played host on Easter Monday to a galaxy of sedate aeroplanes and ferocious motor cars. Although the aeroplanes were the object of the exercise, the cars could hardly be ignored; their decibel output alone could well precipitate an epidemic of hara-kiri within the Noise Abatement Society . . .

The principal aerial activity was a display of business aircraft. . . . Subsequent rip-roaring was undertaken at ground-level by those remarkably dangerous-looking cars – substantially faster, noisier, and (in one instance) of better take-off performance than most of the eighty-seven visiting aircraft.

*   *   *

OCTOBER 8th, 1960: THE WHOLE TRUTH

[The Whole Truth was a regular series of articles detailing the construction numbers, registrations and subsequent histories of individual aircraft of a particular type. At the end of the series on the Miles Whitney Straight appeared this comment: – Ed.]

We are thus once more in the market for reasonable suggestions as to the next "Whole Truth" subject. The subject should be substantially civil in character, and of restricted lunacy. A grisly fate awaits the first reader to suggest Tiger the Moth *[sic]*.

[In the next issue promptly appeared the following:]

That sinister character "Tiger the Moth" who was found skulking among the italics on page 74 is neither an escapee from a strip cartoon, nor a cousin of Chip the Munk. He is merely the product of a technical hitch . . .

[Thank you so much, Denis, for keeping us so well informed and amused throughout those fascinating years – Ed.]

CHAPTER 29

CAVOK

by

ANN TILBURY

[NOTES ON THE AUTHOR: Ann Tilbury joined 'FLIGHT' magazine in 1957. She was the photographic archivist and through this work met many of the aviation characters of the time, for almost anyone writing a book on aviation went to 'FLIGHT' for pictures, and many of the characters who decided to turn their hand to autobiographies were included in that number. Ann later moved to Hawker Siddeley at Kingston where she worked in the Market Intelligence (Military Aircraft) Division. Leaving there to start a family, she found many of her previous contacts still begging her to help them locate pictures. Her husband, desperate that she should not sink to having only babies and housework to talk about, decided that even fuel sloshing would be more interesting than food sloshing, and so encouraged her to become a freelance.

Whilst with 'FLIGHT' she had done the picture research for the film 'Those Magnificent Men and Their Flying Machines', and had assisted many artists with pictures. She continued in both these fields while freelancing: working for films and assisting artists by supplying reference pictures. One of her first jobs in freelancing was to locate the majority of the pictures used at the Guinness World of Records at the Trocadero and she did research for various other museums. She also compiled indexes for books such as Sir Peter Masefield's 'To Ride the Storm' and Gp. Capt. T. Mahaddie's autobiography 'Hamish'.

In addition she wrote articles, mainly on aviation subjects, and two of her books for children on the Battle of Britain have been published. Her articles have appeared in 'AEROPLANE MONTHLY,' 'AIR MAIL,' 'ARMADA INTERNATIONAL,' 'BORN IN BATTLE,' 'DEFENCE INDUSTRY DIGEST,' 'FLIGHT INTERNATIONAL,' 'FLYPAST,' 'RAF NEWS,' 'WORLD WAR AERO' and others. For three years she was editor of 'AIR MAIL', the magazine

Members of the Fakenham Flying Group admire their newly-arrived
Tiger Moth G-ANCS at Docking, July 1st 1957 (D. Kirkham)

The Fakenham Group's three Tiger Moths G-ANFM, G-ANFO & G-AOIP
take off from Little Snoring in formation en route to the 1958 Oulton
Broad Regatta (D. Kirkham)

Douglas Bader's Gemini 3A at Wolverhampton, c. 1950 (R.R. Paine)

The Speed Six shows clearly the emblem of the 'Throttle Benders' Union' at the 1951 'Daily Express' race (via R.R. Paine)

The cartoonist Wren's interpretation of the members of the 'Throttle Benders' Union' ('Cyril' Alington should read 'Geoffrey' Alington) (via R.R. Paine)

A set of six handmade glass goblets depicting the aircraft raced by the six original members of the T.B.U. (via R.R. Paine)

Taylorcraft Plus D G-AHVR which was flown to Switzerland early in 1960; it is seen here whilst with the Southern Aero Club at Shoreham c. 1953 (T.R.V. Foster)

Lewis 'Benjy' Benjamin in the single-seat Super Tiger G-ANMZ (the 'Canon'), c. 1960 (via L.J. Benjamin)

The 1959 London-Paris race (both photos via L.J. Benjamin).
Above: Hugh Tansley climbs aboard Tiger G-ACDC at Croydon
Below: Hugh bravely mounts his French-registered lawn mower
at Toussus for his final rattle to the finishing line at the Arc de
Triomphe

Familiar Tiger Club faces (both photos via L.J. Benjamin). <u>Left</u>: 'Bish', C.A. Nepean Bishop, the Club's CFI from 1957-1963 <u>Below</u>: Chairman Norman Jones (left), Margo McKellar (in car), Vice Chairman Lewis Benjamin (partly in car)

of the Royal Air Forces Association.

More recently she has branched out into interviews, and most of her subjects have been from the world of entertainment, although her first interview was with the then Chief of the Air Staff, Sir Peter Harding.]

Firstly, if you are wondering about the heading to this waffling collection of anecdotes, it stands for Cloud And Visibility O.K. It stems from a time when I was welcomed on board a small yacht and the elderly crew gave their toast as "Force Threes." I asked friends to let me have a suitable toast for Flying Types. It was Fred Marsh, who flew Formula I racers, who came up with CAVOK.

When this proposed new book was first mentioned to me by Peter Campbell, who asked me to contribute, I pointed out to him that I had never been a pilot; this he knew – Peter and I go back a very long way, having met at College at Guildford in 1956. Indeed, he encouraged me to take an interest in aircraft even then.

My enthusiasm in flying was first whetted when a club to which I belonged organised a visit to our local airfield, Fair Oaks, just to have a look around. I was particularly intrigued as my mother had worked there during the war and "WingCo" Arthur, who had known her at that time, was still working there as the Club's CFI.

It was during that period that I started work on 'FLIGHT' but that was almost by accident. I replied to an advertisement which merely stated that the vacancy to be filled was on a magazine, and it was not until I was told that I had the job that I was informed it was on 'FLIGHT' – did I happen to know anything about aircraft? So I cited my mother's wartime job (which was secretarial, with the ROC) and the fact that my cousin had done his National Service in the RAF. That, and the fact that I lived just about under the Fair Oaks circuit and could therefore recognise a Tiger Moth, known locally as a 'Chobham Chaser', was the sum of my knowledge of aviation at that time. I stayed with 'FLIGHT' for some 17 years!

At the time I started on 'FLIGHT' the editor was Wing Commander Maurice Smith DFC. He had been a Pathfinder, but since the war his interest in cars had overtaken his love of flying, and soon after I joined he became not only Editor-in-Chief of 'FLIGHT' but also Editor of her sister journal 'AUTOCAR'. H. F. (Rex) King was the editor of 'FLIGHT.' My other colleagues included W. T. (Bill) Gunston who was the technical editor and is now known for his prolific authorship of books on aviation: C. M. (Mark) Lambert, who went on to become editor of 'JANE'S ALL THE WORLD'S AIRCRAFT': J. M. (Mike) Ramsden who succeeded Rex as editor and became editor of The Royal Aeronautical Society's

'AEROSPACE' before his retirement: Alastair Pugh, who moved to British Caledonian and did rather well at the time of the take-over but never lost his charm, or his interest in old cars (I remember visiting his home in Woking soon after the birth of his son when there were bits of Frazer Nash spread out on the sitting room floor): Humphrey Wynn, who went on to the Air Historical Branch: Roy Casey, who was the most wonderful sub-editor any paper could have had: and a cast of hundreds. So many people in the business of aviation journalism have done time on 'FLIGHT,' and they were all 'aviation types': they knew their subject, enjoyed it, and wrote about it well. And they stayed at the job for years; nowadays such longevity in a post would suggest lack of ambition. In that period it meant contentment in their work and there was a certain amount of loyalty not only by the employee to the company but the other way around as well. Things do not always change for the better!

At this time I also met John Yoxall, who had been the chief photographer on 'FLIGHT': I inherited his desk. He had moved to become the head of the photographic department for all of Iliffe Press. I remember he got me to type letters to his friends when he retired. He was not looking forward to leaving work and suggested he would be like a snail on the compost heap of life looking on as others raced past. In fact he was even busier in retirement than in employment, and he did much with the Caravan Club and wrote many articles for them, illustrated, of course, with his wonderful photographs. He told me how he had been taken aloft by George Bullman of Hawkers. I believe it was in a Hart and that it was the occasion John took the famous aerial view of Brooklands race track. The camera was large to say the least. It was the days of glass plate negatives so it was not a case of putting a few spare rolls of film in the pocket: a box of negs was pretty cumbersome. Often he would take off his harness in order to turn in the cockpit and aim his camera over the side. Not realising what was going on, George decided to entertain John with a few aerobatics. I don't know whether it was a loop or a roll: probably John didn't, either. I do know that the plane was inverted, with the unharnessed John desperately spread-eagling himself in order to stop falling out, shouting at George and worried as to what his employers would say if he lost the camera (losing his life did not seem quite so important at the time!).

My very first flight almost exactly coincided with my starting work on the magazine. It was in October 1957 at Fair Oaks, and was in an Aeronca, G-AETG; the pilot and owner was Bill Cobbett, who still lives in Horsell village near me. Legend had it that Bill had cannibalised a couple of Aeroncas to rebuild it, and that it was powered with a lawnmower engine, so that if one heard a celestial grass-cutter it was more likely to be Bill flying overhead than a crew of gardening angels. In fact the 'cannibalising' story was quite true, but the 'plane was actually powered by a 37 h.p. Aeronca JAP J.99 engine.

I was soon smitten with the idea of flying and started working in the Fair Oaks canteen at weekends, not for money, but for vouchers which I intended to redeem for flying lessons. As luck would have it, I became enamoured of a charming rogue and gave up the kitchen work – and never redeemed the vouchers. This was a great shame for, while the affair spluttered to a finish after a couple of years, my interest in flying was still there. But never did I get around to taking lessons. Luckily during that period at Fair Oaks I met a lot of people who were prepared to take me up.

One was Henry Pelham, who flew me in the Taylorcraft Plus D G-AHLJ to Bembridge, where we took tea and scones and flew back again. I was enormously impressed! An experience only eclipsed some years later by being flown with friends to Le Touquet for a weekend in an Apache piloted by the Marquis of Headfort. I flew quite a few hours with Henry later in his Magister G-ALUX.

I was given an RAF log book in which I entered those of my flights I could recall, along with photographs of the actual aircraft. I have a note that I flew in an Auster in June 1958, although I have no note of type or registration [it was Universal Flying Services' J/1N Alpha G-AIGU – Ed.]. I do have the pilot listed as John Symonds, and apparently also on board were Peter Campbell, Jeremy Gray and Mike Creavey, although as the aircraft was at best a four-seater I think my notes must be awry! I do remember being told to put my hand out of the window and being astonished at the effect that that small amount of drag had on the aircraft.

I am still in contact with Ranald Porteous, who for many years was Auster's chief test pilot. He was 80 last year and is still invited to shoot at Bisley for his old school. So once a year he makes a sort of Royal Progress from his home in Ayr, visiting various friends on the way down, staying with us after his shooting, and then, as often as not, calling on Ann and Lorne Welch in Farnham before continuing on his very indirect way back up north.

At the time I joined 'FLIGHT', they operated a Miles Gemini 3A G-AKHC. Several of the staff had licences, and once I flew with Mark Lambert from Croydon to Little Snoring for an open day at Fakenham. Mark was a marvellous man about whom I learned much more (as is so often, sadly, the case) at his funeral in 1994. He had just retired from the publishers Jane's, and had moved house with everything planned for a cosy retirement with Anna when, in the space of weeks, it seems, he became ill and died. He learned to fly with the Oxford University Air Squadron, having spent his National Service in military intelligence. He flew Meteors – all sorts of Meteors. I remember him flying the Prone-Pilot Meteor and writing it up for 'FLIGHT'. He had a knack of being technical and at the same time conveying his enthusiasm for the aircraft he wrote of. With his linguistic skills he could take 'FLIGHT's aircraft, fly to somewhere in Europe, interview the relevant people in their own language, flight-test the aircraft in question – any type of fixed- or rotary-wing aircraft – and then write it up in elegant and lucid English. He was also a dab hand on the Spanish guitar: a wonderful man.

Humphrey Wynn also flew me in G-AKHC for a most interesting flight. Also on board was L. W. McLaren – known as Mac – who was 'FLIGHT's photographer. The Duke of Edinburgh had entered a Turbulent for the King's Cup Race in 1959 and it was to be flown by his then equerry, John Severne. Being on an air-to-air photographic sortie is fascinating, especially when the backdrop is Windsor Castle and Ascot Races.

My other trips were outside the fifties era, but perhaps you will forgive my including a few of them here. In 1966 I had gone down to Yeovil to visit Harald Penrose at Westlands. Harald, who died in 1996 aged 92, was chief test pilot for Westlands and flew some 400 different types and variants of British and foreign aircraft. It was he who advised the Duke of Edinburgh on the feasibility of flying a helicopter into the grounds of Buckingham Palace – I think he was in fact the first person to do so. Harald had taken me to lunch at a charming country pub and then told me he had arranged a flight for me because he knew I'd never been up in a helicopter. The machine was a Widgeon, G-APWK, and the pilot was R. R. Crayton. They did everything for me: forwards, backwards, left, right, up, down, hovering. I had a cine-camera with me and to make my filming easier Ron opened the door. Now there was nothing between me and the back of a cow a good many feet below me! He asked me where I wanted to go; I did not know at the time that a village from which a line of my family had come a couple of hundred years previously was just a few miles away. I suggested Montacute, which Harald had shown me from the ground. I was totally fascinated by the symmetry of the grounds; more so when considering that the planning had all been from ground level and without the benefit of the sort of sky-hook I was currently dangling upon.

Through my work on 'FLIGHT' I had been helpful to the RAF at Finningley and so they asked me up for their Battle of Britain Day in 1969. I am including this story because the pilot and the 'plane concerned were both going strong in the previous decade. I told the RAF I would love to accept, but how was I to get up there?

"Fear not," said they, "we have a gentleman who is going to take part in our display; if you can get to Ongar he will fly you up here."

The man in question was Squadron Leader Neville Browning. He was flying a Zlin G-ASIM. He kept it in a barn walled off from livestock by a barrier of hay bales. His runway was a path of mown field. It was on a hill so the take-off was somewhat akin to taking off from an aircraft carrier (something I have never tried but am game to have a go at, should anyone with any clout be reading this!). When landing the ploy was to run up the hill, thereby improving the stopping distance considerably. The touchdown had to be made before reaching an overhanging tree. When I suggested removing or at least pruning the tree, he told me that then *anyone* would be able to land on his strip – which he did not want to encourage.

Our journey up to Finningley was also interesting. He passed back to me a map. I thought we were following the M1 but couldn't see it on the map; I later discovered that it was too old to include the road! We also flew over some American AF base, which did not seem to bother either Neville or the USAF. It transpired that he had drawn a straight line from Ongar to Finningley on an out-of-date map, and was duly flying that route, regardless of anything else. I later watched his flying display from the comfort of the viewing enclosure. Neville, no 'chicken,' was putting on a fairly hair-raising exhibition and kind friends were offering me alternative methods of getting home should the expected happen! It did not and Neville and I got safely back to Ongar.

Another favourite pilot of mine was the late Thomas Foxworth, or Junior as I called him, he having been born a good two weeks after me. He was a Pan Am pilot and member of the Tiger Club. He was instrumental in making me a passenger member of the Tiger Club; Michael Jones seconded his proposal. When he was in England he would often take me flying, usually from Redhill, which was the Tiger Club base. He particularly liked the Stampe and I also flew in Tiger Moth G-ACDC doing aerobatics. Junior took part whenever possible in the Tiger Club Dawn to Dusk event and took meticulous care researching his route, often following the route of some famous flight of long ago, such as the King's Cup.

I must confess that I enjoy aerobatics. Possibly the most hairy trip I have done was with Brian Lecomber in his Pitts Special. This was at Denham; it was a Press Facility and I was editing 'AIR MAIL,' so it is well out of the fifties era but is a tale of the pleasures of aerobatics with an expert.

Soon after my arrival at Denham I was asked whether I would like to fly with Brian. I agreed, but at that time ITN were filming him. He was flying two aircraft, a single-seater and a two-seater. Not flying them simultaneously although, if you have ever seen Brian fly, you might agree that there is little reason why he should not fly them both at the same time. The TV people were loving him and taking air-to-air shots from a chase aircraft and with a remote camera on his wing. So my husband and I went to the Biggles Restaurant for refreshments. It was obvious that Brian was not going to be able to take me up so I downed my disappointment and a gin and tonic – and another. Then we went in for lunch, which was very well done, with a change of wine with each course. I was just pigging into a chocolate gateau when Brian came in, had a glass of water and a lettuce leaf and said: "Right, Ann, ready to fly?"

And so we did. I was in the front open cockpit. All I could see of him was a foot by my seat. We did everything: Cuban Eights, loops, rolls off the top. My husband, both feet firmly on the ground, said he had never seen an aircraft fly backwards the way that one did! I found myself singing 'Land of Hope and Glory' at the top of my voice, safe in the presumption no one could hear me.

This was actually some years after my first aerobatics in jets. Again this had resulted from a contact made through 'FLIGHT' and resulted in my visiting RAF Manby where the MACAWs aerobatic team flew Jet Provosts. There Flt. Lt. John Wingfield took me up solo, just to make sure I wouldn't be sick. I had been warned about having to clean out all the tubes and equipment if I sullied them. I had been checked out on the ejector seat and signed the blood chit.

The experience was wonderful. Again I had my trusty cine-camera with me and John snatched it from me at the top of a loop and placed it in front of my face so it just hung there with the negative 'g'. Not trusting such technicalities I snatched it back pretty quickly. As I passed with flying colours I was allowed to fly with the entire team later that year – 1971 – when the leader was one Flt. Lt. Brian Hoskins. Brian went on to lead the Red Arrows but was not leading them when I flew with them in 1972. I flew in the No.3 slot Gnat with Flt. Lt. Al East. We did a practice of an entire routine and I was airborne for 35 minutes with them, longer than the sort of routine seen at air shows. I worried Al somewhat by discovering something on the instrument panel which looked like a doll's eye and winked as I breathed. Not realising he had a duplicate on his panel, I was panting away making this eye blink until poor Al asked me whether I was alright as he presumed me to be hyperventilating.

Flying with a sizeable formation is entirely different from flying an air-to-air photographic sortie. Although the Arrows' performance from the ground seems quite faultless, when you are up there within the formation there is quite a bit of pitching and yawing; it really is like one large aircraft rather than a formation, for each pilot is formating on his neighbour and only the leader is, well, leading. When some years later I flew from RAF Valley in a Hawk I was asked whether I had flown in fast jets before. I mentioned the Red Arrow flight but confided that the flying in the Pitts Special was also 'hairy.' So the pilot did his best to combine the two styles of flying: the result was breathtaking!

I suppose I've really been very fortunate to have been able to do all these things in the course of making a living. As with most things, and especially in flying, it is the people who make the experience good or bad and, thank heavens, I cannot recall a bad airborne experience. Thank you, one and all! CAVOK!

CHAPTER 30

A WINTER FLIGHT TO SWITZERLAND

by

CAPT. E.A.M. FOX-PITT (WELSH GUARDS)

&

LT. E.H. FANE (COLDSTREAM GUARDS)

[This article was first published in 'THE HOUSEHOLD BRIGADE MAGAZINE' for Spring 1961, and is reproduced here by kind permission of Capt. Fox-Pitt, with recent additions by him; Lt. Fane died in 1970 – Ed.]

This is the story of an adventure that lasted only sixty days. It began last February (1960) when two officers bought an Auster aeroplane *[Taylorcraft Plus D G-AHVR – Ed.]* and decided to fly out to Switzerland in it for a skiing holiday.

We drove to Hendon airfield north of London to collect the aeroplane. The pilot had just qualified for his licence on a pre-war biplane and the co-pilot had just started learning to fly on the same biplane, so our experience on monoplanes was nil. To remedy this deficiency we had arranged for the previous owner to show us how to work the Auster. When we arrived at the airfield, finding it deserted, we rang him up, only to find out that he was unable to come due to an engagement. However, he volunteered some instructions over the telephone, adding that there was a barrel of petrol in the hedge and that a painter, living close by, would swing the propeller for us. Needless to say, our first flight was horrific, but once up, better to stay up, so we set off for Hampshire, calling in at Fair Oaks near Woking en route.

Three days later, as we drove across Salisbury Plain to Thruxton Aerodrome near Andover, it was a hazy and overcast morning, with snow clouds blowing up from the north, but a good forecast and a fleeting glimpse of blue sky in the east speeded our departure.

Every spare inch of space was filled with suitcases, ski-boots and odds-and-ends, and it seemed most unlikely that this tiny aeroplane would lift this mass from the ground. Minutes later, as we dashed towards the boundary fence with frightening speed, the co-pilot allowed his feelings to be surreptitiously transmitted to the joystick on his side, endeavouring to raise the nose. The pilot, who was trying to keep the nose *down* to gain sufficient speed to clear this very obstacle, complained of the stiffness of the controls. But he also noted the absence of colour in the co-pilot's face, and defined most clearly with a few well-chosen words our subsequent duties.

At Lympne we cleared customs, refuelled, and on hearing of the two latest non-arrivals from across the channel very carefully examined and inflated our 'Mae Wests'. As we climbed up into the blue over Folkstone, haze completely hid the French coast. At 4,000 feet we set our compass, put our nose down, and headed at full speed for France. Fifteen minutes later Cap Griz Nez appeared through the haze immediately below us. So began a lasting trust in our compass. After a quick inspection of Boulogne Docks we landed at Le Touquet, cleared customs and headed off inland hoping to reach Beauvais before dark. On the way we discovered that we did not have the map covering most of this hop and were again forced to put all our faith in the compass. But Beauvais proved a prosperous town and we were welcomed many miles out by a beacon flashing out across the darkening sky.

The next day, after a late start, we had an opportunity when arriving at Troyes of proving conclusively the range of our seven gallon petrol tank. After 140 miles we had to forego the luxury of a practice run-in, and on landing we checked the fuel to find that there was at the most two pints left.

Pontarlier, the Franco-Swiss frontier town, lies right up in the Jura Mountains, just below the main ridge. Ever since we left Dijon we could see the forbidding peaks away to the east, and the closer we approached the wilder the country became. At first there had been a mere smattering of snow here and there, but now all was white except for the rocks. The town of Pontarlier lay below us but there was no sign of an airfield. We circled lower and lower until we realised that a large snowfield covered all over with little black dots must be the landing ground. We swept in over the railway station and down onto the field. There was a series of violent shocks through the aeroplane, and snow poured over the windscreen as we careered wildly on through a maze of molehills. Those were the dots that we had seen from the air. Somehow the wheels and undercarriage had stayed intact. St. Christopher, we concluded, must have been working overtime that day.

On complaining about the state of the runway we were told that the aerodrome was closed for the winter. We determined to leave early the following morning while the snow was still frozen, but the slowness of the Customs thwarted this plan. So again we had to fight our way through soft snow and slush. The runway in fact was not straight. You take a sharp left-hand turn half-way down it at about 30 m.p.h. and then accelerate to take off. At the first attempt we failed to leave the ground. At the second shot the co-pilot stood holding back the aircraft by the tailplane until the revs had got up, then dashed forward and jumped into the moving aircraft. We weaved in and out of the huge puddles and crops of molehills, left the ground and started turning hard at only a few feet above ground in order to avoid the rockface ahead.

We climbed up over the Jura in dazzling sunshine. Higher and higher we climbed and suddenly there before us was the Lake of Geneva with the Alps rising magnificently behind. We put the nose down, cut the engine and glided down across Lausanne, Montreux to the Rhône Valley. Here the pilot remembered seeing a small airfield when on holiday some years before. There was no mention of it on the map, and search as we might, we could not find it. We tried to land at Lausanne but a man ran out waving his hands, which after our experience at Pontarlier the day before we read as "airfield closed, do not land." So we returned to a tiny private airfield at Yverdon, which was the only place free of snow. There was no snow here because the canal had flooded most of the aerodrome, and we touched down on the driest patch we could find. The field was deserted so we parked the 'plane and walked the mile or two into the town, and called in at the police station.

The excitement our arrival caused was unbelievable. The customs man was sent for, the president of the local flying club appeared, and we were driven back to the aerodrome in a huge American-style police car. With much shaking of hands we took our leave. As we took off we were so busy waving that we all but disappeared into the ploughed field at the end of the runway. This time we found Bex airfield with ease, landed, garaged the aeroplane and left for ten days skiing.

After the holiday, we returned to Bex, where we were advised that the runway was too short for the aeroplane to take off with us both on board, so it was arranged that the pilot should fly east up the Rhône Valley to Sion, a Swiss Air Force base near Zermatt, and collect the co-pilot. All went well to start with, but as we hurried back along the valley from Sion, the river below us and the mountains rising up to 15,000 feet on either side, the wind became extremely strong and gusty and we were blown back and forth, up and down, like a leaf. Now as we were passing over Bex again and heading for the Lake of Geneva, the sky became darker and darker. Rain and snow spattered against the windscreen. We decided to press on, bad though visibility was, until out over the middle of the Lake of Geneva we ran into a wall of cloud. Having no radio or navigational aids except a compass, we turned about hard and dashed back up the valley which was now half closed by low clouds, and landed in driving rain back at Bex.

Most of the day was spent lying up in a hay-barn belonging to a farmer, whose wife supplied us with lunch. We had visions of being stuck at Bex for days and days, for in these mountains the storms often hang around for a very long time. Suddenly in mid-afternoon the clouds opened and blue sky came through. Despite the warning about the runway length, we both climbed in, the pilot opened the throttle and we sped down the runway, left the ground a few yards from the end and climbed away to the west, avoiding a maze of electricity pylons as we went. Back over the Lake of Geneva, and then we turned north towards Berne. As we flew on, the clouds were forming fast 3,000 feet below us and now we were above where we hoped Berne was. Only the snow-clad peaks jutted out through the sea of white. By chance the pilot caught sight, through a funnel in the clouds, of the sun shining on the river Aar. He put the little Auster in a vertical dive, and she weaved down, down, down through the fast-closing gap until there, 500 feet below, were the spires and roofs of Berne.

The next day the clouds were low again, so we slipped though to Basle on the Rhine by one of the passes through the Jura. Now the worst was past. Across the French Plains to Paris. A night of *joie de vivre*. Le Touquet in a 50 m.p.h. gale and an escort of the aerodrome fire engine. And so over the Channel and across southern England to Andover in the setting sun.

A month later, on the 23rd April, we flew down to a party and dance near Torrington in North Devon which was being given for the daughter of some friends of ours. On the following day, someone asked for a lift up to London in the aircraft and Edmund Fane was seeing how much margin there was for taking off from the field when he got blinded by the sun and hit a bank. These Devon banks can be quite big, but fortunately he stepped out unharmed! However the same cannot be said for our beloved Auster, which was a write-off. I remember that a man gave us £70 for the bits, but apart from that I have no recollections of what happened to the wreckage.

So ended a brief sixty-day love affair with an Auster!

251

CHAPTER 31

MY LIFE WITH TIGERS

by

LEWIS J. BENJAMIN

The last quarter of the decade was for me the opening of a new world, of a freedom to fly that perhaps will never happen again. In the last days of 1957 – I was back in London again – I joined the Tiger Club.

I spotted the brief reference in an October issue of 'THE AEROPLANE.' The Tiger Club had a few vacancies for pilot members: the minimum qualification 100 hours as pilot in charge of a light aircraft. Please contact the CFI C.A. Nepean Bishop. Not that I had a clue what the Tiger Club stood for, but presumably they flew Tiger Moths, and come to think of it, who didn't at that time? It was enough that they flew, Croydon was local and I needed to fly again. I wrote off at once. Of course the Tiger Club still thrives but back in 1958 when I first began to fly with it there were only some thirty or forty members (it was to grow at one stage to over 800). To understand the thinking within the Club, it is important to appreciate the ease with which we flew in those last remaining years of the fifties and indeed into the sixties, but to venture there is to exceed my brief.

We flew from Croydon but not without difficulties. The easy informality of operations in 1958 deteriorated in '59 as the authorities twisted our arms as they tried to move us, but the difficulties had nothing to do with radio which none of us used or had, but the long trudge up to the Tower to get clearance. Nothing complex, mark you, just a friendly word to the duty controller that we would be away from the airfield for thirty minutes. A nod, a smile, and down we'd traipse again.

There were no runways at Croydon, it was grass in all its glory; a pause on the threshold into wind, a glance up at the Tower in case of a red, and in its absence we took off. I remember if we hung around too long we might get a green, not in reproach but a gentle reassurance that someone still watched over us.

'Bish' had written at the time: "Whatever you may have heard on the radio or what you may have read in the newspapers it may be categorically stated that at the time of writing (summer '59) the Croydon Branch of the TIGER CLUB is still operating at Croydon Airport and hopes to do so for as long as flying is permitted from the site. It is quite true that all 'pleasure' and instructional flying has now been banned there, but as the TIGER CLUB normally teaches no one to fly and exists for the purpose of giving displays it does not come under the present ban, all its flights being of a business nature."

I wrote later in a book on the Tiger Club: "Flying rates in 1959 went up for the first time, although by today's standards they were still extraordinarily low. For the first time – and the last – a differential was allowed between Full and Associate membership. Lucky Full Members now were asked to pay £6-5s (£6.25) an hour for the Jodel, which was then top of the range, £6 for the Jackaroo, £5-15s for the D.H. Hornet Moth, and the Tiger came in at a round £5-10s. It still only cost £1-10s to fly the Turbulent. Associate members paid 10/- an hour extra. Duty flying remained at £1-10s, and since most of our flying was duty rate anyway, no one worried too much. The Club finances were decidedly thin. Every now and then Norman Jones would write a Chairman's letter urging either prompt payment or more utilization in order to keep head above water. The Club was, I suspect, never to pay its way, and we the members were far too busy flying to pay much attention. I expect if we had thought about it all, we could only have felt reassured by the knowledge that the Boss was then the head of a vast printing business, Samuel Jones, which in those days was very much a household name with their famous 'Butterfly' brand on just about everything that one could write or stick on."

*   *   *

Not only were we introduced to the discipline of giving air displays but I was to encounter my first circuit racing.

I asked for, and got, the mount of my choice for the 1959 National Air Races: Tiger Moth G-APRA, the 'Sue Burges'. When I had presented myself at Baginton, Coventry, the venue for the races, I hadn't a clue about this racing business. I'd never flown a race in my life and my only qualification was a Competitor's Licence, which had been awarded for the asking. So I approached a most successful racing pilot and asked his advice. Dennis Hartas viewed me suspiciously: he always took racing seriously, and saw me as a possible rival, which with my knowledge was laughable.

"Well," he said reluctantly, "what do you want to know?"

"I've got a new and unhandicapped Tiger," I replied; "it's faster than most, but I don't want to let on in the heats. I want to keep something in hand for the final race. What would you do, what would you suggest?"

"Don't hold back," said Dennis airily. "Go flat out all the way."

"Thank you," I said humbly, because he was very well known and had been Air Racing Champion for two years. He must have seen me coming.

We had a day of practice circuits, as much to find our way as anything, and the next day the race for real. I've never been so excited in my life. I won. Not by a head, not by yards, but by miles. I had been so determined that I had opened my throttle and had nearly bent the thing keeping it open. I didn't even think to look back and check where everyone else was. I got carried away. I was fêted. Cameras clicked, press men crowded round my Tiger, and the very next day all my friends and family learned the great news – provided of course they read the Guardian, and I couldn't think of one who did. As it happened the press photo which showed me grinning inanely over the sill of the cockpit at Bev Snook with his Tiger Tim helmet on was the last of that occasion to reach an eager public. That evening the National Press went on strike.

There were two more rounds which I didn't win, not surprisingly since the handicappers, peeved at letting me slip through their fingers, clobbered me. Nothing though could detract from my fun. And I flew, lower I think than anyone else. I went through gates and gaps in trees, having a whale of a time. In my eyes I was the cat's whiskers. I loved every minute of every race. My every moment between races I spent either polishing my Tiger or trying one of a dozen different schemes I'd watched others do.

Someone said: "Put lots of air in your tyres; you get off quicker."

I did so.

Another said: "Have you changed your plugs for a hard set?"

"What is a hard set?" I asked.

"I don't know, but you can get a set fitted free – go over and ask them at the Lodge tent."

I asked and I got.

"What oil have you got in?" asked another lunatic.

"The usual," I said.

"Get it out quick – Esso have some real thin stuff. It's alright," he assured me when my face started to show concern, "they'll flush out the old and put in the new all for nothing."

I tried that too. In fact everything was on the house. The Shell tent was home to all of us with constant food and drink the whole weekend – even to those of us who were using free Esso products.

My conscience wasn't that troubled.

At the Dunlop caravan – I'd gone there to ask advice and get my tyres pumped up – I ran into my old Commanding Officer, S/Ldr. Wispy Turner. It was a great reunion and we repaired to the Shell tent to celebrate. Wispy had with him Dunlop's Chief Instructor who was dying to take a look at the circuit. I immediately agreed to take him, delighted to have an important chief instructor as my passenger.

I swept him away and into the Tiger. He was obviously unfamiliar on type for he tried to get into my cockpit and got all confused with the harness. Used to modern aircraft I thought and helped him. He even found the helmet a bit strange but I readily understood. Who flew these days in an open cockpit? I was so at peace with the world I'd have forgiven anyone. We flew off.

The course was now well known to me, so I concentrated on impressing my passenger as to my flying ability. I did all the things thinking pilots do when they have another pilot at their mercy. I kept my top needle dead centre, my every turn was tight, full of 'g', low and not climbing, and since I didn't have to worry as I would with a non-pilot I got even lower than before – whistling the wheels through the daisies and taking every short cut I could find. It was the most exhilarating trip I'd made to date. I was bubbling with joy when we taxied in and stopped.

My passenger sat low in the cockpit, not moving. I leant in and clapped him on the shoulder.

"Like it?"

He didn't answer at once, he just sat there like a sack of potatoes.

"No," he whispered at length.

Wispy and I helped him out.

"Wispy," I said in a hoarse whisper, "what's the matter?"

"I don't know," replied Wispy irritably, "but he looks frightened to me."

"A chief flying instructor?" I queried incredulously.

"Chief *driving* instructor," corrected Wispy.

*　　　*　　　*

Not all our races were circuit-bound, and it certainly wasn't the King's Cup that people wanted to know about in July '59. For there was another race just a week after the Nationals that had all of Britain on their toes with excitement. The Press, Radio and the TV gave the Blériot Anniversary Race a degree of coverage that set new records.

The '*Daily Mail*' had offered £10,000 to the winner of the

fastest time between London and Paris. It was later labelled the Race of the Century. It was. It must have been. The efforts of the challengers between the city centres were daring, sometimes funny, and often dramatic, and caught the imagination of the World. Their split-second adventures made headlines everywhere. The tense battles between crack service teams using jet fighters, helicopters and powerful motorcycles were followed by millions.

Somewhere in all this fuss and tension were several Tiger Club pilots. Quite what they did, and how they did it, is now hazy in my mind. I recall for instance that Norman flew a Turbulent. So did Joan Short. Jon Hutchinson flew too, but took a tiny motor scooter along with him, and the journey took just under three hours. He said it only cost him £2. But I thought at the time, if you believed that you'd believe anything. I know beyond any shadow of doubt that I was a member of a team that went by lawnmower.

Clem Pike, who was then CFI for de Havillands at Hatfield and a Tiger Club member, phoned Bish and asked him if there was a member willing to fly in the coming race. That's how I got in on the act. Hugh Tansley, who was then studying at the Hatfield Technical College, had got the sponsorship of Ransomes the lawnmower people, with the offer of mowers for transport at each end of the course. I would fly Hugh over the Channel in the oldest Tiger 'CDC and so connect the two.

It took nearly four bone-shaking hours to trundle the motorised lawnmower from Marble Arch down to Croydon. Once there everyone seemed to be in the grip of a madness in their haste to get us airborne in the shortest possible time. We cleared Lympne down in Kent in an atmosphere of pure panic. A flashing green light from the Tower urged me down ahead of a circling DC-3 scheduled flight which they held up above. A line of helpers led me at a fast taxying pace right up to the pumps where Customs men were waiting to *run* with me to clear formalities. In vain did I plead that there wasn't any real hurry. They only knew we were in The Race, and no one was ever going to say that the boys at Lympne weren't helpful. We were airborne in minutes. It was unreal.

Over at Toussus, a small airfield near Paris, there was a huge contingent awaiting us, along with a fresh lawnmower. We made the Arc de Triomphe in the remarkable total time of 10 hours 44 minutes. Crowds had lined the streets to cheer our slow, oh! so slow, cavalcade of cars escorting one tired and collapsing mower averaging some 3½ m.p.h. No one had considered the effect of the French pavé. Blériot undoubtedly crossed the Channel first 50 years earlier, and in doing so went a darn sight faster than many of us, but I bet he didn't enjoy it half as much.

I'm not saying such an event couldn't happen today, but reflect on the freedom the Tiger Club gave to its members. To use the Club's aircraft as if they were our own, with no prior permission from anyone, was a gift beyond belief.

*   *   *

The fifties were drawing to a close, an era was folding, and as one door closed, another was about to open. Late that autumn of 1959 Croydon closed to flying and the Tiger Club moved to Redhill to start a new and exciting period that was to last some twenty-five years. However, I can't possibly close this chapter without a glance back at two men who were the personification of that decade: Norman Jones and his loyal CFI Nepean Bishop.

Bish's pride in the Club knew no bounds and it is only with hindsight that his organising genius and love of his task is apparent. I can't recall at the time that he made anything of his dedication, but that he had the Club on his mind every waking hour is obvious now. His quiet drive and ever-positive presence was truly instrumental in welding this remarkable Club in its formative years, as indeed examination of the early documents shows.

Nor do I think the teamwork between the Founder, Norman Jones, and his henchman Bish has ever been recognised. Time had no meaning for either man. I know for a fact that Norman would ring Bish very early every weekend morning to plan the day. Nor was Norman, of whom we all stood in awe, adverse to 'phoning others at the same hour. I'd be dragged from my sleep around seven by the Boss, stifling a groan as I immediately prepared to jump to it at that unearthly hour.

Norman Jones was a man of action: his practical support to our sport of light flying is now legend. Name what aspect of our flying you like, Norman had a hand in putting it on the post-war map, whether it be aerobatics, glider towing, formation flying, air displays, air touring or his open-handed approach to air racing that in the late fifties saw over half of all entrants in the Nationals flying his small air force of exciting aircraft – and all if you please at £1-10s (£1.50) an hour.

If you will forgive a year's excursion beyond the fifties, let me offer up a delightful cameo of the late Norman Jones (he died on the 13th April 1991 aged 86). I bet if he reads this in heaven, where I've no doubt he's busy organising cloud flying, he'd give a wicked grin and nod his approval.

Redhill lies very near London Gatwick. That busiest of international airfields is only a matter of a few miles away, yet the two airfields have lived in harmony for over twenty-five years. Albeit there has been the odd occasion of infringement, but never anything serious, but then Gatwick wasn't always that busy.

The big airfield was still little used and far from finished in the January of 1961, and so to encourage movements they opened their vast runway and all their facilities to General Aviation, and all was free. The date I first took advantage of that offer is still vividly in my memory. In my log book it's an entry for New Year's Day '61, a date which I suspect was their official opening to the flying world. I was unaware of this on that cold clear morning down at Redhill.

All I knew was that Norman bore down on me and in his abrupt naval manner said "Get in," and pointed to the Jodel Ambassadeur G-ARFT; "we are going to Gatwick."

"Yes, Sir," I said and got aboard.

He settled into the left-hand seat, started the engine, and without any further ado or another word taxied out and took off down the long west runway. We climbed briefly to around 500 feet, and still at full chat turned left towards Gatwick. I began to feel uneasy when the Boss showed no inclination to climb any higher. We sped on at 500 feet. I couldn't very well just say to the Chairman: "Hey, Norman, you're approaching a huge unknown, what about getting at least to circuit height?" so I reverted to subterfuge and, leaning forward, tapped at the altimeter as though the needle had stuck.

Norman never missed a thing. "What's the matter, Benjamin?"

"Do you not think we are a bit low, Sir?"

"Hm," he grunted, and went up another 100 feet.

Over our nose appeared the massive ramifications of a big complex beyond which the new runway loomed alarmingly. We tore on at 600 feet. My eyes were everywhere, all we needed now was someone on approach, and worse, what on earth were they thinking of us down there? I squirmed in my seat. I suddenly remembered – the radio of course.

I leant forward and switched it on and said as calmly as I could: "Perhaps they are calling us."

Norman put on earphones and looked to me expectantly. I didn't know what to say but something had to be said and quickly.

I said: "Say 'Gatwick, this is Jodel Foxtrot Tango – permission to land, please.'"

My radio procedure was pretty zero in those days. We'd seldom used it in the RAF, and for the last several years I'd lived, breathed and enjoyed the peace and true responsibility of radio-less aircraft.

Norman spoke firmly into the swing microphone. "Gatwick, this is Norman Jones, we are coming in for tea."

He turned and smiled at me with pleasure. After all these years I must be forgiven if I don't recall the exact words, but please believe me when I say I'm not far out. Conversations like this are all too priceless to be forgotten.

Gatwick Air Traffic were imperturbable. They came back smoothly like the top professionals they are, gave instructions to let down over South Base and to call finals.

"There!" said Norman triumphantly, and he nodded his head to indicate he understood.

"Norman," I hissed urgently, "tell them. Say 'Roger, will call finals.'"

If he heard me he made no sign. We tore over the new terminal still going south at 600 feet. The term 'South Base' was new to me but whilst I was still grappling with the unknown, Norman swung sharply left and then left again.

"Call finals," I cried in alarm.

But the Boss had the bit between his teeth and in a flash we were lined up with the greatest runway I'd ever seen . . . it seemed to disappear over the horizon.

Norman tore towards it happily. As we approached, ATC turned on all the runway lights. I burst out laughing. It was a wickedly delightful gesture. Norman beamed. His face was a picture of achievement.

"There," he exclaimed, "they are welcoming us."

And of course so they were, but the welcome wasn't to the aircraft but to one of the most remarkable men in aviation – The Boss.

EDITOR'S POSTSCRIPT

I hope you have enjoyed reading about the dreams, achievements, adventures, escapades and occasional mishaps of just some of the fascinating people who were involved with aviation in the 1950s.

For me, putting this book together has been mainly a labour of love, but it has provided many benefits, some hoped for, some completely unexpected – for example, a number of personal questions which remained in my memory unanswered for over forty years have now been resolved. As an added bonus I have had the opportunity to talk to (and in some cases meet) the many contributing authors. Some of their names were familiar to me, and, I suspect, to most other enthusiasts of the time, and it has been a privilege to learn from them; others I knew personally way back then and it has been good to re-establish contact.

May I say "Thank you" once again to everyone who has contributed in any way to the book. And if anyone has any ideas for a sequel, I might possibly be persuaded to consider taking it on!

PETER CAMPBELL
